20TH-CENTURY COMPOSERS
Claude Debussy

Claude Debussy

by Paul Roberts

Phaidon Press Limited
Regent's Wharf
All Saints Street
London N1 9PA

Phaidon Press Inc.
180 Varick Street
New York, NY 10014

www.phaidon.com

First published 2008
© 2008 Phaidon Press Limited

ISBN 978 0 7148 3512 9

Cover illustration by Jean-Jacques Sempé
Designed by HDR Design
Printed in Singapore

Frontispiece, Debussy at
Pourville in the summer of
1904, during the period in
which he completed *La Mer*

Contents

Preface

In terms of greatness, there is no doubt about Claude Debussy's – his greatness, that is, as a composer. But was he a great man? His life manifested none of the epic, star-status qualities, and little of the altruism, of such a figure as Franz Liszt – a man who defines a concept of greatness, not only as a composer and performer but as a compassionate human being. Liszt's antithesis is Richard Wagner, a composer of colossal power and influence, but an odious man. Between these two poles – between the gleaming Liszt and the glowering Wagner – lies the shadowy Claude Debussy: a feline, sensual and enigmatic figure of dubious background and equally dubious morals, who quietly but single-mindedly changed the course of music history. Like the Impressionist painters just before him, with whom he is famously identified, his vision, and his execution of that vision, was such that nothing could ever be the same again. His compositions demanded a new way of listening, just as the Impressionists' paintings demanded a new way of seeing. The music of the twentieth century, in all its wide-ranging originality and complexity, was born from him. Perhaps that is enough greatness for one human being.

I have long been fascinated by Debussy. In my childhood I had singled out his portrait from a row of composers' heads above the walnut upright piano in my teacher's studio. I was impressed by the domed brow and beard and the arrestingly sensual eyes, which I found both frightening and kind. The large head and the pointed black beard made the shape of a triangle, which in my child's mind I associated with the strange sound and the alien shape of the name written underneath – Achille-Claude Debussy. Then in my teens came the haunting piano piece *La Fille aux cheveux de lin*, with its sensuous sonorities and frissons of archaic romance. How could such music come from one who was considered, I soon learnt, rude and unpleasant? I needed to trace such rumours, which I refused to take at face value, to their source.

I became more intrigued by the personality the more I got to know the music. I liked him, and I knew this feeling came in some vital way from what I heard and played. But how? What kind of man could produce music so startlingly original, so shockingly sensuous, so unerringly expressive of sensual experience? The extraordinary power of *Prélude à l'après-midi d'un faune* was intimately connected in my teenage imagination with the erotic splendour of the green-eyed Gaby, Debussy's long-suffering girlfriend of the 1890s, described in all the biographies. But I gradually came to realize that this power rested upon an intellectual rigour, a precision of detail and structural cohesion that had nothing to do with self-indulgence. And finally I discovered that the polarized demands of the intellect and the senses were central to Debussy's existence as an artist and as a man. His personal life was spent finding deeply uneasy compromises between the two; as an artist he allowed no compromise at all, forging instead a sublime unity.

I am especially indebted to Roger Nichols for setting me on the right path in my quest with his compilation of contemporary accounts *Debussy Remembered*. It was in this book that I first truly found the man whom I sensed through the music. Lockspeiser's painstaking *Debussy: His Life and Mind* is without equal, and has to be a mainstay for any biography, but it never quite revealed to me the living personality that came across so powerfully in the contemporary memoirs – and of course in the letters. Debussy's letters are fine literary creations in their own right, although today English readers are largely prevented from appreciating them as no translation is currently in print. But readers of French at last have the complete correspondence, in a magnificent new work of scholarship recently published by Gallimard (though too late for me to draw on the large number of previously unpublished letters, including relevant letters from the correspondents themselves). Here, in one compendiuosly large volume, is a final confirmation, if one were needed, of the centrality in Debussy's life-story of the written word – his own. He appears to have written as he would have spoken: quietly, fluently and idiomatically, with a natural sense of style and pace and a habitual irony. For so private a man, so famously reticent and self-protective, his letters are remarkably revealing. Apart from his journalism, rather too self-conscious and mannered to be reliably the true voice of Debussy, his letters are all we have, in biographical terms, of the authentic man. It is for this reason that I have quoted extensively from them in the following chapters.

I embarked on this biography having spent most of my adult life performing Debussy's piano music. I wanted to see whether I had anything to offer from my intimate knowledge of the music that might lead to an intimate knowledge of the man. 'Art is a reflection of life or it is nothing,' the literary critic F. R. Leavis wrote. For me, as a performer, Debussy's music reveals similar insights to those inherent in great literature, the ability to probe with clairvoyant understanding the experience of being alive. As a biographer I hope I have been able to convey something of what it must have been like for a composer of true greatness to be at the same time the all-too-human Claude Debussy.

It remains for me to record my special thanks to the Guildhall School of Music & Drama for providing me with the time and the funds to bring this enterprise to fruition. Over a number of years I have had the unfailing support and encouragement of the Guildhall's Head of Research, George Odam, to whom I am deeply grateful.

Paul Roberts
Robertsbridge

I

An etching of the stairway in
the courtyard of Debussy's
birthplace, just before
conversion into the Maison
Claude Debussy in 1982

'*Those around me refuse to accept that I could
never live in the everyday world of things and
people. Hence the irrepressible need I have to
escape from myself, and go off on adventures
which seem inexplicable because no one knows
who this man is — yet maybe he's the best part of
me! Anyway, an artist is, by definition, someone
used to living among dreams and phantoms.*'

Claude Debussy

The Quest for Debussy 1862-1918

Biography in our time feeds a voracious appetite. We want to know, we need to know, we are impelled to satisfy an intense curiosity as to the larger-than-life existences of others. For what purpose? 'Never trust biographies,' wrote Anne Michaels, in her novel *Fugitive Pieces*. 'Too many events in a man's life are invisible. Unknown to others as our dreams. And nothing releases the dreamer.' Yet, in part, biography is history, and the appetite and necessity for history need little justification. This aspect of biography *is* trustworthy, at least in so far as history and its multiple interpretations can ever be. So in the case of the present subject – Achille-Claude Debussy, French composer, born 1862, died 1918 – we might see his art, though born from the perceptions of the man, as defining an age. In a famous phrase, concerning the essence of language, T. S. Eliot said that 'sensibility alters from generation to generation in everybody, whether we will or no, but expression is only altered by a man of genius.' Where language goes, music follows, or at least it does in Debussy's case – he for whom poetry and literature were the wellsprings of his creative imagination. He absorbed the sensibility of his age, and through his music gave voice to it. He also incontrovertibly altered musical expression.

Historical evidence is considerable concerning the life of Debussy. Even the material facts of much of his world are still with us: the Parisian streets and houses in which he lived, the old music conservatoire (now a drama school) which he attended for over a decade from the age of ten, and the famous iron bridge, the Pont des Arts (restored in 1981), leading across the Seine from the École des Beaux Arts to the Palais du Louvre. It was on this bridge, in 1884, that the 22-year-old awaited the result of the prestigious Prix de Rome. Nearby his fate was being decided. 'I was quite relaxed,' he recalled years later, 'and wasn't thinking about anything to do with Rome, for the pleasant sunlight was playing on the rippling water, with that special charm which keeps idlers on the bridges for hours on end, making them the envy of all Europe.' On the Pont des Arts we can still watch, as Debussy did then, 'the coming and going of the

Le Pont des Arts by Pierre Auguste Renoir (1867). The Academie Française, from where the Prix de Rome was adjudicated, is the domed building on the right

bateaux mouches on the Seine'. Idlers are there still, painting, hawking, strolling. Europe remains envious. Debussy's Paris survives, in part, for those who will seek it.

But what of the spirit of those times? Can we ever recover the fecundity of the age in which the composer was nurtured? And how far can biography reach into the inner core of an artist's existence – the subtle motivations, the self-deceptions – and reveal those invisible events, diagnosed by Anne Michaels, which nourish the creative imagination? 'An artist,' wrote Debussy, 'is, by definition, someone used to living among dreams and phantoms.' How, *pace* Anne Michaels, can we release the dreamer? The answers must lie in the art, in the music itself. Somehow the man is defined by his art; and through the complex processes of cause and effect, the art in turn defines the age.

The biographer's dilemma might be put thus: if we need the music to find the man – 'one of the most original and adventurous musicians who ever lived', as the American scholar William Austin has put it – to what extent do we need the man to find the music? If the question can be answered, we have first to establish what of the man there is to find. If at the end of the exercise we turn to the music with a willingness to explore further, then the biographer should be content.

So to begin the life at the life's beginning: Debussy was born in Bread Street – rue au Pain – in a tiny room above a china shop in the town of Saint Germain-en-Laye, just beyond the suburbs of Paris to the north-west. The date was 22 August 1862. Those at least are trustworthy, if dull, facts of biography. Other facts of his early life are more difficult to discern, although there is evidence of considerable insecurity and disruption: the conventional happy childhood was certainly not his, and early periods of it must have been deeply unsettling. The boy who became the composer Claude Debussy was deeply affected by this early life, but aware as we are of the turmoil, we would be wrong to conclude that he was neglected or starved of affection. And a child's imagination, certainly this child's, can provide a haven against the ravages outside, an inner existence in which vital nourishment and growth continue unchecked. His sister Adèle recalled that, at around the age of eight, he would often spend 'entire days seated in a chair dreaming about no one knew what'. The dreamer, we note, appeared early. It was his means of survival.

In Saint Germain-en-Laye, the newborn's newly married parents were renting a narrow, graceless house on three floors. They ran the china shop below. When I first found the place – 38 rue au Pain – in the early 1980s, it was dilapidated and vacant, apart from the shop at street level. Remarkably it still sold china, but I could find no evidence that it had continuously done so. Today the shop is gone, but in its place, and indeed in the whole building, is a museum devoted to the life of the genius who was born there. It is small, tastefully quiet and touchingly beautiful. A room upstairs has been converted into a tiny concert hall where music students are allowed to practise.

Plans for Maison Claude Debussy were only in embryo on my first visit to Saint Germain-en-Laye. Then the only visible evidence of one of the world's greatest composers was a modest stone plaque on the wall above the shop, almost unnoticeable: *'A Claude Debussy, d'un Groupe d'Admirateurs Anglais, 1er Juillet 1923'* ('To Claude Debussy, from a Group of English Admirers, 1 July 1923'). I had pushed at the heavy-timbered door next to the shop to discover a tiny courtyard with a wooden staircase leading to the floors above. It was behind the door on the top floor, I was informed, that Debussy was born.

From above the courtyard I had looked down over the balcony rails, trying to imagine the child's young parents entering from the street. In early portraits Monsieur has an attractive, rather daredevil appearance.

Debussy's father Manuel and mother Victorine before their marriage in 1861

He wears the uniform of the Marine Light Infantry, and wears it well. Madame comes across with less aplomb, appearing severe and tight-lipped, although this is probably no more than a determination to appear respectable. In this she was to be sorely taxed.

The commemorative plaque is no longer on the wall above the shopfront, but has been placed instead in the courtyard. The English admirers have been moved into the background.

The small town of Saint Germain-en-Laye is today highly fashionable and monstrously expensive. The rue au Pain is a busy and attractive street for shopping, with a smart clothes shop just down from the museum called Children's Corner, an appropriate name: Debussy's small daughter Chouchou (who inspired the piano pieces *Children's Corner*) was always impeccably attired in the latest English fashions. The town stands high above the river Seine, and from the formal gardens – whose gravel walk-ways run right up to the point where the cliff falls abruptly to the river below – one can make out the tip of the Eiffel Tower. On that warm autumn of my first visit, another famed birth was on my mind. Louis

XIV had also been born in Saint Germain-en-Laye, just the other side of
the ornate railings edging these gardens, where the Hotel Henri Quatre
now stands. He had later built a palace here, more dear to him even
than Versailles, and had his celebrated gardener, Le Nôtre, lay out the
grounds where I was now standing. Revolutionary events in French
history had meant that this most illustrious of all France's sons, the Sun
King, was unrepresented on the country's bank notes, while the head of
the retiring Claude Debussy, *musicien français* as he liked to be known –
in life impecunious to the last – graced the twenty franc note, albeit the
lowest denomination.

I had come to Saint Germain-en-Laye as an adjudicator of the
Debussy International Piano Competition. Biography was then far from
my mind – or at least the actual making of one between covers, for
I had long been intrigued by the relationship between this composer's

The once ubiquitous twenty
franc note with Debussy's
head on the front and back.
The design is based on a
portrait by Marcel Baschet,
painted when Debussy was
a Prix de Rome laureate in
1885. The original portrait
is reproduced on page 147

life and his music, ever since seeing his photograph in my piano teacher's studio when I was a boy.

I realize now that the photograph in question must have been one of the formal poses taken by Félix Nadar in 1909, Debussy's forty-eighth year. Debussy is said to have hated having his portrait taken, but he must have liked those done by Nadar, as he took the trouble to say so in a letter to the venerable old man: 'My dear Monsieur Nadar... if ever posterity should care to preserve the memory of my features I would ask the honourable lady to address herself to you alone.' Even making allowances for polite flattery, at which Debussy could be adept, this is graciously put. In the photographs we see a respectable member of the middle classes, suitably buttoned, not over smart, enigmatic. The shape of the head and shoulders suggest something 'of the early Egyptians', as the conductor Henry Wood noticed when he first met him in London just the year before. This is a striking comparison, and suggests that the inscrutability and the ageless immobility of Nadar's portraits are not just due to the exigencies of early photography, but that they convey the very essence of the man. Nadar specialized in the unadorned, the simple record, allowing the face to speak for itself. In a full-face portrait he recorded the 'deep, soulful eyes' that Wood also remembered, which have an almost Mona Lisa-like intensity. The close-up image and the direct gaze have the life and movement of fine sculpture, suggesting the composer is about to smile or speak.

Nadar had photographed many of the great personalities of the previous century. At 89 he was already a legend, not only for his photographs, caricatures of celebrities and his journalism, but for his balloon exploits and heroism in the Franco-Prussian war of 1870. The Impressionist painters held their first notorious exhibition in Nadar's studio in 1874 and he had photographed many of them. He had also photographed Edouard Manet and Eugène Delacroix, composers such as Gioacchino Rossini and Guiseppe Verdi, and such giants of French nineteenth-century literature as Gustave Flaubert, Victor Hugo and Charles Baudelaire. The old man must have brought with him echoes of the Second Empire and the faint aura of artists whom Debussy revered.

If the photographic record is fascinating, the reality for those meeting Debussy for the first time was extraordinary. Like Henry Wood, the composer Alfredo Casella was intrigued by the strange head: 'The enormous forehead bulged forward, while there seemed something

missing at the back of the huge skull', which gave the composer's features an almost triangular effect. For the singer Georgette Leblanc, 'the most remarkable thing about Debussy was that his body was built for strength, but to all appearances did not contain it... His strength had been drained away by his genius.' The English singer Maggie Teyte, who took over the role of Mélisande in 1908, gives an even more startling image of him, a reversal of the usual impression of languor and sensuality: he had 'immense physical power and primitive vitality,' she recalled; 'one was always conscious of that powerful, nervous force at work, directing and controlling.' Unknowingly, something of Debussy's intrinsic power must have been what frightened me as a child, contemplating his photograph.

Another acquaintance, the critic Émile Vuillermoz, noted that those who knew him only from photographs had 'no way of guessing that his presence was transfigured by a single attribute: his voice – his unique unforgettable voice... His vocal chords produced sounds that were strange, slightly veiled, articulated with a light staccato that separated the syllables, imperceptibly dampened by an invisible mute. Debussy rarely removed this velvet mask which served him well throughout his life.' Igor Stravinsky recalled that 'the ends of his phrases were often inaudible – which was to the good as they sometimes contained hidden stings and verbal boobytraps.'

The writer André Suarès, an acute contemporary observer of Debussy's circle, seems to me to capture most vividly the full complexity of the artist, the contradictions, the spirit, the sensitivity: 'His ironical attitude was innate, as was his inclination towards pleasure; his teasing spirit was full of wit, and he made no secret of his appetites. There was a droop about the corner of his lips, and a certain nonchalance in his speech was matched by the delicate charm of his gestures.' Suarès too noticed his 'fine eyes, caressing and inclined to mockery, sad and full of languor, passionate and thoughtful, like those of some accomplished and powerful woman, eyes such as artists sometimes have, as though they had themselves been women in some previous life. His gaze could also take on a strange heaviness, an extreme concentration – the gaze of some French poet who continues to analyse even in reverie and whose understanding is never at rest.' It is this gaze which is so strikingly captured by the photographic portraits of Nadar.

There are several informal photos of the younger Debussy from the 1890s, taken by one of the closest of his friends, Pierre Louÿs. In these

Opposite, a photographic portrait of Debussy by Félix Nadar, taken in 1909 during the height of the composer's fame

there is a marked air of languor, the eyes are sleepy and Debussy seems never to be without a cigarette. (He was known for the delicate precision with which he rolled the tobacco in the paper, and for his disdain for the dandy's cigarette holder, 'as ridiculous', he said, 'as kissing a woman on the mouth by telephone'.) Comparing them to the Nadar photos of fifteen years later, we can see what a profound change had come over the composer's life in the interim. The contrasts are inevitable: laid-back bohemianism gives way to respectable celebrity, youth gives way to age. But the photographic record captures more than the passing of time. There was a watershed in Debussy's life created by his sudden celebrity following the première of his opera *Pelléas et Mélisande* in 1902, and the subsequent break-up of his first marriage. He was in his early forties. 'Not that he changed,' wrote his friend René Peter; 'but despite himself, despite all of us, he moved into a different category of being.' In other words, he did change. And he exchanged his bohemian existence for the wealthy milieu of the Avenue du Bois de Boulogne (where he, nevertheless, remained chronically short of money). The process had been foreseen by the young Debussy on that day on the Pont des Arts when he dreamily watched the boats on the river Seine, and awaited the result of the Prix de Rome. He was brought the momentous news that he had won the prize. 'My heart sank,' he remembered; 'I had a sudden vision of boredom, and of all the worries that inevitably go together with any form of official recognition. I felt I was no longer free.'

This 'different category of being' creates problems for the biographer. On the surface the new middle-class Debussy, the husband and father walking his dogs, seems a less exciting figure than the penniless unknown artist, of dubious background, who is challenging the very foundations of his art and rubbing shoulders with the poets and painters of the Parisian avant garde. Compared to the outwardly settled artist in his maturity, the youth is in a state of ferment and growth, open to challenges and influences, finding his path in a kind of heroic quest, an altogether Romantic figure. The sexual challenge and the creative are intermingled, wonderfully expressed in Debussy's case by his orchestral tone-poem *Prélude à l'après-midi d'un faune*, by the Baudelaire and Paul Verlaine songs of the 1880s and 1890s, by the erotic *Chansons de Bilitis*, and by the *Proses lyriques* (settings of Debussy's own poems, beginning 'The night has a woman's softness'). And in setting Maurice Maeterlinck's play *Pelléas et Mélisande* Debussy created his only completed opera

Debussy in a characteristic bohemian setting in the home of his close friend, the writer Pierre Louÿs, in 1897. On the left is Louÿs's Algerian mistress, Zohra Ben Atala

from the very conflict of youth and age, of freedom and responsibility, that had tapped him on the shoulder nearly a decade earlier.

'I feel nostalgia for the Claude Debussy who worked so enthusiastically on *Pelléas*,' he wrote in 1904; 'I've not found him since, which is one reason for my misery, among many others.' Certainly the younger man whom we will glimpse is far more of an extrovert, a more entertaining personality, than the brusque, taciturn figure we find later on. But if the outer man noticeably changed, the inner genius of the later years remained the same. After *Pelléas* and fame, the artist still sought the unknown with a determination that was no less than heroic. But he no longer had the shield of *being* unknown. He retired inside himself, and repelled most intruders.

The complex interrelation of life and art which we will explore in the following chapters was summed up by Debussy himself, when he wrote that 'life is a compromise between instinct and civilization.' Biography can assess the compromise. Debussy's life exemplifies ego-bound genius coming to terms with wider responsibilities. The dilemma is caught for us in that snapshot of the young composer on the Pont des Arts feeling he was 'no longer free'.

So we need now to retrace our steps to rue au Pain in Saint Germain-en-Laye, to the hopeful Victorine and handsome Manuel Debussy, and their baby Achille-Claude, just entering the courtyard of number 36, behind the china shop.

2

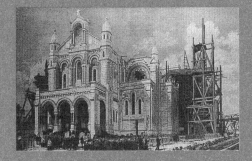

The Sacré Coeur in Montmartre, built to atone for the carnage of the 1871 civil war in Paris. The church took several decades to complete; this shows the building around 1890

'Ah! I forget nothing.'

Claude Debussy

A Boy's Life 1862-80

The new family were not long in Saint Germain-en-Laye. It seems that the near-bankruptcy of Monsieur Debussy forced a hasty departure. His first-born remained unbaptized for two years, an irregular state of affairs for a purportedly respectable family, and by the time Achille-Claude was five the family had moved house four times. (Known as Achille from his childhood, and 'Chilo' to his family, it was not until the age of thirty that the composer determinedly called himself Claude.) Before he entered the Paris Conservatoire at the age of ten, the young Debussy appears not to have had any formal schooling.

The signs point not only to flight from debt but, within two years of his son's birth, the disappearance of Manuel altogether. For a time, it seems, this attractive male was attracted elsewhere. By 1867, however, the family turn up in one piece in Paris, in the rue de Vintimille, not far from the hill of Montmartre. They have become a family of five, with a daughter, Adèle (born 1863) and another son, Emmanuel (born 1867). The drifting Manuel now works as a travelling salesman, and his much put-upon wife, even more tight-lipped than she appears in her portrait, supplements the family income as a dressmaker.

The relationship between husband and wife during Debussy's earliest years would have been uneasy, and most likely highly confrontational. In 1870, when the child was eight years old, things became far worse. Now began the events which led to civil war in Paris, massacres in Montmartre and the near-engulfment of *la famille* de Bussy, affairs in which the 35-year-old Manuel played a significant minor role. The events of these years left scars on his eldest child well into adulthood.

It was Debussy's strong-minded mother who held the reins throughout this trauma. Victorine had already shown herself to be perfectly capable of managing an errant husband and a growing family. She has been treated harshly by several biographers, offended because she left two of her offspring, Adèle and Alfred (born in 1870), to the care of her easygoing sister-in-law, Debussy's Aunt Clémentine. But this was normal practice in this period, a sensible response to a dire lack of money and

Achille-Claude, 'Chilo', as a
five-year-old

space, and Clémentine was childless. In addition, the mother has been
censured for her appearance: 'wary eyes, straight hair, thick nose, not
ugly certainly but not charming either, and possibly hot-headed,' wrote
Marcel Dietschy, on the evidence of one undistinguished portrait. 'She
gives the impression of being only slightly maternal, passionate, violent,
and very independent.' However, there is a snapshot of Victorine and
Manuel together in 1906 (both then over 70) in which she appears come-
ly and attractive, while her short and stocky husband – with cigarette
between his fingers and a watch chain across his belly – is still remarkably
good looking. He now has silver hair and whiskers, and the air of some
genial Parisian barman. Debussy has his arms across their shoulders,

and his mother has been caught looking the wrong way, just having spoken a word or two. It is a conventional enough family photo, depicting affection and pride: past problems are dim memories, the famous son has brought the parents together, the family has survived.

'Mme Debussy was passionately attached to her son and a very excitable person,' recalled Paul Vidal, a close friend of the composer in his student days.

> *Every letter she received from him when he was away was a real event in her life. She was very kind and spoilt me thoroughly; she was an excellent cook and was fond of preparing delicious side-dishes, which also appealed to Debussy's highly developed gastronomic tastes. She and her husband came from a very modest class, but could not be labelled as belonging to the masses because they were interested in everything and well-informed. They went to all the latest theatre productions and liked discussing them.*

Debussy's parents were able to overcome the strains of the early years of their marriage. This family snapshot comes from around 1906

Of course they did belong to the masses, if that is taken to mean the general working population represented by their immediate ancestors: Victorine's mother had been a cook, her father a wheelwright, while on both sides there had been locksmiths, carpenters, cabinet-makers, mushroom growers, dressmakers and wine dealers. But since Napoleon I education had been one of the hallmarks of French Republicanism; the French Catholic Church, too, especially during the periods of Royalist restoration in the nineteenth century, had a strong influence over educational provision. So the 'masses' were not always as ignorant as is popularly supposed. Debussy's gifts were exceptional, but they were given fertile soil in which to take root, despite his early lack of formal education.

In this regard, an important influence was Aunt Clémentine. She ran a small dressmaking business, Maison Debussy, Couture, from her parents' house in Paris. She was of a different stamp from her sister, becoming the mistress of a wealthy Parisian financier, Paul Arosa. The pair became Achille's godparents when he was finally baptized at the age of two. On the baptismal register Clémentine, a devout churchgoer, signed herself Octavie de la Ferronière, a revealing mixture of judicious disguise, confident flamboyance and pretension. She would doubtless have hoped that Arosa's respectability and means would ensure some measure of security for her brother's first-born, which proved to be the case. Aunt Clémentine is a significant figure in Debussy's early background, embracingly feminine, affectionate, and tinged with the faint glamour of sexual adventure that lies just within the realms of respectability. Perhaps only Balzac's *Comédie humaine* could do full justice to her inimitable blend of compassion, easy morals and piousness.

By the mid-1860s her relationship with Arosa had ended and she was living in Cannes, even then a highly fashionable holiday resort. In June 1871, at the age of thirty-six, she respectably married the manager of a Cannes guest house, one Alfred Roustan, eleven years her junior. Achille and his mother visited Cannes several times during this period, and it seems that the boy was left with Clémentine long enough for him to begin piano lessons. He enjoyed picking out chords on the piano, and he would try to reproduce music he had heard, amusing himself on the instrument that graced Roustan's guest house. (An upright piano was a sign of respectability, reaching even into the artisan classes, in this golden age of domestic music-making.) Probably he sang too, for vocal mimicry was later to be one of the hallmarks of his exceptional youthful talent, along with his improvisations at the piano, and his outrageously unconventional chords – all delivered with such boisterous spirit that his friends and fellow students would be laughing and daring him further.

So it is in Cannes that the earliest flickers of Debussy as the future artist appear on the narrative screen. It was here that his sister recalled him spending 'entire days seated in a chair dreaming, about no one knew what'. The conventional picture of young genius discovering music at the piano now becomes that other familiar image of the artist as dreamer, in this case just eight years old, unconsciously absorbing the material that would later inform and mould his art. And these dreams of the child, immersed in a southern warmth and fragrance so different from Paris, are suddenly made vivid for us through the telescope of Debussy's own recollections some forty years later:

> *I remember the railway passing in front of the house and the sea on the distant horizon, which made me believe sometimes that the railway came out of the sea, or went into it (as you chose). Then, also, there was the road to Antibes, where there were so many roses that in all my life I've never seen so many at the same time – the perfume along that road never failed to be 'intoxicating'. I hope they've left the railway… and the roses.*

The sea, distance and space, abundant flowers and their perfume, and the surreal vision, peculiar to a child's perceptions – the imaginative world of Debussy's music is already foreshadowed. He even recalled 'a Norwegian carpenter who sang from morning to night'.

This is a rare glimpse of Debussy's childhood from his own account. Many other events he repressed. He never spoke of the events that so affected him when he was ten years old, apart from a remark he let slip in a letter of 1914, when the cataclysm of the First World War was just unfolding: 'As you know, I have no *sang froid*, and even less military spirit – never having had occasion to handle a gun – added to which my memories of '70 somewhat dampen my enthusiasm.' The reference to '70' here pertained to the Franco-Prussian war, which led to the siege of Paris in September of that year. The capital was cut off and encircled by 250,000 of Bismarck's soldiers, leading to the abject surrender of the French. But scarred on Debussy's memory would also have been the events that followed, culminating in his family's disaster the following spring, 1871. His father was nearly executed for treason.

With the two world wars of the twentieth century dominating our historical horizon, it is easy to forget the depth of humiliation France suffered in the previous century at the hands of Bismarck and what had just then become Germany. The armistice was signed in the Palace of Versailles, the symbol of the power and prestige of the once mighty Bourbon Kings. The reparations enforced by Bismarck were brutally harsh, among them the loss to France of the whole of Alsace and most of Lorraine, committing one-and-a-half million French to the rule of Germany, and a war indemnity of billions of francs, the like of which had never been demanded before. France was in no position to refuse, but for decades a desire for revenge – *revanche* – was a strong undercurrent in French politics as well as in the collective consciousness of the people. This is the background to Debussy's famed chauvinism and his barbed criticisms of German culture. His later rejection of Wagner (and Beethoven) was not entirely on aesthetic grounds.

But for the people of Paris the desire for revenge was first directed at their own country's leaders. When a new government attempted to restore normality after defeat, it only succeeded in leaving 150,000 Parisians bankrupt. After six months of war and siege the people were faced with penury and starvation, and the clamp-down on political opposition was angrily resented. The Parisian National Guard was suspected by the government of supporting the discontent. When, on 18 March, loyalist government soldiers were sent to confiscate the heavy armour in the Guard's possession (stored at the large gun park on the hill of Montmartre), they were surrounded by furious crowds and two generals were murdered. Revolt was ignited, formalized, and Paris declared itself an autonomous commune. The communards, believing history was on their side, were convinced that where Paris led the rest of the country would follow. This time, however, they were wrong.

Debussy's father, Manuel, had been working at a print works in the First Arrondissement, which placed him right at the centre of the political agitation. In the turmoil of the siege, businesses collapsed and the economy of Paris largely ground to a halt. Families withheld rent and pawned possessions, or else relied on the wages of those who joined the National Guard. Manuel joined up. He may well have got caught up in the subsequent events by accident, although equally revolution could have been in his blood. During the French Revolution of 1789 his grandfather, Pierre de Bussy, lived in Bellevue (today a suburb of Paris), one of the centres of the uprising. Pierre's son Claude-Alexandre – Manuel's father – then moved to Paris just at the time of the revolution of February 1848. Manuel, as a boy of twelve, would have seen the rioting and the barricaded streets around his home. Subsequently he became not only a witness to revolution but a participant. Though there is little doubt that he was wantonly incapable of providing for his family, and that he was an opportunist with dubious associations, from the official account of his part in the 1871 uprising there is evidence of some determination in his character and bravery in his actions.

When the fighting was imminent Manuel's revolutionary credentials were enough for him to be promoted to sub-lieutenant, then to captain. The archive report on the events which ensued reveals in meticulous detail Manuel's involvement. On 8 May 1871, at two o'clock in the morning, Captain de Bussy reported for duty at Issy as the head of his company. One hour later the batallion commandant, having been kicked by a horse, handed over command to Captain de Bussy, ordering him to attack the fort at Issy, occupied by troops loyal to the government. The captain led the attack, but his men proved less resolute, abandoning him as soon as the first shots came from the heavily armed fort. Manuel gave himself up and was immediately arrested. The Commune was defeated some two weeks later. Manuel escaped the firing squad and, sentenced to four years' imprisonment, ended up in the notoriously harsh Satory prison. His wife pleaded with the military authorities in an attempt to explain the extenuating circumstances: poverty, she said, had alone dictated his actions. He was released after a year's incarceration, stripped of his citizen's rights.

Even compared to the violence that was to follow in Europe in the next century, this moment of French history in the spring of 1871 was horrifying. The bloodshed was of a scale unmatched elsewhere in Europe during the nineteenth century: some 22,000 were killed by government troops, whose own losses were less than 1,000. Debussy remembered it, although quite what he experienced as a ten-year-old is difficult to say. He may have been sheltered in Cannes during the worst of the upheavals, but he would still have keenly felt the woes of his family And as a consequence of his father's imprisonment, the boy was again uprooted when his mother moved into a tiny flat in the rue Pigalle, as grim an area then as it is today. In 1875, on the steep hill of Montmartre just nearby, the first stone was laid of the Basilique du Sacré Coeur, endowed to atone

Opposite, La Barricade by Edouard Manet (1871). The Commune of that year, an attempt at setting up an alternative revolutionary government in Paris, was brutally suppressed. Debussy's father only just escaped execution

for one of the bloodiest events of French history. Its white walls and dome still dominate the north-west of Paris for miles around.

The piano lessons in Cannes, arranged by Aunt Clémentine, had provided an education of sorts for the boy – although Debussy later said that his teacher, an Italian named Cerruti (actually a violinist) 'noticed nothing remarkable'. But it was a fateful meeting of Manuel's that led to Debussy's musical advancement. Years later Debussy recalled the event, in that matter-of-fact way that one relates the tiny twists of fate whose effects are momentous. He regretted, he said, not having had a career that was distinct from his leisure activities. His interlocutor must have raised an incredulous eyebrow. 'I mean it,' Debussy protested, 'because then I wouldn't have had to live all the time with myself. It nearly happened. My father intended me for the sea. Then he met somebody… I don't know how it happened. "Ah! He can play that? Very good. But he must be taught music… etc." So my father then got the idea that I should study just music, he being someone who knew nothing about it.'

That 'somebody' was a café pianist and composer of popular songs by the name of Charles de Sivry. His mother was a piano teacher who was supposed to have been a pupil of Frédéric Chopin. It is significant that Debussy did not know how the meeting between the two men had come about: de Sivry had been arrested as a communard one month after Manuel. They were thrown together in the squalor of the Satory prison. De Sivry was pardoned in October 1871 (Manuel had to wait for another eight months) and on his release at once arranged for Achille to play to his mother. The good lady's Chopin connection was in fact as false as her aristocratic name – Madame Mauté de Fleurville – was spurious. Achille seemed destined to rub shoulders with mountebanks. Already there had been intimations of aristocratic heredity in his own family's arrangement of the name 'de Bussy', and Aunt Clémentine calling herself 'Octavie de la Ferronière'. Now he had a piano teacher who not only pretended to have been a pupil of Chopin, but who also claimed to have been married to one 'Marquis de Sivry' (in reality the son of a hatter); and whose first husband, she let it be known, had been a landowner (in fact the son of a grocer, who had owned little more than an allotment).

But it seems that Madame Mauté was not quite a charlatan, despite the evidence against her. In her defence is Achille's successful entry into the Conservatoire after barely a year's lessons with her. Could this rapid progress otherwise have been the result of piano lessons in Cannes, and the influence of Aunt Clémentine? Debussy later remembered Madame Mauté as 'a small fat lady who threw me into Bach and who played him as no one does nowadays, making him come alive', clearly implying that she was an inspiring teacher of some quality. And it was Debussy who remembered her as a pupil of Chopin. He had grown up believing it. In the household of the proud parents Victorine and Manuel, who had been encouraged to consider a career for their son as a virtuoso pianist, much would have made of the supposed Chopin connection.

Madame Mauté's son Charles called her 'a musician who was curious about all musical oddities', so it is likely that she took up the Debussy family as a cause. And Achille's lessons were free of charge. What a remarkable figure to have crossed his path: Antoinette-Flore Mauté de Fleurville, a woman with a harmlessly false history, philanthropic and motherly, and with the air of some faded, dotty aristocrat. Like Aunt Clémentine, the 'small fat lady' appears to have stepped straight out of the *Comédie humaine*.

In October 1872 Achille entered the Paris Conservatoire, his fees (as was the norm) paid for by the state. He was one of the youngest pupils, one of eight successful candidates for the piano class out of thirty-eight applicants. He had just turned ten years old, his father was newly out of prison. What bewilderment the boy must have felt in the sombre corridors of the venerated Conservatoire – yet another baffling change in a life already chronically unsettled. Fellow pupils later remarked on his intense shyness and unsociability. 'His clumsiness and awkwardness were extraordinary,' recalled Gabriel Pierné, later a fellow Prix de Rome laureate. It is not difficult to see why. In later life Debussy developed a certain feline charm, but his awkwardness remained.

From now on there was to be another pressure on him: parental expectations. Commentators have tended to disparage Manuel and Victorine's hopes for their first-born, as if dreams of fortune for one's offspring are somehow immoral in those who have no fortune them-selves. Debussy was very proud of the celebrity he finally achieved, not so much on his own behalf, but because he knew how much it meant to his parents.

In that autumn of 1872 the wheel of fortune appeared to be turning in their favour. Victorine's favourite son, now affectionately called

Chilo, was proving to be as exceptional as she had always felt him to be. Manuel's plight was lightening, and his incarceration seemed not to be a stigma on him, maybe quite the contrary – to have been a communard would have added to his swagger. Within a few months he had found a job as assistant bookkeeper at a factory in the rue Caumartin. In the spring Victorine was expecting her fifth child, and by the autumn of the following year, 1874, the family had moved to a flat in the nearby rue Clapeyron, where they were to stay for fourteen years. Some sort of stability had arrived. Yet it is probable that something died within Debussy's father in Satory prison, and that he was never the same man again. Manuel now stayed at home; he kept his job.

At the Conservatoire Chilo enrolled in the piano class of the venerable Antoine Marmontel, someone who really did know his Chopin, and who had heard the master's recitals. (Marmontel had once owned the famous portrait of Chopin by Delacroix, which now hangs in the Louvre.) Marmontel had been a brilliant pianist, but now at fifty-six his

An engraving from the mid-nineteenth century showing the entrance to the Paris Conservatoire, which Debussy attended for over a decade from 1872

reputation rested on his fine teaching and an intellect and depth of cultural experience that denoted the sage. From this point in Debussy's life there is no doubt as to the quality of teaching he received, and the influences that were brought to bear on his awakening imagination. Throughout Debussy's career at the Conservatoire, Marmontel was working on several books on pianists and pianism whose references to Chopin read uncannily like a commentary on the future art of Debussy:

If we draw a parallel between Chopin's sound effects and certain techniques of painting, we could say that this great virtuoso modulated sound much as skilled painters treat light and atmosphere. To envelop melodic phrases and ingenious arabesques in a half-tint which has something of both dream and reality: this is the pinnacle of art; and this was Chopin's art.

Portrait of Chopin by Eugène Delacroix (1838), once owned by Debussy's piano teacher Antoine Marmontel

It is clear that the seeds of what later became known as musical 'Impressionism' had a long gestation.

Alfredo Casella, who knew Debussy towards the end of his life, recalled the wonderful way in which he played Chopin, 'whose every secret he marvellously divined'. Debussy told him of his early lessons with 'a pupil of Chopin's… and he explained how considerable a part this instruction had played in his musical formation, not only as a pianist, but also as a creator.' This does not seem credible if it was only Madame Mauté he was referring to. It seems likely that Debussy's later recollections of his lessons with her became mixed up in his memory with advice from Marmontel. (This contention gains support from the recently published Paris Conservatoire records, which show that Debussy performed seven large-scale works of Chopin during his years with Marmontel – by far the majority composer in his studies – including the F minor Fantasy, the G minor Ballade, the Scherzo from the B minor Sonata and the first movement of the F minor Concerto.)

Marmontel spotted Debussy's exceptional qualities early on, noting in January 1874: 'Charming child, true artist's temperament; will become a distinguished musician; great future.' The epithet 'charming' comes as a surprise, when so many accounts speak of Achille's boorishness. Clearly the boy would lose his shyness in the presence of the patient and kindly Marmontel, who instinctively knew how to break through Achille's fierce defences. Here begins the pattern seen clearly throughout

Debussy's life: awkward unsociability gives way to charm and high spirits whenever friendship is established.

Chilo did not fulfil his early promise as a pianist, although Marmontel maintained his opinion of the child's artistry throughout all the setbacks. Despite a newspaper report of 'this budding Mozart' (when he was thirteen), the rigours of technique and preparation were not for him. His exceptional gifts for quick memorizing and reading at sight soon began to take the place of hard work. His energy and verve at the keyboard were noted by all who heard him, although even Marmontel had to admit he was often 'scatterbrained and inaccurate' *('étourdi', 'inexact')*. Fellow pupils in the class were frequently amused, occasionally shocked, by his bizarre playing. 'He seemed to be in a rage with the instrument,' recalled Gabriel Pierné, 'rushing up and down it with impulsive gestures and breathing noisily during the difficult bits.' But there were compensations: 'These faults gradually receded and occasionally he would obtain effects of an astonishing softness. With all its faults and virtues, his playing remained something highly individual.'

The career of a virtuoso was not at all suited to his temperament or his true talents. That 'rage with the instrument' sounds like revenge for enforced hours of practise at home and occasional slaps from his mother, as he ruefully remembered, to keep him up to the mark. (The piano at home was an old rosewood upright, 'with its keys covered in cigarette burns'.) His frustration would also have been directed at the constant rounds of public competitive examinations (complete with newspaper critics) that were a feature of French Conservatoire life, and still are today. Debussy was never to win a first prize for piano, although in 1875 he gained a 'First Certificate of Merit' for a performance of Chopin's G minor Ballade (he came fourth out of fourteen competitors), and two years later a Second Prize with the first movement of Schumann's G minor Sonata (fifth place out of twenty-one). While admirable achievements, these are hardly the signs of a future concert pianist. In the intervening year, 1876, came a significant failure with the first movement of Beethoven's last piano sonata, opus 111, an especially daunting challenge for a fourteen-year-old. This experience perhaps fuelled his famous antipathy towards Beethoven, subsequently the target for many barbed remarks in his journalism and public utterances.

Yet when he chose, and especially when not under the pressure of publicly assessed performance, Debussy could be an incomparable pianist. This was especially true later when he demonstrated his own scores at the piano, 'providing not only the illusion of an orchestra but an extraordinary impression of life and movement', recalled Raymond Bonheur, a fellow pupil who also noted the character of his singing voice, 'rich in emphasis and expression'.

So a budding pianist maybe, but what of the budding composer? In 1872 Achille also enrolled in the rudiments class of Albert Lavignac, a highly cultured young teacher who had just joined the staff of the Conservatoire. Lavignac taught Debussy the fundamentals of his craft: the boy began without any knowledge of basic rudiments, but was soon to carry off the third, second and finally the first annual prizes for *solfège*, a system of pitch recognition learned through musical dictation and sight-singing (and still the staple of music education in France). Lavignac was also a sympathetic mentor. He introduced Achille to what were to be two of the most important influences on his future development: the radical music dramas of Richard Wagner, at that period still frowned upon in conservative circles in Paris, and musical systems beyond Europe. He encouraged the use of modal scales – the ancient precursors of major and minor – and he was later to write extensively on the subject. Lavignac also wrote two books on Wagner, as well as the first book devoted specifically to the art of piano pedalling (another significant detail in the early life of the composer who was to write some of the most original piano music of the twentieth century).

From the beginning Lavignac found the young Debussy an excellent pupil, 'intelligent, a worker, and particularly well-organized musically'. But as his mastery of the subject developed, Achille began restlessly to resist the discipline imposed and to question the rules. Lavignac dutifully recorded his pupil's failure to follow correct procedures, noting that the fourteen-year-old was 'perfect in reading and dictation but still careless in theory, though he understands it perfectly'. Again that word *étourdi* – careless, feckless, scatterbrained – appears in the reports, although here Lavignac seems less exasperated than increasingly interested in the boy's originality.

There were similar battles in the harmony class of Émile Durand, as Paul Vidal recalled: 'He did not see eye to eye with [this] teacher in the sense that, instead of coming up with harmonic realizations which the latter was expecting, he always went one step further, inventing solutions that were ingenious, elegant and delightful but totally unacademic; and

Durand, who was a good teacher but rather inflexible, had harsh words
to say on the subject.' The harsh words were followed by angry pencil
marks on the boy's manuscript paper, followed by a period of silence
as Durand read the work through again, only to murmur, 'of course,
it's all utterly unorthodox, but still, very *ingenious*.' Durand's end-of-
year reports show that he admired Achille's gifts from the start, but
found him 'unsteady' *(léger)* and 'distressingly careless' *(d'une étourderie
désespérante)*. Interestingly he criticized his propensity for 'mischief'
(brouillon). But in 1880 he noted that 'this year his progress has been
very great'.

Achille won no prizes in Durand's classes, although he excelled in
the sight-reading component and in 'advanced practical harmony' –
harmony at the keyboard, score reading, polyphonic improvisation.
In 1879 he entered the accompaniment class of Auguste Bazille and
at the end of that academic year, approaching his eighteenth birthday,
he won the first prize. Once freed from the inhibiting discipline required
on manuscript paper, at the keyboard the boy's brilliance at sight-reading,
his natural feeling for improvisation and his perfect musical ear proved
his almost Mozartian facility. And as this was what he enjoyed doing,
he did it with a will. (Remarkably, had Debussy not won a prize that
year, 1880, he would have lost his place at the Conservatoire: the rules
stated that a student who had not won a prize or certificate after three
annual attempts would be removed from the rolls. Debussy won
nothing in 1878 and 1879.)

His first compositions date from around this time: Vidal recalls
hearing the songs *Madrid* and *Ballade à la lune*, two settings of Alfred
de Musset probably from 1879. The first survives as a fragment, the
second, if indeed it was ever written down, has been lost – clearly his
first compositions existed more in his head and fingers than as finished
objects. For Achille, coming to terms with the discipline of formal
composition was a slow process. But in 1879 he managed the Piano
Trio in G and he dedicated it, in triumph one feels, to his teacher
Durand. A year later came one of his most celebrated early songs,
Nuits d'étoiles (his first setting of Théodore de Banville), which in 1882
became his first published composition.

In 1880 Achille also briefly attended the organ class of César Franck,
although the old *maître*'s repeated exhortation of 'modulate, modulate'
soon came up against the now familiar refusal of this self-willed student

to be led where he had no desire to go. 'But why should I modulate,' he is reported to have said, 'when I'm quite happy with the key I'm in?' Coming from the composer who was to alter the course of western music, this might be taken for a profound comment; but it could equally have been the remark of an imbecile. Few, however, would have viewed the young Achille as that.

The rebellious youngster besting his academic elders, the anarchic pupil delighting his friends with brilliant pranks, the misfit who refuses to be tied down by rules – these are all stereotypes of young genius, but to what extent do such anecdotes present the true picture of the developing composer? Other examples abound, such as Raymond Bonheur's recollection of a four-part harmony exercise set for the class by a newly fledged composer (and Prix de Rome winner) who was standing in for Durand. Faced with Achille, 'he was so disconcerted by the charming spontaneity of the young beginner's solution that, in a rare and elegant gesture, he took his own realization and tore it up in front of us.' This episode was to be neatly mirrored during the period in which Debussy was himself preparing for the Prix de Rome in 1884: Achille as stand-in teacher mesmerized the other students with audacious harmonies, and 'chromatic groanings in imitation of the buses going down the Faubourg Poissonnière'. The lesson was brought to an abrupt end by the Conservatoire supervisor. 'Debussy was a dangerous "fanatic" and we were ordered to be off,' recalled his fellow student Maurice Emmanuel.

Debussy's own recollections, however, were more sober:

[The Conservatoire] wasn't the best time of my life, but it was no more disagreeable for me than for anyone else… The teaching of harmony seems to me quite misguided. I can assure you I did nothing very remarkable in the harmony class. It was the custom of my time for the professors to teach their students by a useless little game that consisted of trying to discover the secrets of a particular composer's harmony. I humbly must confess that I could never discover them and it wasn't hard to console myself.

He admitted that most of the time he worked by the rules in order to get by, while contriving to do exactly as he wanted. 'But don't imagine for a second that I ever said anything of this. I kept it to myself. Until the time when I could give proof of my ideas, it didn't worry me not speaking about them.'

The authentic, and arrogant, revolutionary stands revealed by these words. Manuel should have been proud of his son, instead of lamenting his fall from grace as a pianist. Achille was biding his time, content to undermine quietly from the inside. Despite our wish to see him as the archetypal outsider, few could have been more on the inside than he. In finally winning the Prix de Rome, some four years in the future, he was to achieve one of the highest awards the French establishment had to offer.

3

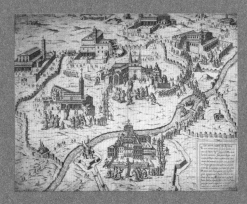

A pictorial map of Rome
towards the end of the
nineteenth century. Debussy
professed frustration and
misery during his two-year
stay in the city, contriving
various escapades back
to Paris

*'I've had enough of the Eternal City… Enough
of music and this endless countryside. I want
to see some Manet and hear some Offenbach!'*

Claude Debussy

The Path to Rome and Back 1880-7

The path to Rome was not exactly arduous. Debussy had all the facility and when he really decided to apply himself he knew what was needed and how to produce it. At the end of 1880 he entered the composition class of Ernest Guiraud, a close friend of Georges Bizet and Marmontel. In some respects Guiraud was the 'wrong' teacher for Achille: Guiraud was a realtively unknown quantity, new to the post, while it was the much-lauded operatic composer Jules Massenet who had all the star pupils. But then the young Debussy was not especially highly rated.

Guiraud's ensuing reports praise his student's intelligence, although he also remarks on his 'bizarre' character and his 'unstable nature', observing at one point that he 'writes music badly'. Debussy was such an original, so possessed of self-knowledge and capable of self-education, that it is questionable what influence the affable Guiraud had on his development as a composer. But over the years leading to the competition in 1884, and beyond, right up to Guiraud's death in 1892, master and pupil became close friends. Bizet said of Guiraud: 'He is so nice, so friendly, but in his approach to life, to playing, to music he is a little soft, a little apathetic. I am trying to liven him up a bit.' No doubt the young Achille also enlivened him. In return Guiraud provided him with the space to find his own way, as well as a friendly, if bemused, ear for his strange ideas.

It was Guiraud who minimized the radical nature of his pupil's offerings to the Rome competition ('he needs to be bridled,' he noted in January 1882). Achille was experimenting, often clumsily but with persistence, with loosening traditional tonal relationships, with flouting the entrenched rules governing which notes or chords should follow which. Even today students are taught that traditional four-part harmony has to avoid the intervals of fifths and octaves moving in parallel from one chord to the next: in strict harmonic practice it is considered dissonant. Achille loved disobeying this rule, not for the sake of disobedience but because he liked the sound that resulted: 'pleasure is the law' he once proclaimed, in defence of his unorthodox procedures. (Parallel harmony, in triadic and multi-part chords, was to remain a hallmark of Debussy's style throughout his life.)

Another of his experiments was with modal scales, imbibed from his earlier teacher Lavignac, which provided him with a means of organizing tonal relationships in a new way. The intervals present in a modal scale differ from those of traditional major and minor, so the chords that can be built from them also differ. The result, a marked characteristic of Debussy's sound world, is that, because the expected harmonic procedures do not occur, a listener's sense of harmonic logic, and hence stability, is undermined. Our sense of time is also affected: in traditional harmony time is partly structured by alterations of harmonic tension and release, of dissonance resolving into consonance, implying forward momentum and arrival. At the root of a listener's awareness of structure – of the way in which we sense music as form and architecture – is a perception of key, the stable centre around which everything revolves. In the traditional tonal language of western music, which had served composers for over two hundred years and whose rules and procedures were the staple of Debussy's conservatoire teaching, the key of a work provided an unassailable gravitational pull. Debussy challenged this force – his weakening of the key centre, the abandonment of which was to be a characteristic of twentieth-century classical music, was one of his achievements and legacies. He sensed early on that, by so weakening it, a hitherto unexplored expressivity could be harnessed, a sound world of floating harmonies and what he later called 'rhythmicized time' – that is, the division of time into freer, more malleable units than those allowed by the laws of periodic phrasing (often in four-bar structures) governed by traditional harmony. He wanted to create, he said later, music 'whose form was so free it would sound improvised.'

Modality, of course, is not the only way in which tonality can be undermined. Later Debussy explored whole-tone and pentatonic scales, an influence from Eastern music, and even the octatonic scale. A preponderance of chromatic harmony can have the same undermining effect, harmony in which dissonant notes are allowed to remain unresolved within the principal tonality. The Wagnerian manner, which had so crucial an influence on Debussy in the 1880s–90s, created a density of chromatic harmony in which resolution of dissonance was delayed: the rule whereby a dissonant note finally had to resolve, or 'correct' itself, became part of a drawn-out procedure in which the chord of resolution would itself set up a new dissonance: one unresolved harmony would resolve into another unresolved harmony, and so on. Debussy worked in this way, but it did not satisfy him for long. His achievement was to explore Wagner's methods and then carve out a distinctly different path. Not only did his music escape the gravitational pull of a key centre, it escaped too from the immense pull of Wagner.

John Clevenger has shown that the three compositions Debussy worked on over the three successive years in which he attempted the Prix de Rome – from 1882 to 1884 – display a progressive 'stylistic regression' as the young composer deliberately curbed his radical instincts. That this *was* deliberate is borne out by a story related by Debussy's close friend Louis Laloy in his biography of 1909. In the early 1880s Debussy was working on a musical setting of Banville's play *Diane au Bois*, and he took the work, with some pride, to Guiraud's class. After reading through the score, Guiraud prounced it 'all very interesting' but advised him to 'keep it for later, or you will never win the Prix de Rome'. In fact Debussy did turn again to *Diane*, while in Rome, and the fragments that remain show the work to be one of his most important and radical early experiments. The writing is confidently chromatic, characterized by the composer's beloved parallel harmonies (now in dissonant sevenths) and a constantly fluctuating tonal centre: throughout the twenty-nine pages of manuscript (for two solo voices, and piano accompaniment with suggested orchestration) the key rarely settles for long. This enabled Debussy to capture the fleeting pastoral dream of Banville's play, a combination, as Edward Lockspeiser has pointed out, of an Antoine Watteau landscape painting and the Forest of Arden from Shakespeare's *As You Like It*. Elements of his later masterpiece *Prélude à l'après-midi d'un faune* are also foretold, especially in the 'dreamy and passionate song of Eros' (Debussy's own stage direction for Diane), intended for a flute 'to which distant horns reply, almost muted' – this is virtually what occurs at the opening of the *Faune*.

The surviving fragments of Debussy's practice cantata for the 1882 competition, *Daniel*, are mostly weak and formulaic, although, as Clevenger observes, they display telling traces of Wagner. (Students would work during the year on practice material suitable for the competition, on which they would be judged for eligibility – in the event Debussy was not admitted to the first round of the Prize in 1882.) Significantly, in Debussy's winning cantata *L'Enfant prodigue* of 1884,

La Fête d'amour by Antoine Watteau (c. 1717). There was a revival of interest in Watteau's paintings in nineteenth-century France, especially apparent in the work of two of Debussy's favoured poets, Verlaine and Banville, as well as in Debussy's music. As a student, Debussy attempted a setting of Banville's play *Diane au Bois,* which inhabits a Watteau-like pastoral world

Wagner's influence is mostly banished, replaced by flattering references to the style of Massenet. The operas of Massenet, of pervasive melodic sensuousness, had an immense popularity and influence during Debussy's time at the Conservatoire. Wagner, on the other hand, was considered in French academic circles as a potently destructive force, as the destroyer of tradition. His music dramas (the term he coined to express the originality of his concept and its affinity with the epic scale of Greek theatre) not only obscured the sacred boundaries of recitative and aria, but gave previously unheard-of emphasis to dramatic meaning, to the mythical significance of narrative, undermining the traditional principal that music should be the sole *raison d'être* of opera. It was not only Wagner's chromatic harmonies which caused offence.

The hostile attitude to Wagner in France at this period (to be replaced within a decade by a reverence akin to mania) was largely based on pique

and chauvinism: Wagner after all was a German, a country of which
France had recent dire memories. French composers would also have
been aware of Wagner's arrogant attitude to the music of other countries
(he had called French opera 'a coquette with a cold smile') and his view
of his own as 'the music of the future'. French academia was also suspi-
cious of the pervasive employment of 'leitmotif' in Wagner's operas,
the ubiquitous recurrence of themes and melodic fragments associated
not only with characters and objects on stage, but even more audaciously
with the ideas and concepts being enacted. Here was music, it was said,
being yoked into the service of what should alone be the province of
spoken theatre, music as symbolism, divorced from purely 'musical' laws.

The young Debussy eagerly seized on whatever he could find of
Wagner's music, and just as eagerly discussed it with his friends and
teachers. Although years later he was to denigrate the Wagnerian leitmotif as a mere 'visiting card', a trifle whose only object was to proclaim the
master's presence, he was one of the first to discern, even as a student, the
leitmotif's deep significance for the nature of operatic expression. (He
was to use the device extensively in his own opera, *Pelléas et Mélisande*,
over a decade later.) Through the subtlest transformations at each occur-
rence, or even simply by the recurrence itself, the leitmotif could bind
music and drama in an ever closer unity. Repetition, hitherto at the service of purely musical structures, now takes on a role that guides narrative
and psychological meaning. The very fabric of the musical composition – the web-like accumulation and complex layering of leitmotifs –
becomes the embodiment of the multiple significances of the text.

Clevenger suggests it might have been the presence of leitmotifs and
the blurring of sectional breaks in Achille's Prix de Rome cantata for 1883,
Le Gladiateur, that pushed him into second place behind Paul Vidal.
However, it was recognized he had made a great leap forward from the
previous year and he was given due recognition. The panel praised his
'generous musical nature' and noted the work's 'gripping dramatic
accents' – but also described his nature as 'ardent to the point of intemperance'. (Doubtless the emotional intemperance of Wagner's music
was much discussed too, another aspect of the German master's work
that was viewed with deep suspicion.) A press reviewer more discerningly
observed that Debussy was 'less expert than Vidal in the technique of
his art,' but seemed to have 'a more original personality.' Achille would
have been more than content with this appraisal. The moral victory was

his – indeed the same reviewer went on to note that 'Debussy's scene was worthy in all respects of the supreme recompense'.

By the following year, 1884, Achille was loath to enter for the prize at all. When he finally won it he even tried to give it up. The supposed rebel assumed the pose of dignified artistic independence, claiming that the minimum two-year's residency at the Villa Medici in Rome, alongside all the other laureates (in poetry and painting as well as music), would simply stifle him. In fact there was another reason, less to do with artistic genius, which was stopping him concentrating on the task in hand. He was besotted with a married woman, some fourteen years his senior, and he could think of little else. Leaving Paris for Rome would mean giving up the gratifications supplied by Madame Marie-Blanche Vasnier, with whom the young Debussy had been having an affair for some time.

His transformation from adolescent to young man had been as sudden as it had been profound. Like most adolescents, he had desperately wanted to grow up. He looked younger than his years, despite his swarthy looks, and at sixteen, at the end of his first year in Durand's harmony and accompaniment class, he was still in short trousers. The family on the rue Clapeyron had little money to spare for new clothes, and this could not have helped the boy's social awkwardness. He would often arrive for classes late and out of breath from running, bringing with him echoes of an unsettled home life. At home he had to contend with an errant younger brother, Emmanuel, who was backward at school and seemed frequently to end up at the police station. And in 1877 another brother, not yet four years old, died of meningitis. Sister Adèle and another brother Alfred, both being brought up by Aunt Clémentine in Cannes, were fortunate not to be involved.

The shrewd Marmontel alleviated some of these difficulties. He found his pupil comfortable summer jobs as pianist to the rich, firstly at the magnificent chateau of Madame Marguerite Wilson-Pelouze, mistress of the President of the French Republic, and then for Madame Nadezhda von Meck, the intimate correspondent and confidante of Pyotr Ilyich Tchaikovsky. In the employ of these formidable *grandes dames*, the one an alluring socialite (and active Wagner enthusiast), the other a forbidding recluse, Achille was introduced to wealth and high society beyond his family's dreams.

Madame von Meck took Achille on the European grand tour, and for three summers some of the leading cultural centres of Europe became

Opposite, Debussy (seated
right) in the summer of
1880 during his travels with
Nadezhda von Meck. He
is with the members of
his piano trio, with whom
he played his Trio in G

his playground. He played his Piano Trio for her, and she duly tried to interest Tchaikovsky in it, along with the boy's piano piece *Danse bohémienne* ('nice… but the form is bungled', was the master's comment). He also wrote a 'symphony' for Russian approval (never orchestrated and later published for piano duet), and arranged several pieces of Tchaikovsky's *Swan Lake* for piano. In Rome, the von Meck entourage passed by the Villa Medici. 'This is your future home,' he was told. He was not over-impressed. One might indeed question the extent of the artistic influences gained on these travels. Debussy's essential formation was to come later, all in a rush. He quickly developed an assured inner self that enabled him to pick his influences with acute discrimination. This was already becoming apparent to his teachers and friends at the Conservatoire. Later he was to find nearly all he needed for his artistic development in the cultural milieu of Paris, among the avant garde.

A photograph taken of Achille during the first of these summers shows his boyish looks. 'He says he's twenty, but he looks sixteen,' Madame von Meck wrote to Tchaikovsky (in fact, he was barely eighteen). His eyes gaze fiercely into the distance, already bearing the stamp that was to be so remarkable later on. The hand resting on his knee seems large and touchingly expressive, characteristics borne out by many later photographs: he has noticeably forthright hands, which match the forthright eyes. As was remarked at this time, on a first meeting 'you felt that here was a personality'.

The von Meck family loved having him, and he loved them in return. 'The little Frenchman arrived, dark, thin, sarcastic, and gave everyone amusing nicknames,' recalled one of Madame von Meck's sons; and to Tchaikovsky, at the end of the first summer, Madame von Meck wrote: 'Imagine, this boy wept bitter tears when he left'. Of his third visit in 1882 she leaves us this image of the composer when he really was a twenty-year-old:

> *Yesterday, to my great joy, Achille Debussy arrived. Now I shall gorge myself listening to music and he will bring the whole house to life. He's a Parisian to his fingertips, a real* gamin de Paris [a lad], *as witty as they come and a brilliant mimic. He takes off Gounod and Ambroise Thomas* [the director of the Paris Conservatoire] *perfectly, he makes you die laughing. He has a good nature; everything pleases him and he affords us infinite amusement. In short, a charming boy.*

By now, however, Debussy was not quite the 'boy' she imagined. He had already met Marie-Blanche Vasnier, unquestionably the most crucial influence on his development during his preparation for the Prix de Rome, and beyond. When he first met her he was eighteen; Marie was thirty-two and had been married for fifteen years. Of immense consequence to Debussy was the fact that she was an amateur singer with a radiantly high voice. Of no less significance was her sexual allure. One only has to look at the pastel portrait of her by the fashionable Jacques-Émile Blanche (a painter who was part of Debussy's circle) to see how she was regarded.

The work arrests our attention with the hauteur of the pose, and a challenging sexuality. But Blanche was highly adept at flattery – it was after all an important part of his trade – and he shows himself fully aware of how the lady herself would like to be regarded. It is a brilliant portrait, the striking red of the lips and the gleaming blue of the sitter's eyes highlighted by the prevailing black of the costume and head-dress. Blanche suggests a tinge of decadence, a style very much à la mode. He personally considered it to be one of the most successful of his works, 'characteristic of the aesthetic woman, rather *Fleurs du mal,* rather Symbolist.'

Madame Vasnier first met Debussy some time in early 1881 when he became the accompanist of a singing class to which she belonged. The class took place twice weekly in the rue Royale, in the heart of the wealthy and fashionable quarter of Paris around the Place de la Concorde and the Opéra. Achille's acquaintance with the *haut monde* was becoming a habit.

Youthful, unpolished no doubt – but Achille would also have shown evidence of unusual sensitivity and inner refinement to those society ladies in the rue Royale with the intelligence to notice. 'He seemed rather withdrawn and distant,' recalled Raymond Bonheur, 'with a marked predilection for everything that was rare and precious. But he was a singularly attractive person none the less.' Refinement is also the hallmark of his manuscripts of this time: the calligraphy of *Caprice*, for example, a song from 1880 which he later dedicated to Madame Vasnier, is exquisitely done, with a confident freedom and elegance that does not at all seem naïve or youthful. And there is taste and discernment in his choice of poets for his songs, especially Banville, whose poetry is rich in musical nuance as well as bold in sexual imagery. 'Debussy and I

Madame Marie-Blanche Vasnier, with whom Debussy had an affair in the 1880s. This pastel portrait is by Jacques-Émile Blanche (1888)

The autograph manuscript of Debussy's song *Caprice*, written in 1880 and later dedicated to Marie-Blanche Vasnier. The text is by Théodore de Banville

became friends through a volume of Banville I found in his hands,' wrote Bonheur, 'a rather surprising discovery in that milieu.' Madame Vasnier, too, would certainly have noticed.

Marie-Blanche Vasnier was the wife of a man eleven years her senior whom she had married at seventeen, and with whom she had three children. Her first-born died at the age of two, and when she became part of Debussy's narrative her surviving children were aged ten and twelve. So she would have been a mother within a year of her marriage, and bereaved by the time she was twenty. Her husband, Henri Vasnier, was a civil servant, politically left-wing, with a wide interest in the arts, archaeology and Hellenic history. He was a decent and cultured man, if unfortunately uninspiring when compared to a young artist of genius. Marcel Dietschy sums up Vasnier as 'cold, secretive, an obsessive worker, a teetotaller', unfairly condemning the man who showed great generosity to the young composer, and who took a keen interest in his artistic development. Vasnier supported and advised his wife's protégé for more than five years, apparently without being aware of their liaison, unless his liberal leanings led him to turn a blind eye.

Achille became a daily visitor to the Vasniers' house in rue Constantinople, a short walk from his parents' flat in rue Clapeyron. At the beginning, with her husband's backing, Madame took up this unusual student as a project needing support. Space was provided for him to work, and most evenings he would compose, either walking around the room singing to himself, or improvising at length at the piano. His first compositions were almost all songs – from 1880 to the early months of 1884 he wrote over forty, thirteen of which were settings of Banville, five of Verlaine and six of Paul Bourget. The songs are mostly in the melodious French operatic style of Massenet and Charles Gounod, effusively expressive, and showing little sign of the originality to come. This is less true of his settings from 1882 of Verlaine, a poet who was then little known, and whose poems were probably introduced to Debussy by the Vasniers. Debussy set, and dedicated to Marie, five of Verlaine's *Fêtes galantes* (now known as *Fêtes galantes pour Marie Vasnier*, to distinguish them from later settings of the same poems). Clearly the greater the poet, the more the young composer exercised his musical imagination. These songs, especially the lively *Fantoches*, are worthy predecessors of the great later Verlaine settings – indeed with only a little revision *Fantoches* became the middle song of the masterly *Fêtes galantes* of 1891. It is worth mentioning here too the Mallarmé setting of 1884, *Apparition* – one of Mallarmé's earliest poems from 1863, written when the poet was twenty-two – which shows similar signs of originality. The confidence of the setting is striking, the manner in which the changing harmonies shadow the characteristic dream imagery, as well as the passion, of Mallarmé's text – here are the unmistakable accents of a new voice. As in *Diane au Bois*, Debussy succeeds in finding a musical language – harmonies, textures, melodic shape – that embodies the meaning and the atmosphere of the poem. Just such an instinct for the conjunction of poetry and music was rapidly becoming one of the hallmarks of his developing genius.

Marguerite Vasnier, Marie's daughter – just eleven when Achille's visits started – recalled him composing with 'his eternal cigarette in his mouth or rolling tobacco and papers in his fingers. Then when he'd found the idea he'd write it down. He never crossed out a great deal, but he searched a long time in his head before writing anything down and was highly critical of his own work.' Her memoir, written over forty years after the event, gives us a detailed insight into the Debussy of the early 1880s:

> *At eighteen Debussy was a large beardless boy with clearly defined*
> *features, with thick, black, curly hair which he wore plastered down over*
> *his forehead. But when, at the end of the day, his hair became unruly*
> *(which suited him much better) he was, my parents said, the image of*
> *a Florentine from the Middle Ages. It was a very interesting face; the*
> *eyes especially attracted your attention; you felt that here was a personality.*
> *His hands were strong and bony, with square fingers; his touch on the*
> *piano was sonorous, rather percussive but also sometimes very gentle*
> *and cantabile.*

Achille was sensitive about his abnormally protuberant forehead, and in his early manhood he took pains to conceal what later so startled all who first met him.

The progress towards intimacy with Marie Vasnier seems to have been rapid. This apparently unpolished youth was soon writing songs for a woman fourteen years older than himself, inscribing them with extravagant and flattering dedications. On the manuscript of *Caprice*, for example, one of a group of songs he dedicated to her which were actually written before he met her, he added the words: 'To Madame Vasnier – These songs somehow conceived in your memory can belong only to you as does the author.' It is difficult to date this dedication precisely, but the gift would most likely have been offered in 1881 or 1882 at the latest. Did he really belong to her by this time? The title page of *Caprice* contains the suggestive inscription: 'Poetry by xxx very unknown/Music by xxx less unknown. Composed in the year 1880.' The Banville poem he set is even bolder in its implications: 'When, pale with fever, I kiss your lips from which a song springs forth / You avert your eyes, your lips remain as cold as ice, / And thrusting me from your arms you say I do not love you.'

By 1882 the two were performing concerts together in public: on 12 May of that year at the Salons Flaxland, Madame Vasnier, accompanied by 'Mr Achille de Bussy', presented two of the latter's newly composed settings of Banville, *Les Roses* and *Fête galante*. ('It appears that he had the idea of calling himself Ach. de Bussy,' writes Marguerite, 'but this little exercise in vanity could not have lasted with someone of his mocking habits.') Six years later he still liked *Fête galante* enough to recast it as the Menuet in *Petite Suite* for piano duet. Out of some forty songs of these early years, nearly thirty were dedicated to Marie Vasnier. When Achille, under protest, left Paris for Rome in 1885 he inscribed a manuscript collection of songs to her – simply entitled *Chansons*, now known as the 'Vasnier Song Book' – containing twelve solo songs and one duet, *Chanson Espagnole*, which they had sung together.

Marguerite's reminiscences, albeit entitled 'Debussy at eighteen', refer mostly to the year immediately prior to the Prix de Rome of June 1884, when Achille was twenty-one – that is, when his relationship with Marie was fully established. Marguerite recalls his daily summer visits to her parents' country home south west of the city at Ville d'Avray:

> *He used to work long hours, but sometimes we went for long walks…*
> *or played interminable games of croquet. He was very good at it, but a*
> *bad loser. Out in the countryside he would sometimes become as carefree*
> *and cheerful as a child. For our walks in the woods he refused to wear*
> *a straw hat, preferring a large, blue, felt one which he wore to one side;*
> *one day, as the eternal cigarette had singed the rim slightly, someone*
> *covered up the hole by sewing a piece of blue velvet over it, and this sent*
> *him into ecstasies. Sometimes he would turn his stick into a guitar and*
> *pretend to be a Florentine singer, improvising ditties or serenades, or*
> *parodying Italian music, which he didn't care for. One day some street*
> *singers stopped in front of the house. He started by accompanying them*
> *on the piano, and with his voice, and then invited them in and made*
> *them play, adding a line in patter which had us all rocking with laughter.*
> *He had moments of extreme gaiety like that, but these would be followed*
> *by hours of gloom and discouragement.*

What the young girl would not have realized is that Debussy's alternating gaiety and gloom would have been the outer signs of the composer's developing intimacy with her mother. The moods and behaviour she describes bear all the hallmarks of fulfilled, as well as thwarted, sexual desire, of euphoria laced with frustration and jealousy when others succeeded in drawing Marie's attention away. 'He was unsociable, and did not disguise his discontent when my parents entertained,' wrote

Salons de MM. FLAXLAND et Fils, Facteurs de Pianos

40, Rue des Mathurins

SOIRÉE MUSICALE

donnée par le Violoniste

MAURICE THIEBERG

Avec le gracieux concours de

Mme VASNIER et de Mr ACHILLE de BUSSY

Vendredi 12 Mai 1882, à 8 heures 1/2 très-précises

PROGRAMME :

1. A. Allegro de la Sonate, Mi bemol majeur... BEETHOVEN
   B. Pensées fugitives, pour Piano et Violon... St-HELLER & H. W. ERNST
   Andante con Variazoni et Intermezzo (Presto) par
   MM. de BUSSY et THIEBERG.
2. Air d'Actéon .... AUBER
   Chanté par Mme VASNIE
3. Concerto en Mi majeur........................... VIEUXTEMPS
   Adagio et Rondo, par M. THIEBERG.
4. A. Nocturno, }
   B. Scherzo,   } pour Piano et Violon............ Ach. de BUSSY
   par l'auteur et M. THIEBERG.
5. A. Adagio du Concerto Militare .... LIPINSKI
   B. Polonaise brillante................... WIENIAWSKI
   par M. THIEBERG.
6. A. Fête galante ....
   B. Les Roses................................ } Ach. de BUSSY
   Chanté par Mme VASNIE
7. A. Berçeuse.................................... REBER
   B. Rhapsodie Hongroise..................... MISKA HAUSER
   par M. THIEBERG.

Prix du Billet : 6 francs

On trouve des Billets chez MM. DURAND et SCHONWERK, place de la
Madeleine 12, et à la Maison FLAXLAND.

Marguerite. 'He usually refused to meet strangers and this meant he could
not come to the house. If by chance he did meet them, and they were
lucky enough to find favour in his eyes, he could be charming, playing
and singing Wagner, imitating and caricaturing some modern composer.'

It was the Vasniers who most encouraged and cajoled Achille into
applying himself in earnest to the Prix de Rome. He was the last to sign
up for the competition in 1884, and had been almost as late the year
before. In 1883 he nearly opted out of the final round altogether, but

Paul Vidal persuaded him to continue that year, and indirectly smoothed his path for the next year's competition. When Vidal won the first prize himself, in 1883, and so had to leave for the Villa Medici, he recommended that his friend take his place as accompanist of La Concordia, a choral society whose president was Gounod. This prestigious old man, on his weekly visits to the rehearsals, got to know the young Debussy well. 'Gounod appreciated Debussy's extraordinary gifts,' recalled Vidal, 'and did not hesitate to proclaim that he was a "genius".' What is more, in his influential role at the Académie des Beaux-Arts, Gounod backed Debussy forcibly for the Prix de Rome.

The conditions of the annual competition were gruelling. For the first round students were shut away, literally, for six days, required to bring their own work-tables and chairs, beds and chamber pots, and to compose without the aid of a piano a four-part fugue and a choral work with orchestra. It seems at first remarkable that Debussy got through this round twice, for his record in the fugue examinations at the Conservatoire had been dismal. His fear of imposed deadlines (which was to dog him all his life), as well as churlishness in the face of academic discipline in general, may have led to deliberate failure, a form of protest. But although fugues held little interest for him, he could produce one when he wished. He could not have passed through the first round of the Prix de Rome otherwise.

The second round, with no more than six contenders, involved isolation for twenty-five days, access to a piano, and the composition of a cantata to an original libretto. The cantata had to be orchestrated and had to include two or three characters, solos, duets and ensembles, complete with linking recitatives. 'The very idea of being shut up for weeks on end filled him with horror,' recalled Marguerite Vasnier of the 1883 competition. 'The contenders received their parents and friends in a courtyard in the garden [of the Conservatoire], where we stayed as long as possible in order to comfort him. He pointed to the window of his room and, when I asked him why there were bars across it, replied: "No doubt because they think we're wild beasts."' Debussy would have needed considerable persuading to put himself through this a second time.

Ten days' grace was allowed for rehearsals before the first performance of each of the works, which was to be in a piano reduction for four hands, with singers. This acted as a dress rehearsal and was held at the Conservatoire. The final judgement was made the following day before the grand jury, press and public, in the hallowed hall of the Institut de France. On 27 June 1884 Debussy's *L'Enfant prodigue* was given its first performance. The next day some of his friends, including Maurice Emmanuel who tells this story, wheedled their way into the Institut, where they sat back, in delighted anticipation, to await the revolutionary score from the Conservatoire's *enfant terrible*.

> *When Claude-Achille's turn came, and the air was filled with the opening chords of* L'Enfant prodigue, *we exchanged delighted glances. But these soon faded. Instead of the scandal we were counting on, and despite occasional signs of agitation from one or two elderly conductors who looked surprised and inclined to protest, compared with the outrageous harmonies Debussy had [previously] served up to us, Claude-Achille's cantata struck us as debonair!… We felt seriously let down that the expected brouhaha had not materialized.*

Their hero's politically correct tribute to Massenet and Gounod won him first prize. His facility rather than his originality won the day, along with his willpower and capacity for endurance, his extraordinary gifts for mimicry and pastiche, and his faultless ear. Yet the opening of *L'Enfant prodigue* is especially ravishing, and the score has many points at which the signs are positively Debussyan: the lazy triplet accompaniments, the floating textures, the sensuality of the sonorities, and at times a confident modal harmony. But if the 21-year-old's brilliant talent was on display, his truly personal language had barely evolved, and no one knew this better than he did. As he admitted later, he was content to keep himself to himself until he could give proper 'proof of his ideas'.

The jury noted a 'very marked poetic sense, brilliant and warm colouring, animated and dramatic music.' In a further example of discerning press criticism (proving perhaps that critical opinion was never as wholly deaf and blind in this period as posterity has liked to assume), one critic observed that 'by making, so to speak, an abstraction of the poetry that was offered to him, he has dared to depict the colour of the poetry.' This was a highly up-to-date judgement – the Symbolist movement and its obsession with the unity of poetry, painting and music, was only just stirring – and a remarkably prophetic one considering the path Debussy was to follow. Another straw in the wind came from a reviewer who criticized the cantata for 'defects that characterize the style of dreamers in music,' noting that such defects arose from tonal and formal disorder. It would seem that Achille's radical musical experiments were not all hidden from view.

For Debussy's delighted parents, whose plans for virtuoso stardom for their pianist son had been thwarted, the prize was compensation enough. There is no doubt that he too had felt the prick of ambition. But now the future home that had flatteringly beckoned when he was last in Rome with the von Mecks was to become a reality. When he first learnt that he had won, as he stood contemplating the river Seine that summer's day on the Pont des Arts, he was filled with dread. As he later claimed, he felt he was 'no longer free'. But he had not been free anyway; he was enslaved to Marie Vasnier.

Paul Vidal, for one, knew the truth of it; he was party to many of the duplicities necessitated by Achille's affair. A letter he wrote a few weeks after the competition reveals how long the affair had been going on:

So our friend Achille has won the prize despite himself! This sinister tale of adultery has been played out over a long period. Last year I had to persuade him to compete in the final round, against his wishes. Then during the winter he told me he wouldn't leave for Rome even if he won, that he was prevented from doing so… Another time his mother accused me of being an accomplice in the affair; he'd used me as an excuse for a whole heap of escapades and I had a job restoring her confidence in me. The tears I saw her shedding because of her son's misbehaviour are not designed to make me side with him when he turns on the charm. Everything you have seen me do for him, I have done for his mother, who is an excellent woman and treats me like a son. I don't know whether anyone will manage to overcome his egoism. He's incapable of any sacrifice. Nothing has any hold over him. His parents aren't rich, but instead of using the money from his teaching to support them, he buys new books for himself, knick-knacks, etchings, etc. His mother has shown me drawers full of them… His succubus is battening on to all his little weaknesses. She's pretty and much pursued by admirers, which pleases her jealous vanity; it appears she's a talented singer (I haven't heard her) and sings his songs extremely well; everything he writes is for her and owes its existence to her… I am sorry to have got mixed up in it all, and not to have let things take their course. His moral sense is undeveloped, he's

Opposite, The first surviving letter by Debussy, dated 30 November 1883. It is a hasty missive to Henrietta Fuchs, the organizer of the choir where he was, erratically, the piano accompanist: 'Family matters obliged me to leave town. I only found your note today; the same matters mean I have to go away again, but I should return tomorrow morning. Allow me, Madame, to take the blame for having arranged things so badly. Once more a thousand pardons…'

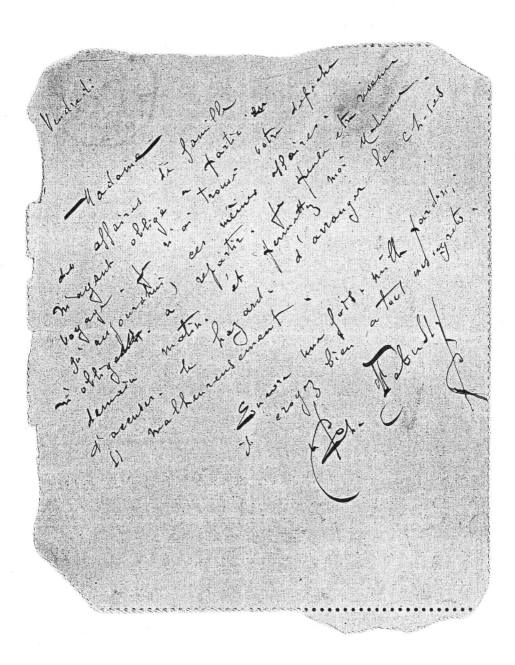

*nothing but a sensualist. I've acted like an imbecile. But, with all that he
has such talent and such a personality!*

The recipient of this letter was Henrietta Fuchs, the organizer of La
Concordia, where Debussy had been accompanist. By this time, July
1884, scandal was hanging dangerously in the air, and the generous but
somewhat strait-laced Vidal was becoming genuinely vexed for his friend
and his already vulnerable reputation. Paris, to an outsider, might have
had the air of a city with easy morals, but in fact this was only the case
in certain quarters and classes. In respectable middle-class circles such
as La Concordia, or in the staid milieu of the Conservatoire, Achille's
relationship with a married woman, if exposed, would have caused
great offence, and his friends would also have suffered by association.
'Massenet won't find it easy to pardon the support I've given him, if he
ever does!' complained Vidal, ever mindful of his valuable connections.
Massenet, Vidal's former teacher, had since 1878 established one of the
most highly regarded composition classes at the Conservatoire. And as
far as this institution was concerned, whatever was thought of the affair,
the greater outrage was Achille's suspected intention of giving up the
highly coveted Prix de Rome.

Debussy was to cause similar moral outrage more than once in his
later life, with graver consequences. This time scandal was avoided, and
persuasion won the day. He left Paris for the Villa Medici on 27 January
1885. His letters home, to Henri Vasnier of all people, are piteous – and
breathtakingly duplicitous. He laments the rain, the lack of stimulating
conversation, the pretensions and deficiencies of his fellow laureates.
He is homesick:

*And then back to my vast room, with a five mile walk between one piece
of furniture and the next. I've been so lonely I've cried. I'd come to rely too
much on your friendship and intelligence and on the fact that you were
interested in what I was doing and were willing to discuss it. I'll never
forget all you have done for me, or how welcome you have made me inside
your family circle. I shall do everything I can to prove to you that I am not
ungrateful… P.S. Please give my best wishes to Madame Vasnier.*

The homesickness, however, is genuine, as well as the keen need for
friendship (a constant refrain in his letters from now on). Debussy had

Debussy (in white jacket, seated lower step) with fellow Prix de Rome students at the Villa Medici, Rome in 1885

indeed enjoyed in the Vasnier household the first true meeting of minds of his adult life, and had had the opportunity to both witness and relish the unaffected cultural confidence of the educated middle classes in which he was accepted as an equal. It is an irony, one of many in Debussy's history, that in this milieu he also became the lover of another man's wife, thus threatening the very middle-class security he so craved.

In Paris there were others on whom Achille relied for friendship, advice – and money. Like Vidal they were to become embroiled in the young man's 'sinister tale of adultery'. Just after the competition, Achille had befriended Count Giuseppe Primoli, some ten years older than

himself, and a relation by marriage of *la famille* Bonaparte. 'Gégé' had
a villa by the sea not far from Rome and he spent much of his time at
the Villa Medici. Before he left for Rome Achille, in typically brusque
fashion, had asked Primoli to lend him money. 'My uncouth ways,' he
wrote, 'have not made me many friends, and that's why I'm turning to
you, as I know you are kind and sympathetic to my problems… I can't
even buy any flowers for *her who loves them so much*. So I'm asking you
to lend me 500 francs… I ask this only because of the friendship I feel
you have for me. And my parents are in such dire straits, I don't want
to be a further burden to them.' The emphasis is Achille's, who knew
instinctively to whom he could confide his love affair. He must have
known too that the impoverished artist, without even money enough
'to afford my Prix de Rome dinner', was not an undignified posture
to assume. It was fully understood that such circumstances allowed a
little sponging, a skill at which he was particularly adept.

Primoli at once introduced him to the Popelins, father and son: the
son Gustave was already a Roman laureate (in painting) and was to
become very close to Achille during his first months at the Villa. The
father, Claudius, a respected and well-connected painter and poet, could
offer sound advice on *les liaisons dangereuses*: he had once been the lover
of Princess Mathilde, niece to Napoleon. Once again Debussy, through
a combination of innate charm and a sense of his own self-worth, was
making his way. Without Primoli, who as well as money gave Achille
the use of his villa near Rome, and without the Popelins, who covered
for him in his affair with Marie Vasnier, Debussy would very likely not
have seen his Roman studies through to the end.

Many of Debussy's letters to Claudius and Gustave Popelin only came
to light in the 1980s. (They were published in 1989.) Compared to the
letters he was simultaneously writing to Vasnier – twelve letters over
two years, which received fatherly advice in return – it scarcely seems
credible that they could be from the same pen. It is not only Debussy's
deception that is remarkable – no 'affair' could very well exist without
it – but that he writes to Vasnier at all, and in such a heartfelt manner.
This might partly be explained by his knowledge that Marie would
also read the letters, but he was writing to her too so he hardly needed
to use this form of code. (She collected her letters from the post office
near her home. None of this correspondence appears to have survived.)
At the same time as Debussy was pleading for Vasnier's friendship,

extolling his kindness and sending polite postscripts to his wife and children, he was revealing another side of himself to Gustave Popelin:

Problems have arisen that will (I fear) considerably delay my trip to Paris. And I cried when I read your phrase 'see you soon', which contained so much joy for me. That joy is over, her last letter received the day before yesterday barely concealed the pain my presence would cause her. Telling me it would be very unwise for us to see each other. You'll understand that, if I have to suffer, I would rather stay here than expose myself to the insane feelings I would certainly experience should I be prevented from seeing her. Though being near her, such a life would be unbearable, given the jealousy that I know is part of me. To force her to act otherwise would mean losing her, but better to lose her, and keep my love's pride, than play the fawning dog that is always left at the door. I ended up telling her I wanted nothing to change, and that she was everything to me. Her answer will show if I did the right thing.

Some of the Popelin letters are difficult to date precisely, but it seems most likely that this letter belongs to the summer of 1885, not a year

La Falaise à Dieppe by Claude Monet (1882). The Vasniers had a holiday home in Dieppe where Debussy, on leave from Rome, secretly met Marie during the summer of 1885

later as the first publication suggested. By the summer of 1886 the young man's passion was cooling.

Achille clearly had the capacity to keep the two relationships, with wife and husband, completely separate. He had no more conception of Vasnier as a sexual entity than a son has of his father. He felt he was in total possession of Marie, and Vasnier's claim did not concern him. This allowed him to treat the older man with genuine deference, and to express quite freely his sense of homesickness, his fears and hopes for the future of his music, and his thanks for Vasnier's gentle encouragement. He needed such a father figure. When Achille spoke of his jealousy, it was not jealousy of Vasnier, but of everything that took Marie's attention away from himself.

The first months at the Villa were misery for Achille. 'He's terribly bored,' wrote Vidal in February, 'and dreams of nothing but going back to Paris. As for me, I'm powerless to stop him. If his mother could do nothing with him, how can I?' And indeed in April he suddenly took flight for Paris. How this was contrived, and where precisely he stayed, is not known (although from the evidence of his letters, the Popelins aided him), but he was back again in Rome by the first week of May In July he returned home again – a formal leave this time, granted by Ernest Hébert, the new director of the Villa. He went secretly to Dieppe on the Normandy coast of France, where the Vasniers spent their holidays, and he wrote the following pleading letter to Claudius Popelin:

You will not perhaps believe that I'm close by. Gustave says he's not spoken to you, and anyway I'm lying low, both very happy and very unhappy. It would take too long to tell you everything. If, friend as you are, you could possibly come to see me, I would be more at ease, as I rather need to confide in someone. Above all someone who loves me a little.

Please know that I am truly ashamed of having to appeal to the goodness that you've always shown towards me, but I am in such a state I don't know where to turn. The people here where I am staying ask me every day for money. Besides that I've seen my parents, who are terribly hard up. That's why I am once again turning to you, in the hope that your friendship will pardon all this new bother. Certainly I would wish it otherwise, and that you no longer had to trouble yourself over me, at least in this way.

When Achille asked for love and money, his friends complied. As an exasperated Vidal earlier commented, 'he's nothing but a sensualist… But with all that, he has such talent, and such a personality!'

Debussy's obsession with Marie Vasnier was the real reason for him not relating to life in Rome, at least for the first nine months. His feelings were inflamed by his protracted absence from her, the first since their intimacy had become fully established. However, he had many distractions at the Villa Medici, despite his protestations to the contrary. He travelled out frequently with M. Hébert and his wife and he became an intimate of their drawing room. He also joined Gégé Primoli at his villa and often stayed there alone for several weeks at a time, composing and simply enjoying the peace and solitude that the place offered him. 'It's a charming spot where the Romans come for sea bathing,' he wrote to Vasnier; 'there's a little port with little boats, all very picturesque and delightful.' So he was not always as disconsolate and solitary as he claimed. Paul Vidal remembered him at the Hébert's soirées, 'playing piano duets and singing his songs, which everyone adored':

There were continual demands in particular for [the Verlaine songs] 'Chevaux de bois', 'Mandoline', *and* 'Fantoches' *(which he later altered – in my opinion to its detriment). He and I spent most of our time together, playing piano duet arrangements of Bach's organ works, which he was passionate about. We also studied closely the two-piano arrangement of Beethoven's Ninth Symphony, Chabrier's* Valses romantiques *etc. It was around this time that we met Liszt at a dinner given by M. Hébert… [With the arrival of another friend] the three of us would spend our evenings giving readings. We read most of Shakespeare out loud, each of us taking a different role. Debussy had a marked predeliction for the Goncourt brothers, Flaubert, Banville and Verlaine, at a time when the last was known only to a small circle.*

Madame Hébert's diary shows that Debussy met Franz Liszt three times, and on one occasion heard the aged master play *Au Bord d'une source* (*'Beside a Spring'*, from Liszt's *Années de pèlerinage*), an intriguing detail for the future composer of works such as *Reflets dans l'eau, L'Isle joyeuse,* and *Jardins sous la pluie*. Debussy never forgot this episode and how, as he recalled at the end of his life, Liszt 'used the pedal as a kind of breathing'. (Liszt also went to sleep, noted Madame Hébert, during Debussy's and Vidal's two-piano rendering of his own 'Faust' Symphony.)

So Debussy's Roman years were not quite as wasted as he proclaimed. For his future piano music, the influence of Liszt was now grafted on to that of Chopin. Debussy was not even as impervious to Italian culture as he liked to suppose, fiercely though he defended, and certainly missed, the culture and the cafés of Paris. He found a few things impressive in Rome, especially the music of Palestrina and Orlando di Lasso, and the little unadorned church, Santa Maria dell'Anima, where their masses were performed. 'I'm truly amazed at the effects they can get simply from a vast knowledge of counterpoint,' he wrote to Vasnier. 'In their hands it becomes something wonderful, adding an extraordinary depth to the meaning of the words. And every now and again the melodic lines unroll and expand, reminding you of the illuminations in ancient missals.'

The young composer also got important work done, important in the sense that experimentation, which necessarily involved failure, gave him a feeling for what he might later be able to achieve. The statutory *envois*, the symphonic and vocal odes laureates had to produce annually

Le Bar aux Folies-Bergère by Edouard Manet (1882). In Rome Debussy felt cut off from the vibrancy of Parisian culture. Some decades earlier Liszt had commented on the lack of culture in Rome: 'Here there is no tomorrow; everything falls asleep.' For Debussy in the 1880s it was much the same

for the Académie des Beaux-Arts in Paris, caused him a great deal of trouble. *Zuleima,* based on a text by Heinrich Heine, he abandoned in exasperation: 'those great stupid lines bore me to death… My music would be in danger of sinking under the weight.' He did however complete enough of it to send back to Paris, for the Académie reported the work 'bizarre, incomprehensible, unperformable' (which makes it all the more a pity that the score is lost). *Diane au Bois,* on a text by Banville after Ovid's *Metamorphoses,* excited him again for a time (the work that Guiraud had advised him to put away for later) but he couldn't 'manage to find a musical idea that gives me the look of her.' He did not submit Diane as an *envoi,* and it is possible that the manuscript which survives actually dates from his Conservatoire days.

Just as interesting as the music of *Diane* were the comments Debussy makes about it – and *Zuleima* – in his letters to Vasnier. Of *Zuleima* he wrote, 'it is not at all the sort of music I want to write. I'm after music that is supple and concentrated enough to adapt itself to the lyrical impulses of the soul and to the whims of reverie.' A youthful and generalized ideal perhaps. But it also happens to be a virtual quotation (unacknowledged) from Baudelaire, from the introduction to the poet's late *Petits Poèmes en prose*:

Who has never dreamed, in our more ambitious moments, of the miracle of a poetic prose, musical yet without rhythm and without rhyme, supple yet concentrated enough to adapt itself to the lyrical impulses of the soul, to the undulations of reverie, to the pangs of conscience?

The young Debussy might have been donning Baudelaire's garments, but such an ideal is surely what, at least in musical terms, the older Debussy achieved.

In the case of *Diane* he confesses to Vasnier that he has 'taken on something too ambitious,' and with extraordinary foresight he proceeds to explain exactly why:

There's no precedent to go on, and I find myself compelled to invent new forms. I could always turn to Wagner, but I don't need to tell you how ridiculous it would be even to try. The only thing of his I would want to copy is the running of one scene into another. Also I want to keep the tone lyrical without it being absorbed by the orchestra.

Debussy's treatment of the orchestra in *Pelléas et Mélisande*, ten years later, and the way in which he kept the vocal lines independent from it, was to be one of his most radical departures from Wagner's practice. In the autumn of 1885, the date of these comments to Vasnier, he would have heard almost no Wagner apart from a performance of *Lohengrin* in Rome (and perhaps the overture to *Tannhäuser* in Paris). His knowledge would have come almost entirely from studying the scores in the Conservatoire's library, and in the study of his teacher Lavignac. It was to be another three years before he would visit the annual Wagner festival at Bayreuth. Yet already he is both drawn and sceptical, and fully aware of the daunting path he had to follow. It should be remembered he was only twenty-three. He gave up the beautiful *Diane* – 'the idea must be beautiful but cold – it mustn't give any hint of passion' – because he knew he simply was not ready: 'Never before has a work filled me with such misgivings.'

The final *envoi* Debussy worked on in Rome was *Printemps*, for orchestra, piano and choir, which he completed in February 1887 just before his departure. It was inspired, he said, by a masterpiece of Italian painting, Sandro Botticelli's *Primavera*. In its use of a wordless chorus it anticipates the third movement of his later *Nocturnes*, but its chief interest lies in the criticism it received from the Académie. Their report employed for the first time the term 'impressionism' in relation to music:

> *Monsieur Debussy… has a pronounced tendency – too pronounced – towards an exploration of the strange. One has the feeling of musical colour exaggerated to the point where it causes the composer to forget the importance of precise construction and form. It is strongly to be hoped that he will guard against this vague impressionism, which is one of the most dangerous enemies of truth in works of art.*

The original orchestration of *Printemps* was destroyed, but it was later orchestrated by the conductor Henri Busser (in 1913, with Debussy's help), allowing audiences today to get some idea of what the fuss might have been about. Pierre Boulez's remark on *Printemps* is interesting in this regard: 'Listening to *Printemps* I can never help thinking of Monet's *Femmes dans le jardin*. Both works have the same freshness, the same lack of sophistication and a sort of delight in embarking on the voyage of self-discovery.' The particular voyage in this instance was in the direction of organic form, an attempt at a freedom of structuring – an

Femmes dans le jardin by Claude Monet, an early work painted in 1866 that composer Pierre Boulez has associated with Debussy's *Printemps*

unfolding of material that appears improvisatory – which was to reach its first definitive expression in *Prélude à l'après-midi d'un faune*.

Debussy's unwilling sojourn at the Villa Medici was, then, by no means as unproductive as might have appeared. He also continued to write songs: the masterly Verlaine settings, later to become *Ariettes oubliées*, were begun at the Villa. But above all, in the empty and silent spaces between one work begun and another abandoned, as he undertook his painstaking formation as a dramatic composer, the ideas came into being that eventually led to *Pelléas et Mélisande*. As early as June 1885, within three months of his arrival, he tries to articulate some half-grasped perceptions to Henri Vasnier:

*I don't think I'll ever be able to cast my music in a rigid mould. I hasten
to add I'm not talking about musical form, merely from the literary point
of view. I would always rather deal with something where the passage of
events is subordinated to a thorough and extended portrayal of human
feelings. That way, I think, music can become more personal, more true to
life; you can explore and refine your means of expression.*

By itself this is far too vague to be a manifesto, yet working back from
Pelléas, from that point ten years later when *Pelléas* became a fact of
musical history, it is momentous. Without *Pelléas* the young man's
meaning is difficult to grasp, it is no more than a half-caught aspiration.
Applied to *Pelléas*, however, these ideas suddenly come sharply into
focus: the literary character of the work (it is after all as much a play set
to music as it is an opera), the 'extended portrayal of human feeling'
as opposed to dramatic action, the distillation of emotion and exquisite
subtlety of musical means by which this emotion is conveyed.

It is an extraordinary irony that it was Vasnier who elicited Achille's
prophetic proclamation, for what eventually enabled the full creation
of *Pelléas* – its explorations of sexual awakening, love and jealousy, youth
and age – was not only the discovery of a suitable text, nor yet the
painstaking development of refined compositional skills, but Debussy's
ability to draw on the 'personal' and the 'true to life'.

There were other distractions in Rome, familiarly 'true to life', that
were slowly pulling at the knots of his enslavement to Marie. At the end
of January, 1886, some smart friends of the Héberts, the Hochons, came
to stay for a month. Achille, in his usual manner with newcomers who
might threaten his security, at first rudely kept himself away from the
dinner table by telling Hébert that he had sold his evening dress to raise
money. 'He thought I was mad, but who cares?' he nonchalantly tells
Vasnier in a letter of 29 January. Achille mentions Monsieur Hochon, but
not Madame – a tiny detail, but one we would now call a Freudian slip.
Ten days later Hébert's wife records in her diary: 'Gégé Primoli tells me
that they have seen Debussy and Loulou [Hochon] kissing in the Villa.'

This episode is given in more detail in the early biography by René
Peter, although it is only through the recent access to Madame Hébert's
diary that the names have been joined together. The story may well have
become more colourful in the retelling: 'His misery and boredom were
enlivened by a few instances of amusement, such as when a beautiful

Parisienne, having heard him play and sing his recent compositions one evening in Hébert's drawing room, stealthily made her way through the corridors of the Villa Medici, tapped at his door and offered herself to him, naked under her long cloak.'

Neither amusement nor work, however, was able to get the better of Debussy's displeasure for long. He departed Rome for good at the beginning of March 1887, having fulfilled the statutory two years' residence, although he would have been expected to stay for three (and to have spent another year in a European musical centre such as Germany – the Prize statute allowed for four years' support). His letter to Vasnier on 24 February contains an explanation of his plight which is direct and convincing:

> *I swear I've put the greatest possible goodwill into my efforts. The end result has been only the realization that I could never live and work here. You'll say that this is rather a sudden decision and that I haven't taken long enough to think about it but, I promise you, I've thought about it a great deal. I know what would happen to me if I stayed – total obliteration. Ever since I've been here I feel dead inside. I really want to work, and to go on until I produce something solid and original.*

Debussy saw Marie on his final return from Rome, but how their relationship ended can only be conjectured. The memoir of Blanche, the artist who painted Madame Vasnier's portrait – and, in his later years of fame, Debussy's – recounts an intriguing tale which reads like a scene from a farce: 'I knew Debussy while I was doing a pastel of Madame Vasnier in Dieppe, where he came on his return from the Villa Medici. She and her husband lived in a little chalet owned by the painter Mélicourt. It was there that one night, coming back very late to Bas-Fort-Blanc, we could distinguish in the shadows a rope ladder: Mme V. at the window, Debussy climbing up.' But then why not? Debussy, as many friends testified, could be 'very extravagant, and could rarely resist any desire or temptation'. Or was Blanche, sixty years on, colouring his memories with a delighted mixture of rumour and the plot of *Pelléas* (especially the tower scene Act III, scene 1)? It is in any case possible that he mistook the year. By March 1887 Achille Debussy's relationship with Marie-Blanche Vasnier had very little time to run.

The account written by Madame Vasnier's daughter, Marguerite –
showing throughout not the slightest awareness of the affair – is probably the closest to the truth: 'When he came back for good, the former
intimacy was no longer there. He had changed, as we had. We had
moved house, made new friends, and he, with his moody unsociable
character and unwillingness to alter his habits, no longer felt at home…
Then gradually, he too made new acquaintances; he stopped coming
and we never saw him again.'

This was written in 1926, exactly at the time when Marguerite also
made available for publication the letters from Debussy to her father.
Had she heard rumour of the affair, then these actions display a wise
manner of dealing with it. In her memoir her family's dignity is maintained to the end. The celebrated intruder, while granted an affectionate place in their family life, is finally banished for good: 'We never saw
him again.'

4

Montmartre at the end of
the nineteenth century.
Here were many of the cafés
and nightclubs that Debussy
so missed when in Rome.
In the early 1890s he knew
Henri de Toulouse-Lautrec at
the Moulin Rouge, and at the
Auberge du Clou and the
Chat Noir he met Erik Satie,
who became a lifelong friend

'When all's said and done, desire is what counts.'

Claude Debussy

From Achille to Claude 1887-93

It is not difficult to reconcile the contradictions at the heart of Debussy's experience in Rome. He was still in his early twenties, still a student, and for all his determination to develop a coherent artistic credo, he only dimly perceived his path. In this he was doggedly consistent – it was only in his personal life that he was impulsive. He was unformed, but his exceptional intelligence meant that when he surveyed the world around him, not least his fellow laureates, he saw he did not fit. And his misery was genuine, although alleviated by his participation in the social life of the Villa.

It was to be another five years before he would begin to feel at one with the adult world. Then, towards the end of 1892, at the age of thirty, he was able to divest himself of the youthful Achille, a name he had always found ridiculous (Achilles, the Greek warrior hero): in a simple act of great significance he dropped all allusions to his first name from his signature, to remain thereafter plain Claude.

Very little is known of his first two years back in Paris. Few first-hand accounts exist and even fewer letters. There is, however, one brilliant and revealing letter (dated March 1887) from Achille to M. Hébert, the director of the Villa Medici, in which the young man expresses in his most winning manner that familiar tone of homesickness we found in his letters to Vasnier from two years earlier. But this time, of course, typical of one with such a deep need for friendship and security, he was homesick for Rome. His amusing self-dramatization betrays his struggle to find an identity with which to face the adult world – but between the lines there is his other voice, serious, sincere and fully aware of the momentous artistic issues he needed to resolve:

> *First of all please forgive me for taking so long to send news of your poor little musician. The first reason is a terrible cold, an Italian one which became French, but whichever, the mother of all colds; fever! coughing fits! exhaustion! The full works! The second reason is that since being back in circulation I have been a bit crazy in the head, at least I was, for today I*

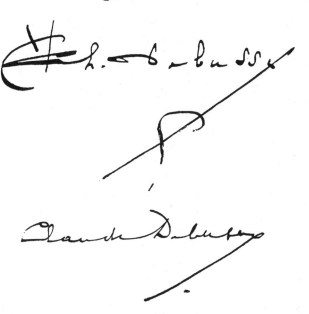

Three samples of Debussy's changing signature from 1884, 1885 and 1893

have good reasons to be more than happy, otherwise there would have been almost as many reasons, despite everything, for regretting the passing of my old life. Arriving in Paris, I felt just like a little boy (God forgive me, I was almost frightened of the carriages!) timidly trying to find his way about. My friends all have the air of people of considerable importance; Vidal, very busy, just manages to favour me with lunch! Leroux arranges to meet me in the street between two other meetings! Pierné! He, I daren't visit at all! In short, all of them treat Paris like a conquered city! How adaptable they are, and how forgetful of their fine rebelliousness of yesteryear!

I find all this a bit upsetting! But my last months in Rome have also contributed to this state of mind; I lived in these months a kind of dream life, wrapped up in my work, everything bent towards the ideal of an exalted art, without ever worrying about what Peter and Paul would think. Now I wonder what I am going to do, with my terrible unsociability, how I will

ever make my way and struggle against this rat-race, and I have this
foreboding of weariness and endless strain. Yes I'm going to miss, with all
my soul, my lovely bedroom, your great friendship, cher maître, *and all*
your warm encouragement. In the end, you see, one can only make Art for
five people at the most, and five people whom one loves! But reaching for
the applause of the world in general, of the man in the street, and all the
empty-heads, my God that would be tedious. But enough of me! I'm ending
up being tedious myself.

This is Debussy at his most lively, and it shows how well, in his letters,
he could capture the complexity of his thoughts and emotions and weave
them into observations of his everyday existence – in short, how well he
could write. The manner in which the amusing sketch of the little boy
lost develops into a critique of his friends, and finally into a deeply felt
analysis of impinging reality, could not be more finely judged, nor more
spontaneously evolved. We notice too the telling detail of 'making Art
for five people'. The esoteric nature of art, art for the initiated few, was
a central belief of the literary Symbolist movement, which had received
its official birth only the year before in a manifesto by Jean Moréas in
Le Figaro. In Rome, Debussy had already become drawn to Symbolist
poetry and found an affinity with its abiding concern with allusion, with
a fluidity of expression that sought to invest words with the abstract qualities of music. In the next chapter we will see how, in the decade following his return to Paris, he made the Symbolist milieu his natural home.

It is possible that he saw Marie Vasnier within two weeks of his
return, if this is what he means by 'I have good reasons to be more
than happy.' (This might lend corroboration to Blanche's story of
Debussy visiting her at Dieppe.) And though he was jealous of the
success of his friends, his frustration was fully justified. Vidal had no
trouble in getting his own works performed, and Pierné was taken up
immediately by the major orchestras, finding an exclusive publisher.
(He later became a conductor of Debussy's orchestral works.) Debussy
had no success at all, a contrast pointed out by Blanche's unkind
description of him at this time as 'that very material-minded fellow…
that sleepy, heavy creature, always on the lookout for music publishers'.

The family moved from rue Clapeyron in 1888 to a larger flat in rue
Berlin, not far away, where Achille had the independence of his own
entrance. But financial conditions were no better than in his student

days, especially as in the month following Achille's return to Paris his father lost the job he had held since recovering from the Commune debacle. The pressure on Achille was now to produce something worthy of a Prix de Rome laureate – and, more to the point, able to earn him money. But two principal works of these years he could only publish by private subscription: the songs *Cinq poèmes de Charles Baudelaire* (1887–9) and *La Damoiselle élue* (1887–8). The latter – a cantata setting of Dante Gabriel Rossetti's *The Blessed Damozel*, in a French translation by Gabriel Sarrazin – was the third Prix de Rome *envoi* required by the Académie des Beaux-Arts. The Baudelaire songs had a print run of 150, and the Rossetti setting, including an illustration by Maurice Denis, a run of 170. Both publications were offered as objets d'art, with fine paper and binding. Truly little more than 'making Art for five people', they at least gave the composer a prized position in elitist Symbolist circles, and both works showed his advanced literary tastes.

Rossetti was one of the founders of the English Pre-Raphaelites, a mid-nineteenth-century movement in the visual arts as well as the literary, which was just then becoming greatly admired in France. The Pre-Raphaelite ideal of feminine beauty, in which the ecstatically sexual is combined with the fulsomely spiritual, became a central strand of visual and literary art in France during the last two decades of the century. The type is illustrated by such a painting as Rossetti's *Beata Beatrix*, as well as by the opening stanzas from his poem *The Blessed Damozel*:

The blessed damozel leaned out
From the gold bar of heaven;
Her eyes were deeper than the depth
Of waters stilled at even;
She had three lilies in her hand,
And the stars in her hair were seven.

Her robe, ungirt from clasp to hem,
No wrought flowers did adorn,
But a white rose of Mary's gift,
For service meetly worn;
Her hair that lay along her back
Was yellow like ripe corn...

The French were also attracted by the quasi-medievalism of the Pre-
Raphaelite manner, the imagery of castles, knights and flaxen-haired
damsels in distress. 'The golden bar of heaven' in the poem is not so much
a spiritual conception as an Arthurian tower (as it would be in Debussy's
Pelléas) where the damsel is awaiting her lover's arrival. Though in heaven,
her physical presence is not in question: we are asked to linger over the
shape of her back, where her yellow hair lies 'like ripe corn', and later we
are told that 'her bosom must have made the bar she leaned on warm.'

Rossetti's *Blessed Damozel* drew from Debussy, in his setting for female
choir, contralto narrator, soprano solo (the Damozel) and orchestra,
the most successfully sustained large-scale work of his apprenticeship.
Its qualities were even registered by the Académie des Beaux-Arts, whose
report was markedly warmer in tone than the previous year's comments
on *Printemps*. This time the 'vagueness of expression and form' for which
they had earlier reproached him, seemed 'to a certain point justified
by the nature and indeterminate character of the subject', and they
noted that Debussy's music was 'neither devoid of poetry, nor of charm'.
Possibly the shade of Massenet in the work persuaded them. Yet *La
Damoiselle élue* is also reminiscent of Wagner, of *Tristan*, and even more
of *Parsifal*. The huge influence, and danger for Debussy, was now at its
height as he became exposed to the full might of the German composer
at Bayreuth in 1888, and again the following year.

And it is *Tristan*, the *Tristan* of unfettered sexual arousal, that pervades
the *Cinq poèmes de Charles Baudelaire*. By comparison the fleshly allusions of Rossetti, and Debussy's delicately textured response in *La
Damoiselle*, seem cool and chaste. Of all Debussy's works the Baudelaire
songs are the most densely and chromatically wrought, to the point
where the work seems to lie outside the development of his characteristic
musical language. The piano part is as flamboyant and richly textured
as any late Romantic piano writing, especially in the first of the songs,
Le Balcon, while all five display a complexity of working-out that is
almost symphonic, a pattern of intricate motivic development that the
later Debussy rejected.

Baudelaire's *Les Fleurs du mal*, in its frank exploration of the duality
of existence – of the spiritual and the degraded as the poles of human
awareness – was the bible of the Symbolist generation. It was also one
of the reasons that publishers wanted little to do with Debussy's settings.
Thirty years earlier the first publication had been confiscated and the

Beata Beatrix by Dante Gabriel Rossetti, one of the founders of the English Pre-Raphaelite movement. The Pre-Raphaelites were much admired in France; their literary and visual images influenced the Symbolist movement to which Debussy was drawn

poet prosecuted for offending public morality. In the 1880s Baudelaire, in the public memory, was still deemed beyond the bounds of good taste.

Although Debussy's *Cinq poèmes* is an early masterpiece without issue, he never lost sight of Baudelaire as the touchstone of his imaginative experience. The title of the piano Prelude from 1909, *Les Sons et les parfums tournent dans l'air du soir* is a quotation from the poet's *Harmonie du soir*, while in 1917 another quotation appears as the title of the last piano piece Debussy ever wrote, *Les Soirs illuminées par l'ardeur du charbon* (from Baudelaire's *Le Balcon*). The circumstances of this tiny piece, which only came to light in 2001, will be discussed in the final chapter.

So Debussy might in the end reject Wagner, but he was never to reject Baudelaire, the poet who, with Verlaine, sustained his creative imagination during that humiliating period when he became piano-duet arranger of the music of Camille Saint-Saëns. As co-founder of the Société Nationale de Musique, Saint-Saëns had become representative of a French tradition which had little time for new ideas. He was ceaselessly obstructive towards Debussy's music and everything it stood for. 'Debussy simply had a name with a euphonious sound,' he once remarked; 'had he been called Martin, nobody would ever have heard of him.'

But not all of Debussy's music was completely ignored. His settings of Verlaine, begun in Rome and completed in 1888, did find a commercial publisher (although this did not mean a market or a public willing to pay attention). The six songs were published as *Ariettes* (to be reissued in 1903, with minor alterations, as *Ariettes oubliées*). And one contemporary at least recognized the quality of these songs: the writer André Suarès, who was to remain one of Debussy's most perceptive admirers throughout the composer's life, noted privately 'a melodic quality that is very subtle', and 'musical writing of incontrovertible mastery'. He also observed that the composer seemed 'to have understood Wagner thoroughly, but he does not copy his technique'. There are indeed Wagnerian echoes in *Ariettes oubliées*, especially in *L'Ombre des arbres*, but it is the difference between these songs and the *Cinq poèmes de Charles Baudelaire* that is the more striking. Clearly the manner of Verlaine's poetry, the subtle irony, the delicate musicality of the rhythms, drew from Debussy a different language, and one that he wished to explore. He was to return three more times to Verlaine, most immediately in the *Trois mélodies* and *Fêtes galantes* of 1891, and later in a second book of *Fêtes galantes* in 1904. Others among his early muses – Banville, Paul Bourget, Leconte de Lisle, fell away. Verlaine remained.

It is significant that the best of the piano music of this period was also Verlaine-inspired: the *Petite suite* for piano duet (whose titles he took from Verlaine's *Fêtes galantes*), and *Suite bergamasque* (where the famous *Clair de lune* alludes to Verlaine's poem of the same name). Both works still hold a popular place in the repertoire, along with the two *Arabesques* published in 1891. Another piano piece from this period worth mentioning is the exciting and unjustly neglected *Danse* (published as *Tarantelle styrienne* in 1891 and re-issued with its new title in 1903). Other piano pieces, written in a desperate quest for money – such as *Mazurka*,

Nocturne, Ballade – sit uneasily with Debussy's confident early genius and he later wanted little to do with them, or indeed any of the piano music from these years.

But it is the songs of this period that should have been heralded by a far wider audience. In their mastery of the rhythms and accents of language, and their imaginative empathy with poetic expression, they already show their unknown composer to be one of the greatest exponents of art song. Their variety is extraordinary: from the deeply erotic frissons of *C'est l'extase* to the merry-go-round whirl of *Chevaux de bois*, both from *Ariettes*; from the luminous water imagery of the Baudelaire setting, *Le Jet d'eau*, to the all-embracing sweep of the sea in Verlaine's *La Mer est plus belle* (from *Trois mélodies*, beginning with the audacious simile 'The sea is more beautiful than cathedrals'). Most are love songs, to which the composer brings a sensitivity to ambiguity that seems clairvoyant, casting a new light on those familiar literary combinations of sadness and ecstasy, love and sorrow, desire and loneliness – as in *Il pleure dans mon coeur* from *Ariettes*, and *En sourdine* and *Clair de lune* from *Fêtes galantes*. And from song to song Debussy rarely repeated himself, a sure sign, for those who cared to notice during those quiet years of neglect, of the seriousness of his intent. His apprenticeship with Marie Vasnier, all those songs written for her and offered to her, bore the richest fruit.

It might be argued that Debussy's style – his essential voice – evolved to a significant degree from the intrinsic qualities of French poetry, above all from the poetry (and the ideas) of Baudelaire, Stéphane Mallarmé (who was soon to inspire one of Debussy's greatest masterpieces) and Verlaine. The qualities are defined in Verlaine's poem *Art poétique*, in which the poet proclaims his standard for poetry: '*De la musique avant toute chose*' – 'Music above everything'. And by 'music' Verlaine means both the sound of words and their rhythm – he continues: 'And so, one must choose the uneven metre *(l'impair)*, hazier, dissolving in air, in which there is no weight, no constraint.' Such an ideal, transposed into specifically musical terms, was fundamental to Debussy's aspirations.

Debussy had first set *En sourdine, Clair de lune* and *Fantoches* from Verlaine's *Fêtes galantes* as early as 1882, when he was probably first introduced to the poetry by Marie Vasnier. In the composer's own *Fêtes galantes* of 1891 he set the first two again, to different music, but added *Fantoches* virtually unaltered (it is a sign of the student's early brilliance that this song effortlessly holds its own against the later songs). Verlaine's poems had been inspired by the paintings of Watteau, the creator of the *fête galante* genre early in the eighteenth century. Through a subtle combination of verbal music and visual imagery, Verlaine renders the delicately coloured pastoral paintings of Watteau in narrative form. Debussy, in his turn, equally as entranced by the paintings, manages to capture the dream-world of Watteau, where youthful love is touched with a poignant concentration of sadness that can catch an onlooker unawares. The *Fêtes galantes* songs of 1891 achieve the ideal interrelation of poetry, painting and music – Verlaine, Watteau, Debussy.

To understand the originality of Debussy's approach to this poetry, his *Clair de lune* from this series might be compared with Gabriel Fauré's setting of the same poem from just four years earlier. Fauré's song, itself a tiny masterpiece in the style of a minuet, is more generalized in its response; the piano accompaniment is cast in seemingly self-generating (and effortless) sequences, the vocal line is altogether more conventionally singable. Debussy's surface is more fragmented and 'difficult'. He appears to meet the poet line by line, point by point. He engages fully, as if he himself were a poet, with the meaning as it occurs within the body and conjunction of the words, and so disallows any easy response on our part. Fauré captures for us the exquisite but more immediate impact of the verses, whereas Debussy's more allusive art explores the inner resonances. Significantly, Debussy reveals the implication of sexual climax in the final stanza, where the mingling and melting of the lovers, the singing and the moonlight, all combine to 'make the fountains sob with ecstasy'. The style Fauré has chosen cannot express this experience. Debussy captures the ecstasy and the subsiding, as well as the poignant suggestion of loss and loneliness contained in the final line, 'the tall, slender fountains among the marble statues'. In *Clair de lune* he combines a mastery of musical language with a profound analysis of Verlaine comparable to that of the finest literary critic. It is almost as if he achieves a new kind of art, a new subtlety of allusion.

The artistic challenge for Debussy, then, in the years immediately following his time in Rome was Wagner: how to use him, how to escape him – indeed how to proceed at all. 'It is *Tristan* that gets in the way of our work,' he said in 1890; 'I don't see what can be done beyond *Tristan*.' The strength of Wagner's embrace is revealed as early as 1887 in Debussy's letter of thanks to Hébert, even before he had heard *Tristan*. (He possessed at this time a score for voices and piano, and later became renowned for rendering the whole of it himself at the keyboard, mostly from memory.) 'The first act of *Tristan and Isolde*, decidedly the most beautiful thing that I know,' he wrote. 'In its depth of emotion, which grasps and embraces you like a caress, it makes you suffer: what I mean is you experience the same feelings as Tristan without doing violence to your own spirit or your own heart.' This act of self-identification, expressed so tellingly in contradictions, was costly, but wholly necessary. No composer of this period came to know and understand the music of Wagner better than Claude Debussy, and nobody was to find a better means of escape. He spent the next decade, dominated by the gestation of *Pelléas et Mélisande*, finding this path.

In his bleakest period at the beginning of the 1890s, Debussy was nearly derailed. He accepted a commission to write an opera, *Rodrigue et Chimène*, on a text by the poet and novelist (and fanatical follower of Wagner) Catulles Mendès. But *Rodrigue*, a version of the Spanish legend of *El Cid*, offered him neither the concise richness of Baudelaire nor the subtle musicality of Verlaine. Nor did the subject have the mystical, erotic aura of Rossetti's *Damozel*. The composer Paul Dukas, the friend to whom Debussy had dedicated *La Damoiselle*, described the libretto of *Rodrigue* as 'totally devoid of interest; a mishmash of Parnassian bric-à-brac and Spanish barbarism'. But Claude persevered for over two years. In January 1892 he wrote to another close friend, the writer Robert Godet: 'My life is hardship and misery thanks to this opera. Everything about it is wrong for me... I'm afraid I may have won victories over my true self.'

It was not that Debussy's acutely sensitive literary antennae had let him down, but rather that he had suppressed his instincts. He was in his late twenties, a Prix de Rome laureate with nothing to his name. Contemporaries such as Paul Vidal were going from strength to strength – that same Vidal who had once been a welcome guest and ally of his mother. The pressures on him at home in rue de Clapeyron must have been unendurable: for a brief period towards the end of 1890 it seems he moved out of his parents' house, as several letters bear the address of his loyal friend Étienne Dupin (who had paid for his trips to Bayreuth and who underwrote the private publication of the Baudelaire songs). It may have been to him that Debussy addressed a forlorn, pencilled note: '*Cher ami*, forgive me, but can you lend me 20fr. until the end of the month: for the urgent necessities of life. I'm ashamed to write this, but I'm *famished*.' It would have been poverty that drove him home again.

There were, however, more positive reasons for his perseverance with *Rodrigue*. Despite himself he achieved some beautiful music, especially in the chorus at the end of Act II and in much of the third act. And it seems Debussy was still toying with the work in the summer of 1893, when he played some excerpts to Paul Dukas: 'The short scenes are delightful,' Dukas wrote to Vincent d'Indy 'and have a harmonic finesse which recalls his early songs.' But the most important aspect of his work on *Rodrigue* was the way in which it primed him for *Pelléas*, quite suddenly beckoning just at the point when *Rodrigue* was seeming so hopeless. Maybe this was the reason he revisited the score with Dukas in the summer of 1893. By then he had seen the first performance of Maeterlinck's play *Pelléas et Mélisande*, and its possibilities were looming in his brain. *Rodrigue* was to be the springboard: Debussy needed to review it one final time, as a warning but also as an encouragement.

Effectively *Rodrigue* was abandoned sometime in 1892, and with it the highly influential Mendès connection and the hopes of Debussy's parents. They had no conception of the path he was seeking, which is hardly surprising. All they saw was indulgence and decadence – extravagant purchases of books, prints and objets d'art (and caviar, according to Blanche), and a seemingly wilful inability to follow through projects that could secure recognition. The abandonment of Mendès was but one of several similar actions. Not long before, Debussy had forbidden a performance of his *Fantaisie* for piano and orchestra by the prestigious Société Nationale de Musique, on discovering that only the first movement was to be given. During a break in the final rehearsal he removed all the parts from the stands. (The *Fantaisie* was also to have been his fourth and final Prix de Rome *envoi*, for 1888, but he never submitted it.) No doubt his action was governed by the cyclic nature of the work, and the necessity for the movements to follow on without a break. He informed d'Indy, who was to have conducted it (and who, since 1890, had been president of the Société), that a performance of the first movement alone 'must inevitably give a false impression of the whole'. Claude Debussy was no longer young, he was unknown, he was penniless. Who at that time, least of all disillusioned and exasperated parents, would have seen such actions as those of a genius?

But some did – and d'Indy remained a supporter, despite being temperamentally opposed to Debussy's music. Debussy had for some years attracted loyal and discerning patrons and friends, who gave not only emotional support but money. In the second half of 1892 Prince André Poniatowski appeared on the scene, full of plans to get Claude to America and a desire to give him 'if not riches, at least the opportunity to work for a year or two in peace'. Poniatowski was part of the *monde*, that wealthy, fashionable milieu of town houses and country chateaux in which artists had to find patronage in order to survive. Debussy was no different from many of his contemporaries in his need to exploit these opportunities.

Poniatowski's idea was for a concert of Debussy's works in New York, and then to 'persuade someone like Andrew Carnegie to take an interest... and to offer him over a period of two or three years the material and spiritual tranquillity which he lacked entirely in Paris'. In retrospect the whole idea seems absurd. It is hard now to imagine Debussy in America – he for whom Rome was a trial, and for whom his native city supplied all the security and inspiration he could possibly hope for – but he went along with it. His letter of acceptance, 8 September 1892, one of the first in which he signed himself Claude Debussy, has an air of unreality – almost as if he was imagining his parents' response to this golden opportunity. But while Claude was playing the role of a good son, he could not help spoiling it by simultaneously asserting an artistic credo not in the least designed to earn fame and fortune:

Now, it's a question of how to calculate my commercial value from the American viewpoint. You mention the names of Rubinstein, Tchaikovsky etc., but they were people who were already well-known, and for whom, may I say, prospects were easy. With me it will be more difficult, being totally unknown, and more to the point one whose art is a little abstruse, which needs listeners to come towards it, and which has always refused to make advances towards them, and with good reason. But my advantage is your influence over there: and from what you say, your considerable financial backing. But I think I should point out that other than the practical and utilitarian side of things, nothing should be taken for granted.

And I have to make it clear that in order to make the trip I will need everything. It's a long time since tailors and shirt makers etc., have been other than characters in a fairy tale. And I wouldn't want you to take on such a great responsibility without my feeling I could give you something in return. Whatever, I am determined to follow this up in every respect, but it's my duty to let you know my scruples despite my huge desire not to look back.

In the event letters went astray (or at least Claude said they did) and the plan foundered. But it also seems as if he eventually came to see the inappropriateness of the whole idea, although in material terms he did get something of what he wanted: in a long letter to Poniatowski the following February, containing not one reference to the American trip, he insouciantly remembers to thank him for a generous allowance – in a postscript. As in his earlier letters to Primoli, Vasnier and Claudius Popelin, he plays the 'poor artist' role; and along with the familiar apologies for not having written, he again brings the hardship of his parents to the fore, a ploy to gain sympathy which also reveals his sense of guilt. It is a fascinating dichotomy and lies at the heart of the complex ambiguity of Debussy's personality:

You are right to chide me for my long silence… I'll try and explain in a few words the reasons: first, my family, in which there have been various regrettable incidents that I've had to deal with, and who then decided I was not pulling my weight where fame and fortune are concerned. So they began a needling campaign against me, on the one hand emotional blackmail, on the other simple nastiness… Add to that the daily grind, the struggles and the worries, and you will have a rough idea of my life.

But despite the tone of persecution in this letter Claude is perfectly aware that his life has not all been like that, as he then goes on to demonstrate in writing of spontaneous vitality. His letters to Poniatowski rate as some of his greatest literary creations, and they reveal, with a typical self-knowledge and ironic detachment, some of the fundamental impulses of his art:

However real one's sufferings are, they look rather quaint and dramatic on paper. Anyway the best thing is not to take all these hardships too seriously. They support what I might call the Cult of Desire. And when all's said and done, desire is what counts. You have this crazy but inescapable longing, a need almost, for some work of art (a Velazquez, a Satsuma vase or a new kind of tie), and the moment of actual possession is one of joy, of love really. A week later nothing. The object is there and you spend five or six days looking at it. The only time the passion returns is when you've been away for several months. It's like the sun, which is so wonderful when you feel it again on an April morning and then all through the summer we're tired of it. You could write down a formula for desire: 'everything comes from it and returns to it.' By a rather elegant piece of trickery, the desire to be happy works pretty much on the same lines. One is never happy except by comparison or by giving oneself a certain limit to aim at, whether it's so many millions in cash or so many children, to provide some relaxation from the onward drive to glory. I don't know whether, like me, you are 'a happiness addict'; that's to say, whether you wish to be happy in a particular way, using your own resources and with the highest of motifs, [but which then] condemns you to be written off for the most part as either a blackguard or a poor idiot. How wise you are to spend your time coping with railways and figures!

Still avoiding any show of effusive thanks for his benefactor's generosity, he goes on to describe, with mounting passion, the frustrations of Claude Debussy trying to assert a new vision:

There's a new star on the musical horizon called Gustave Charpentier, destined, it seems to me, to achieve glory, riches and complete freedom from aesthetic considerations... The work that has just endeared him to the populace is called La Vie du poète. *The faded romanticism of the title tells us something about it but what you cannot possibly imagine is the work's total absence of taste – what you might call 'the triumph of the Brasserie'. It smells of tobacco and there are whiskers all over it... And of course all the little snobs, terrified for being taken for lifeless cretins, cry, 'What a masterpiece!' It's suffocating! But music, don't you know, is a dream from which the veils have been lifted. It's not even the expression of a feeling, it's the feeling itself. And they want to use it to tell lurid anecdotes, when the newspapers do that perfectly well! It's not easy to put up with this sort of thing. It's like being arm in arm with a beautiful woman whom you love and seeing her other arm being taken by a lout! It amounts very nearly to a personal insult.*

Debussy's frustration was justified; his predictions of fame and fortune for Gustave Charpentier were to be proved correct. By the end of the century Charpentier was being hailed as 'the saviour of French music'; his opera *Louise* was a box-office triumph, while one of the great masterpieces of opera, Debussy's *Pelléas et Mélisande*, was still, after five years, awaiting its first performance. 'I may not be any more talented than these people, but at least I can say I adore music,' rails Debussy, and he proceeds to give Poniatowski an example of exactly what it is he adores:

> *These last few days I've found some consolation in a very satisfying musical experience. It was at Saint-Gervais, a church where an intelligent priest has taken the initiative in reviving the wonderful sacred music of earlier times. It was extremely beautiful. They sang a Palestrina mass for unaccompanied voices. Even though technically it's very strict, the effect is of utter whiteness, and emotion is not represented (as has come to be the norm since) by dramatic cries but by melodic arabesques crossing with each other to produce something that has never been repeated: harmony formed out of melodies! (When you're next in Paris I promise I'll get you to come and hear it – better than my prose, which can't possibly do justice to miracles like this!)*

But of course his prose does do the music justice. And Debussy kept his promise.

A Sunday pilgrimage to Saint-Gervais had become a fixture for the group of poets and painters who gathered around Stéphane Mallarmé, who by the late 1880s had become the guiding spirit of literary Symbolism. Drawn to this milieu, Debussy took Poniatowski one Tuesday evening to Mallarmé's small apartment in the rue de Rome. These regular 'Tuesdays' provided the poet with an audience for his scrupulously refined – and mystically inclined – philosophy of art. 'To name an object is to suppress three-quarters of the enjoyment of a poem,' Mallarmé wrote in 1891; 'to suggest it, this is the dream.' Suggestion, dream, capturing presence within absence – such were the tenets of the Symbolist movement, in poetry, painting, drama, and in the music of Debussy. Such was the source of Debussy's own credo, as expressed in his letter to Poniatowski, and drawn from him by his vivid recollection of the music of Palestrina: 'It gives one courage to go on living in one's dream! And the energy to go on searching for the Inexpressible which is the aim of all art.'

A portrait of Stéphane Mallarmé painted by Renoir around 1892, at the time of Debussy's association with the venerated poet

'I attended the Tuesday meetings only rarely,' Poniatowski recalled:

> *I felt awkward there, occupying a place merely out of curiosity, among those young people who came in the spirit of apostles. But I continued to see Mallarmé outside his salon, at my house on the rue Balzac. The first time he came there was on a Sunday morning, after a mass at Saint-Gervais where Debussy had taken us to hear Gregorian chant* [actually the music of Palestrina, Victoria and Josquin]. *Very soon these Sunday morning sessions at Saint-Gervais became extremely popular. Indeed the numbers of our group grew to such an extent that the parishioners complained to their curé, because their seats were taken every Sunday by crowds of people who, it had to be said, listened to the sacred chants in exemplary silence, but usually with their backs to the main altar.*

Another of Debussy's favoured haunts was the Librairie de l'Art Indépendant, a tiny bookshop in the rue de la Chaussé d'Antin run by Edmond Bailly, a small-time publisher and composer. In addition to these interests, Bailly had a passion for Symbolist literature and the occult. 'Now there's someone I can recommend to you,' Debussy wrote to Poniatowski. 'If you only knew what erudition this little man hides within, what truly artistic ideas, and as for his intransigence it puts mine in the shade.' (Debussy was, however, in two minds about 'making tables talk', as he told another new friend, the composer Ernest Chausson, after attending an evening seance at the bookshop: 'Despite the interest afford-ed by such beyond-the-grave revelations, I had rather hear your conver-sation any day.') It was Bailly who had published, in limited editions, Debussy's *La Damoiselle élue* and the Baudelaire songs. He also published one of the most select Symbolist literary reviews of the day, *Entretiens politiques et littéraires*, edited by the Symbolist poet Henri de Régnier. At Régnier's suggestion Bailly published in this review two of the poems Debussy had written himself for his new collection of four songs, *Proses lyriques*. Debussy, in turn, was planning a set of orchestral pieces based on Régnier's *Scènes au crépuscules* (a project which in its original form came to nothing, although it eventually developed into the *Nocturnes* for orchestra at the end of the century).

During this period Debussy would arrive at Bailly's almost every after-noon around five o'clock. 'One went there,' Régnier recalled, 'to talk about literature' – but so congenial to Debussy were the surroundings and the conversation that he could easily be drawn into playing his latest compositions on the piano at the back of the shop. Bailly himself showed prophetic judgement in his estimation of his new composer friend: 'Yes young man,' he said to René Peter, 'he is one of the greatest and noblest, and he will be the most famous of them all.'

In the manner so characteristic of the multi-faceted Symbolist époque, Bailly's friends and customers would discuss their respective art forms and the way in which music, poetry and painting overlapped. One day Debussy played the piano score of *L'Après-midi d'un faune* to Régnier 'which he found as hot as a furnace,' as Debussy wrote to Chausson:

He also loved the way it gave him the shivers! (add that together if you can). But when he talks about poetry he becomes extremely interesting and shows a really refined sensibility. We got talking about certain words in the

Opposite, title page of the first edition of the songs *Proses Lyriques*, for which, with the encouragement of Symbolist poet Henri de Régnier, Debussy wrote his own poems

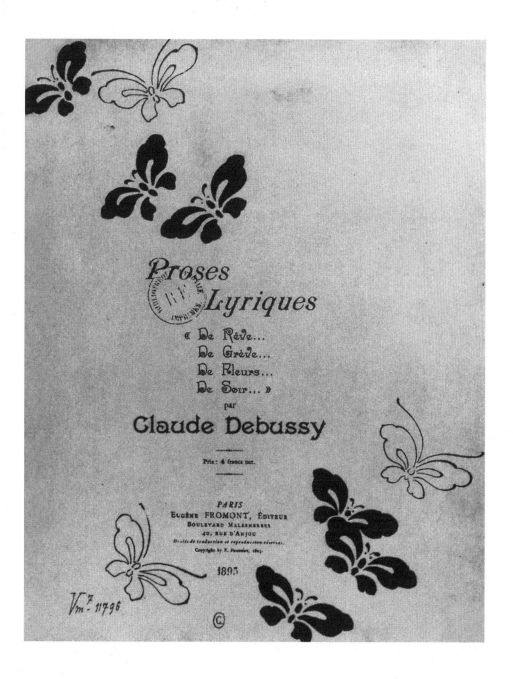

French language, and he said that their gold had been tarnished by overuse and brutish ignorance, and I thought to myself it was the same with the sound of certain chords, made banal by mass production; not a deeply original thought, I know, unless I add that these chords have lost their symbolic essence at the same time.

Régnier and Debussy shared a deep appreciation of Verlaine, whose delicate musicality echoed from many of Régnier's own poems. The erotic symbolism of such a poem as Régnier's *Le Prisonier* has a remarkable affinity with the images of desire which, as we shall see in the next chapter, caught Debussy's imagination in Mallarmé's extended poem *L'Après-midi d'un faune* and Maeterlinck's play *Pelléas et Mélisande*. Régnier's poem begins 'You have slipped away from me, but I saw your eyes when you slipped away' – and it goes on to describe 'the taste, the colour, the line and the curve of your body, pursued by my desire.'

When the artist Debussy humorously praised the businessman Poniatowski for the way in which he spent his life 'coping with railways and figures,' he could hardly have drawn attention to a lifestyle more removed from his own. The composer's milieu of the 1890s was what is usually described as 'bohemian', a term associated with a hand-to-mouth existence, transient love affairs, and intellectual discussions in cafés and nightclubs. The flavour of this existence is captured in an account by Vital Hocquet, a poet friend who performed at the Chat Noir cabaret under the pseudonym Narcisse Lebeau. The following recollections come from around 1892, at the time when Debussy had just started living with his girlfriend Gaby Dupont, the 'charming companion' Hocquet refers to:

Debussy couldn't afford to clothe or feed himself. Lunch consisted of a small bar of chocolate, such as schoolboys eat, and what was, in those days, the classic petit pain costing a sou. Dinner was, sometimes, more solid: Lebeau, who earned 500 francs a week as a plumber, would come and fetch his friend and the young woman who then shared his life and take them to some modest neighbourhood dive: Boilesve's place on the rue Monthyon, near the Folies-Bergère or, when 'the stars were touching' – that's to say when their pocket was practically empty – to the Cabaret du Clou on the rue Trudaine.

*At the Clou the food was far from being as appetizing or as copious as
at Boilesve's! The 'ratatouilles' – which is the best word to describe the stews
they served up there – were sometimes so uninviting that Debussy asked for
the plat du jour to be replaced by 'omelettes with sugar and jam', because he
was keen on his food and incredibly keen on sweet things of all sorts. Often
Claude Achille's charming companion would bring some sweets, which the
three of them would divide up as unequally as they could.*

*Debussy adored watching games of billiards and going to the circus;
he was particularly fond of the Guignol on the Champs-Elysées or at the
Folies-Bergère, where there were often billiard matches.*

*The room on the rue de Londres was a sort of panelled garret, untidily
filled with a rickety table, three cane chairs, a sort of bed and a splendid
Pleyel, on loan naturally...*

*In this room, where everything had to be done, Debussy wrote master-
pieces. He was collaborating then with the poet Catulles Mendès, for whom
he felt a profound antipathy, on the confection of a Cid, in a style far removed
from that of* Pelléas: *a romantic work, full of concessions...*

*The material difficulties under which Debussy laboured had no impact
on his artistic intransigence. He refused to give piano lessons at twenty francs
an hour on the pretext that the pupil was untalented. I mean! Twenty francs!*

*Lebeau permits himself to steal from Debussy's room a piece of Japanese
silk, representing a stream with tree stumps and carp. Lebeau admits his
theft and, after a discussion, it's agreed that in exchange for the Japanese
silk he will hand over an umbrella. Delighted to have an umbrella, Debussy
presents Lebeau into the bargain with a copy of the* Cinq poèmes de
Charles Baudelaire *on Holland paper, with this inscription: 'To Vital
Hocquet, who stole my fish, but for whom I feel a special affection'.*

This is surely an accurate impression of the surface colour of Debussy's
existence in the early 1890s – 'a time of destitution and youthful enthusiasm' as Hocquet called it – but along with the 'bohemian' label, such
accounts can also be misleading. It was not just youth and enthusiasm
that produced his masterpieces of these years, the String Quartet
(1892–3), *Prélude à l'après-midi d'un faune* (1892–4) and *Pelléas et
Mélisande* (broadly complete by 1895), any more than it was destitution
that provided the necessary pressures under which art is supposed to be
created. The pressures on Debussy in this regard were intellectual ones,
chief among which was the inhibiting presence of Wagner. Hocquet's is

Debussy adored circuses
and frequently attended the
Medrano or the Fernando
in the 1890s. This painting,
L'Écuyère au Cirque
Fernando, was painted in
1888 by Henri de Toulouse-
Lautrec, a painter whom
Debussy knew and admired

a Romantic portrait. Destitution hurt, despite Debussy's ability to
bounce back from it. Hocquet also fails to mention (or even notice)
the suffering caused by incomprehension, and the general neglect
of Debussy's genius which, towards the end of the 1890s, would lead
him to contemplate suicide.

But Debussy's artistic determination in this period was formidable,
and barely recognized by even his closest friends. At the same time as
entertaining them in cafés and cabarets, he was single-mindedly educat-
ing himself. He absorbed not only *Tristan* and *Parsifal*, but the novels
of Balzac, Charles Dickens, Leo Tolstoy and Flaubert; not only the
gamelan music of Indonesia (heard at the Exposition Universelle of
1889), but Modest Mussorgsky's *Boris Godunov*. He had already read
Shakespeare, Verlaine and Baudelaire, and he now added the philosophy
of Arthur Schopenhauer, the poetry and short stories of Edgar Allan Poe
(translated by Baudelaire and later by Mallarmé), the English poets
Shelley, Rossetti and Swinburne, as well as Mallarmé, Auguste Villiers de
l'Isle Adam, Joris Karl Huysmans and Jules Laforgue. As impecunious as
he was, he bought oriental objets d'art, Pre-Raphaelite prints, Art
Nouveau knick-knacks; he attended exhibitions and art galleries and,

with the sculptress Camille Claudel (Auguste Rodin's model and mistress), marvelled at the 'miracles of composition and paradoxes of perspective' (according to Robert Godet) in albums of Japanese prints, one of the most crucial influences on the Impressionist painters.

Many of Debussy's closest friends and mentors from this period were far from bohemian. He was quite able to lead a double life, as he had in Rome when writing letters to the husband of his mistress. Despite his awkwardness and shyness ('I'm really just a bear,' he told Marcel Proust), he could when he wished display a natural charisma that gave him entry to affluent circles: just as he had once been a welcome guest of the Vasniers, he was to become an intimate of Ernest Chausson, wealthy, cultured and truly representative of generous bourgeois respectability. The consequences of this friendship will be recounted in the next chapter. Then there was the family of Alfred Stevens, a painter whose grand career had been formed in the upper reaches of Second Empire society. Debussy was for a time close to his son, Léopold, also a painter, and daughter Catherine, god-daughter of the painter Edgar Degas. In 1895 he proposed to Catherine Stevens. Quite how serious he was is difficult to say, but Catherine had great beauty and, according to the Goncourt brothers' *Journal*, 'sweetly wanton eyes'. Debussy was rejected with the gentle admonition that he should get *Pelléas* performed first, after which his proposal might be reconsidered. It seems that, as welcome as he undoubtedly was in this milieu – and notwithstanding the profound influence he could assert on those around him – his complete social acceptance depended on a wholesale abandonment of his risqué background, and an increased income to match. Unfortunately the bohemian life of Claude's had a habit of breaking through the surface of his new respectability.

In Chausson's household for example, it would have been virtually impossible to introduce Gaby Dupont. (When introductions were needed, Gaby became Gabrielle Lhéry, a name with pretensions far removed from the ubiquitous Dupont.) Mistresses, lovers, a free lifestyle untrammelled by tedious middle-class norms – these were quintessential aspects of the bohemian existence. If painters had their models, so poets and composers had their muses. Contemporary accounts suggest that Gaby was a formidable partner, 'the least frivolous blonde I've ever had the pleasure of meeting', according to René Peter. 'Her most remarkable feature was her eyes, which were a blazing green. She had a powerful chin, strong limbs and a resolutely feline manner, and she accepted with stoicism, one might even say sublimity, the management of their destitute life together.' She remained with Debussy for eight years – living with him for six – which is serious by any standards. In view of the circumstances and his repeated infidelities, it was heroic. 'While he was lost in thought in company with his genius,' Peter dryly observed, 'Gaby would be out raising money on knick-knacks at some sordid pawnshop.'

There were considerable reasons for her to stick with him, not least his fundamental kindness and compassion, often only recognized by his closest friends. And with her 'strong opinions' (according to Peter) she would have relished the intellectual and artistic challenge of Debussy's circle. As for him, master of the unconventional and usurper of tradition, he would have appreciated Gaby's originality, and the courage with which she faced down the stares of respectability. Furthermore, he would have craved the emotional and domestic security she gave him. Finally, not least for the sensualist, there was her physical allure. Vital Hocquet recounted a tale of a meeting with Gaby in the company of the Comte de Balbiani, with whom she began a liaison post-Debussy: 'Dear friend,' she began, addressing the Count, 'this is Vital Hocquet; I have never slept

Debussy's girlfriend of the 1890s Gabrielle Dupont, known as Gaby. The photo was taken by Debussy's close friend Pierre Louÿs

Erik Satie in his room in Montmartre in 1890, painted by Santiago Rusiñol. Satie and Debussy had a lifelong friendship and it was partly through their discussions on music and contemporary culture that Debussy's aesthetic direction came into focus

with him.' The count replied, 'I am sorry for you, Monsieur, for you have missed out on something very special.'

Another special companion in bohemianism was Erik Satie, whose carefully cultivated eccentricity as artist-tramp would likewise not have comfortably fitted Chausson's drawing room. 'Satie was in the position of a man who knows only thirteen letters of the alphabet,' wrote his friend, the writer Contamine de Latour, 'and who decides to create a new literature using only these, rather than admit his own deficiency.

For sheer bravado, it was unparalleled at the time… [though] he admitted "I have to commit *tours de force* to get one bar to stand up"'. Satie
and Latour collaborated on a ballet, *Upsud*, 'a conglomoration of every
extravagance likely to astonish the public,' wrote Latour. The first
performance of 'half a dozen musical phrases, which he grandly called
his "score"' was given by Satie on the bar piano of the Auberge du
Clou, 'in whose basement thrived the intellectual life of Montmartre':

> *In the middle of the tumult caused by this rendition, one man remained*
> *impassive. Beneath his stubborn, bulging forehead, two little dark eyes*
> *shone like carbuncles; with his arms crossed he smiled silently under his*
> *faun-like beard. It was Claude Debussy. He had realized at once what*
> *a fund of seriousness, of boldness and sensitivity lay under Satie's outrageous*
> *clowning… Soberly, without excitement or self-satisfaction and with the*
> *authority that was already his, he explained the curious stamp of Satie's*
> *musical personality and the hopes it gave rise to for the future.*

'The authority that was already his' – this was in November 1892, just
at the point when Claude was finally shaking off Achille, as well as the
weight of *Rodrigue et Chimène*. He was already working on *Prélude à*
l'après-midi d'un faune and the String Quartet. Among the discerning
avant garde he was making a reputation, although as yet he had to be
content, as he had written some years earlier to Hébert, 'to make Art for
five people at the most'. Only the month before he had inscribed a copy
of *Cinq poèmes de Charles Baudelaire*, one of the mere 150, 'For Erik Satie,
gentle medieval musician, lost in this century for the benefit of his good
friend Cl. A. Debussy.'

Erik Satie was a continual presence throughout Debussy's great creative maturing of the 1890s. He witnessed it, worshipped it, and to a large
extent was involved in it, although it would be absurd to suggest that
without him Debussy would not have developed as he did. But undoubtedly Claude admired and respected Satie's originality, and did everything
in his power to promote his music. Claude was also influenced by Satie's
example (he called Satie 'the precursor') – his single-handed creation of
a musical style which was the antithesis of the Wagnerian manner, at
once spare, minimalist, emotionally drained and profoundly witty.

Their friendship lasted to the end of Debussy's life – a remarkably
sensitive achievement on his part considering that Satie fell out with

almost everybody. 'I wanted to be near him all the time,' recalled Satie, as if speaking of a love affair; 'for thirty years I was lucky enough to be able to fulfil this desire. We never had to explain things to each other – half a sentence was enough, because we understood each other and, it seemed, had always done so.' (In 1917, however, Satie became deeply offended by Debussy's apparent disegard of *Parade*. They became briefly estranged, but were reconciled just before Debussy's death the following year.)

'Among my memories as a guest [at his house],' Satie recalled, 'I cannot forget the delightful lunches I had, over several years, with him while he was living on the rue Cardinet. Eggs and lamb cutlets were the centre of these friendly occasions. But what eggs and what cutlets!… Debussy had the secret (*the innermost secret*) of these preparations. It was all washed down, gracefully, with a delicious white Bordeaux, which affected us somewhat and happily predisposed us to the joys of friendship.' We can be sure that 'the innermost secret' of Debussy's cookery was something over which he was as intransigent as his music, and certainly more boastful. René Peter too recalled such simple but unique culinary delights, the 'sausages and scrambled eggs, which he cooked to perfection, juicy and golden'.

Those who have suggested that Debussy's attitude towards Satie was patronizing miss the point. Any such hint, intended or accidental, and Satie would have been off. He probably knew Claude better than anyone, the good and the bad (some of his more acerbic comments after Debussy's death show this) and the length and depth of their friendship were a direct result of this knowledge and the trust it created. René Peter observed: 'It seems that Claude's feeling of being a benefactor took his mind to some extent off his own troubles. In this way Claude unwittingly manifested one of the most unjustly ignored facets of his character: that sort of proud goodwill which he hid even from himself under a rough, despotic exterior, better suited, in his view, to the real person he was.'

In June 1893 Satie wrote to his brother that the Société Nationale de Musique – 'the famous Society of Franck, Saint-Saëns, Vincent d'Indy & Co.' – was going to include several of his 'orchestral pieces' in a concert (such as the *Gymnopédies* and *Gnossiennes*, not in fact orchestrated). 'Debussy has shown some of my works to Chausson, who almost fainted, and it is that which has persuaded them to play my pieces.' In fact the concert did not happen until four years later, when Debussy undertook to orchestrate two of the *Gymnopédies*, the only orchestration he ever did of another composer's music. For a brief time, then, through the good offices of Claude Debusssy, it seems that Erik Satie did gain admission to Chausson's drawing room.

Satie later claimed responsibility for turning Debussy away from Wagner in the 1890s:

> *I explained to Debussy how we Frenchmen needed to break away from the Wagnerian adventure, which did not correspond with our natural aspirations. And I told him that I was not at all anti-Wagner, but that we needed our own music – without sauerkraut if possible. Why not make use of the representational methods of Claude Monet, Cézanne, Toulouse-Lautrec and so on? Why not make a musical transposition of them? Nothing simpler. Are they not alternative means of expression too?*

This is a tantalizing glimpse into the table-talk of two of the most important figures in early twentieth-century music. One yearns for more details of how 'the representational methods' of contemporary painting might be applied to musical composition, and details of Debussy's response. Nevertheless what ensued – whether in response to Satie or not – was *Prélude à l'après-midi d'un faune* and *Pelléas et Mélisande*, two works that were to change the course of western music. Satie, meanwhile, had written *Gymnopédies*, tiny pieces which, as influential as they were to become, not even he would have placed in the same company.

5

Boating on the river Marne, 1893: (l to r) Ernest Chausson, Raymond Bonheur, Claude Debussy, Madame Jeanne Chausson

'The bell has tolled now to mark my thirty-first year, and I'm still not confident that my musical attitudes are right; and there are things I can't yet do (write masterpieces, for example, or, among other things, be completely serious).'

Claude Debussy

Masterpieces 1893-5

While it will be forever arguable as to whether or not Debussy followed
Satie's advice and made a 'musical transposition' of the painters – of
'Monet, Cézanne and Toulouse-Lautrec' – it is certain he made one of
the poets; the creative collaboration is there for all to see. It was done with
concentration and immense discipline – with the artistic 'intransigence'
of which Debussy spoke to Poniatowski. To some observers, however –
those who witnessed him on the fringes – Debussy's failure to make a
mark in the years following his return from Rome was a sign of laziness.
His painter-friend Jacques-Émile Blanche did not even notice the
colossal effort involved in the gestation of *Pelléas*:

> *Work on* Pelléas *was slow, and we despaired of him ever finishing it.
> Having to give music lessons irked him. Indolent as he was – a dreamer,
> a sensualist, a voluptuary – a thousand outside amusements distracted him
> from an arduous task which meant his staying at home. His needs were
> imperious and frenetic. His friends did their best to satisfy his besetting sin:
> greed. How many times have I come across him leaving Cuvillier's with
> a bottle of port and caressing a pot of caviar, which he would then consume
> alone in his unheated apartment. After our meetings, someone would take
> him off to dinner at a restaurant; then we'd go on to the circus or the music-
> hall – but under no circumstances the theatre – and he would finish the
> evening with a long walk until dawn.*

But then Blanche recorded Debussy's 'extraordinary intellectual development' since his Roman days, without noticing that indolence could
not possibly have produced it. The composer Charles Koechlin gave
a different and rather more sympathetic interpretation of Debussy's
working methods: 'People have said he was lazy, or at least unreliable,
and only sat down to compose every now and again. That would have
been his right; he paid posterity in royal coinage. But – as far as I can
judge – this reproach smacks of philistine injustice, and Debussy certainly did not deserve it. It was simply that he belonged to a generation

which had a horror of hustle and making do. Finishing a song took him a long time.'

The main problem affecting the pace of Debussy's work was his meticulous self-criticism. He refused to exploit what Dukas called his 'angelic facility' for the sake of public acclaim or for desperately needed financial reward. Even *Rodrigue* is not an exception in this regard: he laboured long, and his admission of defeat came from self-knowledge. What Debussy was seeking was not natural facility, which he had in abundance, but a way, as it were, of divesting himself of it. He sought a technical mastery which would cut through the conventions of musical language, especially those of the nineteenth century, so as to allow him to get at 'the feeling itself' (his words to Poniatowski), which he knew was a near-unattainable goal. When he finally achieved technical mastery, in the great works of the 1890s, he spent the rest of his life trying to escape it. As he said to Dukas at the end of his life, he wanted to remove from his music 'all the marks of professional virtuosity'.

Debussy's turning year was 1893. By the end of it, voluptuary or no, his achievements quite suddenly looked considerable. This year saw the completion of *Proses lyriques* and the masterly String Quartet, as well as substantial work on the *Faune*. For his reputation, however, the most important event was a performance, at last, of *La Damoiselle élue* in April. This was arranged by the Société Nationale de Musique, an organization that Debussy had assiduously courted. (His refusal to have his *Fantaisie* for piano and orchestra performed under the society's auspices the previous year appears to have done him little harm.) He was finally becoming noticed. Reviewing the première of *La Damoiselle*, the critic of *Le Figaro* remarked on its abundance of life, how it was 'very insinuating and extremely modern… very sensual and decadent, rather corrupt in fact, but it has pages of sparkling beauty. How refreshing is a touch of youth!' So even at thirty-one, Debussy could get away with being a young composer after all.

Blanche's account of Debussy's indolence was far from the mark. Another vivid impression of him at this period, this time as a serious composer and thinker, comes from a memoir by Raymond Bonheur, his friend from conservatoire days:

It is well-known what an incomparable player he was of his own works, providing not only the illusion of an orchestra, but an extraordinary impression of life and movement. His hollow voice was rich in emphasis and expression, and those who have not heard him in the terrible scene with the hair in the fourth act of Pelléas *can have no suspicion of its real tragic power. But it was when he played from a still uncertain sketch, with the fever of improvisation still more or less upon him, that he was truly prodigious – 'How I envy the painters,' he used to say, 'who can embody their dreams in the freshness of a sketch.' I shall always remember how dazzled I was when he showed me* L'Après-midi d'un faune *in its original state, rippling with light, aflame with all the heat of summer, giving off a blinding radiance which was to be resisted in certain quarters for many a year …*

I have often heard it since, but no performance, however perfect, can make me forget those few minutes. In the same way, when I think of Pelléas, *I like to remember the various episodes not in the dusty scenery of the Opéra-Comique, but in the charming atmosphere of that apartment on the rue Gustave-Doret where I saw them being born and transformed, one after the other. It was usually on Saturday afternoon that I would climb the four storeys and I could be almost certain of meeting some friendly face there; Satie, in any case, would be sure to heed the summons and would come from Arcueil, always on foot, and would be particularly punctual that day because he would have the use of the piano in the house until evening. Debussy would begin by preparing tea with minute care, then, between a joke and a morsel of gossip, would sometimes let fall a brief, penetrating remark about the art he was then aiming at – but undogmatically, since he had no leaning towards the solemn, professorial tone. This art was one free from all formalism and any building-up of empty complexities, an art made of perpetual sacrifice, everything being subordinated to the single-minded search for expressivity.*

The artistic issues that propelled Debussy towards the *Faune* and *Pelléas* were foreshadowed in his letter of February 1893 to Poniatowski. 'The Cult of Desire', as he articulated it there, lies at the centre of both works. 'You could write down a formula for desire,' he wrote; '"everything comes from it and returns to it."' Debussy is defining desire in its broadest sense, as a compulsion for possession, an 'inescapable longing, a need almost', for an object: 'the moment of actual possession is one of joy, of love really.' In both the *Faune* and *Pelléas* desire is explored in a specifically sexual context. At their imaginative core both works are concerned with the artistic expression of desire and, in the case of *Pelléas*, the consequences that desire has for human happiness.

In the early 1890s Debussy had begun a collaboration with Mallarmé on a stage presentation, with incidental music, of the poet's first book, his extended poem *L'Après-midi d'un faune* (published after several rejections in 1876). First announced as *Prélude, Interludes et Paraphrase finale pour L'Après-midi d'un faune*, this original plan foundered, although it remains significant that Debussy's *Faune* began life not as an orchestral tone-poem but as music for the stage. Poniatowski has related that the collaboration resulted in 'long meditations in the course of which the musician received from the poet his conception of the role of music.'

The first line of Mallarmé's *L'Après-midi d'un faune* suggests a dream of perpetual pleasure: 'Those nymphs, I want to make them permanent.' The breath of the faun, as he plays on his flute, is also the warm breath of desire: implicit in the poem is the Syrinx myth, where, at the point when Pan attempts to ravish the nymph in the reed bed, she turns into a reed, which he plucks and plays as a flute. From desire music is born. And music for Debussy, as he wrote in 1893, 'is a dream from which the veils have been lifted. It's not even the expression of a feeling, it's the feeling itself' – surely an allusion to his *Faune*, on which he was then working.

Debussy's music is not programmatic, not least because Mallarmé's poem hardly offers a discernible narrative. The poem, through a combination of verbal images and verbal music (and even the visual appearance of the words on the page), aims to create an impression in the reader's mind in the manner of a dream. The music, in turn, 'is the general impression of the poem', as Debussy remarked in a letter to the critic Henri Gauthiers-Villars, adding that 'perhaps it's what remains of the dream within the depths of the faun's flute.' The languid flute solo at the outset announces the faun's presence as well as the dream landscape in which he is himself dreaming. Debussy unerringly transposes into music the intensity of the faun's desire and the keenness of his erotic visions:

Those nymphs, I want to make them permanent.
                                                                So clear
Their light crimson flesh, that it trembles in the drowsy air
Dense with sleepiness.
                                                I loved a dream?

In his apprenticeship as a composer Debussy had ample experience
of capturing this 'languorous ecstasy, this fatigue of love' (the opening
lines of *C'est l'extase langoureuse*, the first song of the Verlaine *Ariettes*).
Yet in the *Faune* not all is inaction. The emotional climax of the music,
which can be overwhelming in a great performance, is surely Debussy's
ardent response to that part of the poem in which the exultant faun
swoons at 'the secret terror of the flesh, quivering like lightning'. The
sexual resonances of both poem and music are palpable, but contained
within an essentially abstract framework that cannot cause offence.
(Debussy's *Faune* finally reached the stage in 1912 as a ballet choreographed by Vaslav Nijinsky. Debussy was appalled. What enraged
him, as we shall see later, was not only the angular modernism of the
choreography, but its sexual explicitness.)

The historical significance of *Prélude à l'après-midi d'un faune* cannot
be underestimated – 'the flute of the faun brought new breath to the art
of music', as Boulez has often proclaimed. Debussy himself spoke of the
Faune's 'disdain for the "science of beavers"', by which he meant the
formulaic, dogged constructional processes of musical composition
that 'weigh down some of our finest minds'; and of how the *Faune* 'has
no respect for tonality!' His remarks are typically to the point, but they
hardly suggest the full scope of his originality, nor the exquisite subtleties
of the score, whose harmonic and structural unfolding seem to defy
analysis. Boulez has spoken for all composers since who have felt the
impact of it:

*What was overthrown was not so much the art of development as the
very concept of form itself, here freed from the impersonal constraints of
the schema, giving wings to a supple, mobile expressiveness, demanding
a technique of perfect, instantaneous adequacy. Its use of timbres seemed
essentially new, of exceptional delicacy and assurance in touch; the use
of certain instruments – flute, horn and harp – showed the characteristic
principles of the manner in which Debussy would employ them in later
works. The writing for woodwinds and brasses, incomparably light-
handed, performed a miracle of proportion, balance and transparency.
The potential of youth defined by that score defies exhaustion and decrepi-
tude; and just as modern poetry took root in certain of Baudelaire's poems,
so one is justified in saying that modern music was awakened by* L'Après-
midi d'un faune.

Opposite, four wood
engravings, by Edouard
Manet for the first edition
of Mallarmé's *L'Après-midi
d'un faune* (1876)

If the impetus behind Debussy's creative development during these years was poetry, his ambition was to put music at the service of theatre: music *for* the theatre and music *as* theatre. He was preoccupied, as he had been since his Rome days, not just with the union of words with music in a technical sense, but with the meaning behind words, the interior landscape and the action implied. (He told Gauthier-Villars that the *Faune* 'follows the ascending shape of the poem as well as the scenery so marvellously described in the text.') It was to remain his life-time preoccupation – he was forever searching for new theatrical projects, although few eventually came to full fruition. Even his purely instrumental pieces, in their visually descriptive titles, manifest a conception of music not as an abstract art but as an art of representation.

In this regard the String Quartet of 1892 lies outside the main stream of Debussy's development. It is an intricately wrought, cyclic structure, employing a continuity of thematic material from movement to movement in the manner of the César Franck school. While it might not quite achieve the startling originality of the *Faune*, it is a work of compelling presence and inventiveness, although it baffled many at its première in December 1893 at the Société Nationale. (The *Faune* was not premièred for another year.) The *pizzicato* section of the scherzo movement is especially audacious, where texture takes precedence over melody and sonority, foreshadowing not only the Sonata for Cello and Piano of 1915, but the quartet writing of Anton Webern and Béla Bartók in the next century. The slow movement, in its allusions to plainchant, manifests a poignant lyricism that was perhaps Debussy's response to the religious music he heard with Mallarmé at the church of Saint-Gervais.

But by the time of the String Quartet's première, at the end of 1893, another operatic project was in view, and this time everything was right about the text and Debussy's capacity to set it. The Belgian poet and playwright Maurice Maeterlinck had recently become a cult figure in the Symbolist circles Debussy frequented, especially since the publication of his first play *La Princesse Maleine* in 1890. In May 1893 Debussy attended the first performance of the playwright's *Pelléas et Mélisande*, and in August, through the good offices of Régnier, he had secured Maeterlinck's permission to set the play to music. Debussy was about to give birth to his operatic masterpiece.

Maeterlinck's play is a retelling of the Tristan legend, so part of its interest for Debussy would have come from the challenge of meeting

Wagner on his own ground. It is about the eternal triangle, about an irresistible and illicit love that ends in jealousy, violence and death. The differences, however, between Maeterlinck's and Wagner's versions are crucial. Maeterlinck's is Celtic in origin, with strong resemblances to Arthurian legend. The play begins as the story of Golaud, the grandson of Arkel the King of Allemonde, who meets a beautiful princess in strange, dream-like circumstances. He marries her and takes her back to his grandfather's castle where the sun rarely shines. Here the princess, Mélisande, falls in love with Golaud's younger half-brother, Pelléas, but at the point where they declare their love Pelléas is killed by Golaud. Mélisande dies from grief, but it is so understated that those around her believe she has died giving birth to her premature baby. For the audience Golaud's tragedy is no less painful. He remains at the end tortured by his act and tormented by not knowing whether Mélisande and Pelléas had actually made love.

In strong contrast to *Tristan und Isolde*, timidity lies at the centre of *Pelléas et Mélisande*, which makes the incipient violence – and its brutal realization – all the more disturbing. The contrast is inherent in the characters of Wagner's Isolde and Maeterlinck's Mélisande, the former passionate and extrovert, the other timid, disconnected, emotionally damaged in some way that is hardly explained. The opening scene, however, suggests obliquely that Mélisande has been raped. This is the implication, although it is often overlooked, of her hysterical answers to Golaud's insistent question 'Has anyone wronged you?' She cries, 'I don't want to tell you, I cannot tell you'. This colours the whole opera and brings to her character and behaviour, otherwise that of the *femme fatale* of male fantasy, a deep psychological realism. (Richard Langham Smith has pointed out that this pre-history, although never explicitly referred to by Maeterlinck, was much discussed by early performers of the opera, who associated Mélisande's story with the ravishment in the Bluebeard legend.)

Nor can Pelléas's desire for Mélisande compete, in Wagner's terms, with the overwhelming passion of Tristan for Isolde – although in the scene in which Pelléas finally confesses his love we can sense he might have got there if he had been allowed: he is killed by Golaud at the very moment when passion takes fire. Debussy makes Pelléas's initial confession, however, timid to the point of extinction (even more so than Maeterlinck), thus creating the ideal antithesis to Wagnerian opulence.

'I love you' is heard in sudden silence. Mélisande's reply, 'I love you too', is barely audible, sung on a low C without orchestra. The protagonists, and the audience too, are transfixed by the terrifying momentousness of it all – 'You said that in a voice which came from the end of the earth,' says Pelléas. Debussy's denuding art, here, is at the furthest remove from the operatic and the nearest to the prose and Harold Pinter-like silences of Maeterlinck's play. ('I've gone looking for music behind all the veils Mélisande wraps round herself,' Debussy wrote to Chausson, 'and a means of expression which I think is quite unusual, namely silence.')

Pelléas and Mélisande do not appear to consummate their love, whereas Tristan and Isolde most definitely do – indeed Wagner's whole musical edifice depends on it. In Wagner's opera sexual passion is explicitly stated and glorified in the music, while the death of the two lovers symbolizes their passion at its most extreme. In the Debussy-Maeterlinck version death is a symbol of nothingness and failure, even though at first it is only the imminence of death that brings passion to life. Neither Pelléas nor Mélisande is transfigured by death: they lose everything and gain nothing. Mélisande's epitaph might be Othello's anguished words as he faces the death of Desdemona, 'Oh the pity of it, Iago, the pity of it' – surely in Maeterlinck's mind when he wrote the words for Arkel, '*Mais la tristesse, Golaud, mais la tristesse de tout ce que l'on voit*' ('But the sadness, Golaud, the sadness of all we've seen').

Another strong appeal for the composer of *La Damoiselle élue* was the Pre-Raphaelite influence on Maeterlinck, although in the playwright's case this was drawn not so much from Rossetti as from the second phase of the Pre-Raphaelite painters – often termed the 'romantic' generation – and above all Edward Burne-Jones. 'The haunting figures of Burne-Jones's pallid damsels,' writes Langham Smith, 'their dilated eyes on the verge of tears, distilling the world's sorrow, were clearly implicated in the genesis of Mélisande, and in *Pelléas*, as in many images of Burne-Jones, these frail figures exist in an atmosphere where violence is never far away.'

Unlike Wagner's *Tristan*, the events of *Pelléas* are not concerned with apocalyptic love, with humanity larger than life, but with people (including a child) grappling with timeless issues of innocence and guilt, youth and age, sexual desire, loneliness, human disconnection, jealousy. As Debussy said, 'Despite its atmosphere of dreams, *Pelléas* contains much more humanity than those so-called documents of real life' (an allusion, again, to the operas of Charpentier). There might be a fairy-tale knight

La Belle Dame sans merci, by John William Waterhouse, an English painter inspired by the Pre-Raphaelites. This painting, which echoes the fairy-tale atmosphere of *Pelléas et Mélisande*, dates from 1893, the same year as the première of Maeterlinck's play

lost in a forest, but we are left in no doubt as to how to relate to him: 'Are you a giant?' asks Mélisande, to which Golaud replies, 'I'm a man like any other.' She might be a princess who has lost her crown in a forest pool, but as old King Arkel comes to recognize at the end, she was 'as poor and mysterious a creature as all of us are'.

Here was the subject and the text the young composer had dreamed of eight years earlier, as expressed in one his numerous letters to Henri Vasnier: 'I would always rather deal with something where the passage of events is subordinated to a thorough and extended portrayal of human feelings. That way, I think, music can become more personal, more true to life; you can explore and refine your means of expression.' Because the playwright's dialogue is so plain, and at times so seemingly disconnected, the emotions of the protagonists are barely revealed by the words themselves. What they fail to articulate is meant to be understood by other means, through symbols, objects and images either present on stage or alluded to in the dialogue. So, for a composer, at 'the point where the word becomes powerless as an expressive force', in Debussy's own phrase, music can take over. He saw in Maeterlinck's play how he could achieve, operatically, a deeply affecting psychological realism by keeping the dialogue unadorned, close to the rhythms and inflections of speech ('more personal, more true to life'), while giving the expressive force of the drama to the orchestra. Music would become the ultimate symbolic expression of meaning. As such, Debussy's tragic opera expresses a universal truth with a force and insight that Maeterlinck's play fails to reach by itself.

One of Debussy's accomplishments in *Pelléas* was the extraordinary balance that he achieved between orchestra and text, and the way in which he allowed the 'expressive force' of the words to control the dramatic action. At the time some considered this to be a deconstruction of the true nature of opera (and a few still do). As Richard Strauss said when he first heard the work in 1907: 'There's no music in it' – by which he meant no 'opera' as he understood it, no lyrical vocal lines supported by rich symphonic development. 'One might as well be listening to the play of Maeterlinck as it was,' he complained, 'without the music.' He had almost put his finger on it, although he failed crucially to hear that this was in fact a profoundly original *musical* process. Allowing the play such predominance – with opera emerging from the pressures and necessities of speech – called for a supreme control of musical means. The composer George Benjamin has said that the fundamental intention of Debussy's style in *Pelléas* was 'to liberate and concentrate the perception of the harmony. No more subtle harmonic language than this has existed, with such extraordinary care devoted to details of register, interval, modality and harmonic significance.'

For a composer so ready to test the limits of music as a means of representation, and music as 'the feeling itself', Maeterlinck's blend of symbolism and realism was ideal material. The symbols are especially effective for the way in which they work in the real world too: forests, darkness and light, the sun (or lack of it), the sea, all sit comfortably in a naturalistic framework, as do crowns and golden rings. The forest and the sea are the constant background images of the play, suggesting non-human power, mystery, fear – and immutability. The forest in the opening scene, where Golaud finds Mélisande weeping beside the pool, also symbolizes their hopeless entanglement, as well as their lost paths

Following page, Act IV, scene 2 of Glyndebourne's 2004 production of Pelléas et Mélisande. Golaud was played by John Tomlinson and Mélisande by Marie Arnet

in life: 'Where are you going?' Mélisande asks at the end of the scene.
'I don't know,' he answers, 'I too am lost.' Water is a celebrated symbol
of the unconscious (with often sexual overtones): so the pool is an image
of the dream world from which Mélisande has appeared; it is shallow, or
it appears to be, for her lost golden crown can be seen gleaming at the
bottom. It would apparently be a simple matter for Golaud to reach in
and retrieve it, but she becomes nearly hysterical when he offers to do so.
The sexual implications are clear, although outwardly Golaud maintains
complete decorum: significantly Mélisande later maintains that Golaud
had tried to kiss her, which is factually untrue. And this moment by the
pool also implies that if Mélisande's dream world, or indeed her past, are
disturbed, then the consequences will be devastating.

In a later reversal of this scene Pelléas takes Mélisande to a well, which
seems fathomless – 'no one has ever seen the bottom'. This time the water
is invaded. Mélisande allows her hair to fall into it, much to Pelléas's awe,
and she drops Golaud's ring into it, a moment of carelessness with
perhaps just a hint of deliberation – the audience is allowed to choose.
Unknown fate, desire, deception: all of these themes are competing
within the offered symbols. But Debussy also captures the simple realism
of the scene – the youthfulness of the pair, their innocence, the hint
of flirtation between them, the silence in which 'one can hear the water
sleeping'. Their awakening love is set against moments of disturbing
premonition (for the audience): when they discuss Golaud, or when
Pelléas dismisses the loss of the ring as trivial, or when Mélisande says,
with such strange inconsequence, 'my hands don't seem very well today,'
we are uneasily aware of the depth of that water.

There is another deep pool, the stagnant depths below the castle vaults
where Golaud takes Pelléas and nearly pushes him in. Here the water is
both a symbol of death and the objective correlative of Golaud's jealous
fears, of the depths of his subconscious where sexual corruption lies.
Outwardly Golaud is nothing less than a gentleman but, like Othello,
when he is sexually thwarted a crude masculine violence breaks through.
The faint premonition of violence in the opening scene, caught from
allusions to Mélisande's past, turns out to have been emanating from
Golaud too. 'Do you never close your eyes?' he asks her, warning us of
his attraction to her. 'Only when I go to sleep,' she innocently answers,
which can only have added to his growing desire. When later he loses
control, it is her eyes that obsess him as a symbol of her guilt – 'Shut

them! Shut them!' he cries – and it is the word 'innocence' that he bitterly
flings at her.

Mélisande's hair is quite simply a symbol of her allure: she unties it for
Pelléas at the well, she combs it from her bedroom window, Pelléas wraps
himself in it (a notoriously difficult moment to stage), a tree ensnares it –
so ensuring the lovers are caught by Golaud – and finally Golaud pulls it
in his bestial rage and drags her across the floor. Mélisande's femininity,
the source of her power and the men's woe, is here finally and brutally
turned against her.

The greatness of Debussy's *Pelléas et Mélisande* allows many interpretations, though a considerable degree of misunderstanding has meant
that it has not always achieved popular recognition in the opera house.
The history of reaction to *Pelléas* has been littered with doubt as to its
dramatic strength, as Boulez has lamented:

> *Since Debussy's ideas about the drama are expressed so pointedly in his*
> *music and the means he employs are defined as precisely as it is possible*
> *to define them, why and how did all the misunderstandings arise that have*
> *so totally perverted the sense of* Pelléas*? It seems to me the very height of*
> *nonsense to associate this opera with a kind of celestial boredom, a pale,*
> *remote, 'distinguished' poetry, and an imagination that is not so much*
> *exquisite as tired, even exhausted. People who use words like 'mystery'*
> *or 'dream' when speaking of* Pelléas *are in fact emptying them of real*
> *significance and indulging in an imagery which is insipid, bland, mock-*
> *modest, and in fact plain silly.*

It was, nevertheless, Debussy himself who spoke of 'its atmosphere
of dreams'. And Boulez's commentary might be placed next to the
composer Robin Holloway's:

> *Because Debussy's manner is to denude his events and emotions, he in*
> *fact succeeds in expressing them with painful and uncomforted intensity.*
> *Not insupportably raw and violent as Wagner would be without music, but*
> *merely excruciating; a poignancy that can barely articulate itself… I have*
> *called the work the perfection of nihilism; few operas manifest a greater*
> *unity of atmosphere, or a more consistent appropriateness of music to*
> *subject and story. In its ability effortlessly to touch upon what is elusive,*
> *mysterious, quietly disquieting,* Pelléas *is without rival.*

Debussy would live with *Pelléas* for nearly ten years before its première in 1902. He was occupied with it in performance, and in endless revisions and retouching of the orchestration, almost to the end of his life in 1918.

The gestation of *Pelléas* occurred at a fascinating point in Debussy's personal life, one which, like the Vasnier episode in the early 1880s, is central to an appreciation of his character and motivation. Since 1888 he had been a member of the Société Nationale de Musique, the body founded in 1871 for the promotion of contemporary French music. For Debussy the society was the principal channel through which he could get his music known – indeed for many years the only one – and it was also where he first became acquainted with Ernest Chausson. In April 1893, following a Société concert which had included the première of *La Damoiselle élue*, Debussy and Chausson developed a close friendship. Debussy also became close to Chausson's brother-in-law, the painter Henri Lerolle. There begins again a familiar pattern: protestations of deep and exclusive friendship, financial help generously offered and freely accepted – and in the midst of this a hectic love affair, this time ending in scandal.

Chausson was a lawyer by training, as befitted a wealthy and respectable background in which sons were not expected to waste their time in the arts. Not having to earn a living, however, meant that he could fulfil his passion for music, and instead of practising law he took composition lessons from Massenet, and later Franck. He also sketched, and wrote short stories, as well as the draft of a novel. Today he is remembered principally for his late-Romantic chamber music, such as the Piano Quartet, and such melancholy songs as the *Chanson perpétuelle* for soprano, piano and string quartet. One of his finest series of songs, the Maeterlinck settings *Serres chaudes* (1893–6), shows the strong influence of Debussy. (The opera to which he devoted his life, *Le Roi Arthus*, is rarely performed.) It is a mark of Chausson's character that he was not offended that the promotion of Debussy's music should be at the expense of his own: one review of the concert in April 1893, which had also included work by Chausson, savaged his music and everything the Société Nationale stood for, with the sole exception of its discovery of Monsieur Claude Debussy.

Henri Lerolle, while largely overlooked today, was one of the most successful of French artists of this period. His deliberate avoidance of academic formulae would have appealed to Debussy, as would his taste

Debussy in 1893, with the Chaussons and Raymond Bonheur

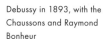

in music and his enthusiasm for the gradually emerging *Pelléas*. He was close to the circle known as the Nabis, led by the painter and theoretician Maurice Denis, and was friends with a number of the Impressionists, especially Renoir and Degas; it was surely through Lerolle that Debussy acquired his taste and fascination for Degas.

Ernest Chausson's home in Paris would have delighted Debussy's keenly visual imagination. (Even as a student, Marguerite Vasnier recalled, Debussy's opinions on visual art were 'completely personal and quite remarkable'.) The decor included painted panels by Lerolle alongside works by those who were to become the elite of French visual art, including Auguste Renoir, Degas, and the Symbolist painters Odilon

Redon and Paul Gauguin. Chausson's salon was host to some of the most brilliant painters, writers and musicians of the day.

The friendship between Debussy, Chausson and Lerolle was a meeting of minds, a rediscovery of youth, and a celebration of an essentially male companionship. Debussy liked to flatter both men by claiming they were like elder brothers – Chausson was seven years older, Lerolle fourteen. From the copious correspondence one gets the impression that the older men were slightly surprised, even flattered, by the strength of their attachment, which was driven by that trait in Debussy's character that could attract people so strongly – his 'extraordinary charm… made up of a thousand things difficult to analyse, but which few men failed to feel', as the writer Gabriel Mourey recalled. However, in later life this charm was displayed to fewer and fewer people.

In the month following the success of *La Damoiselle* Debussy was twice invited down to the chateau Chausson rented at Luzancy, on the idyllic river Marne. The first visit produced a letter of thanks which sounded that poignant note of loss, like homesickness, that was so characteristic of Debussy when his affections were aroused: 'I feel sad at being separated from you, and the assurance of your friendship is all I need to wipe away the slightly disconcerting memory of your departure, just when everything was going so well… I'd rather just say that I'm very fond of you and that your support is certainly one of those things in my

Baigneuse allongée sur le sol by Edgar Degas (1886–8). Lerolle owned this painting, so it is highly likely that it would have been known to Debussy. Robert Godet recalled that Degas was 'the only artist constantly on Debussy's lips' at this time, an interest no doubt imbibed from Lerolle

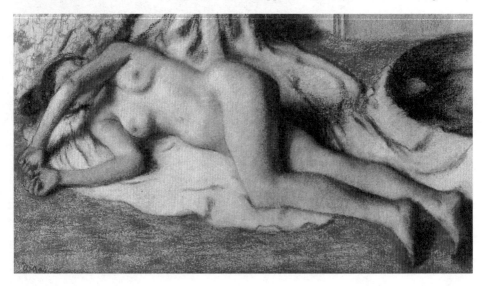

life I care most about!' The second visit to Luzancy at the end of May was to a big house party. 'There will not be just us this time,' wrote Chausson, looking forward to Debussy's arrival; 'the Lerolles, six of them, will also be there, but that doesn't matter, they are as nice as anything… Bring something to do.' Debussy at once got on with Lerolle, performed Mussorgsky and Wagner at the piano, played billiards, went boating, and was surrounded by 'dear little children, making a noise like half a million thunderstorms', as he later recalled to Chausson. He must have enchanted the company at Luzancy, just as he had ten years earlier at the Vasniers' country retreat outside Paris. 'In truth I'm

An engraving showing the painter Henri Lerolle, the brother-in-law of Ernest Chausson and, for a time, a close friend of Debussy

amazed,' wrote Chausson on 4 June, when the party was all over and
Debussy had departed. 'Ball games, and wooden horses!!! How old am
I then? I hardly like to think; but it seems that this spring has turned
me into a child again… I am deeply touched by the affection you have
shown towards me. I am so sure of this, that you are without doubt one
of those – perhaps the only one – with whom I can talk freely, because
I feel I've nothing to fear with you, and can show myself as I am, even
my bad side. And that is one of the great and rarest charms of friendship.
You know you can count on mine absolutely.'

Chausson had high ideals, both of behaviour and art, and he wel-
comed Debussy's friendship as an antidote to his own earnestness.
Debussy would bring out a different side: 'You'd knock me about a
little, and all would be well,' Chausson confessed to him. And it seems
Chausson also accepted trenchant criticism of his own music: 'You
don't let yourself go enough,' Debussy wrote, 'and in particular you
don't seem to allow enough play to that mysterious force which guides
us towards the true expression of a feeling, whereas dedicated, single-
minded searching only weakens it.' Debussy could be speaking of his
own struggles, and the dawning of his artistic maturity.

In the light of the subsequent rupture in their relationship, Chausson's
protestations of absolute friendship take on a heavy dramatic irony. He
writes at one point, having previously ventured a criticism of Debussy's
life-style with Gaby (to which Debussy had taken offence), 'if you could
have read my deepest thoughts you would have seen that there was
nothing there but affection, and not a trace of distrust. This is a very
nasty word which must never be uttered between us.' But in March 1894
distrust of Debussy becomes, for Chausson, the only course to follow.

The exact reasons are not entirely clear. In 1959, seventy-five years after
the events, Chausson's daughter, Madame Etiennette Lerolle-Chausson,
suggested to Edward Lockspeiser the following: 'Financial questions
played a part in their estrangement, particularly as there appeared to
be an element of double dealing… My father was also annoyed by the
strange engagement, fortunately but very unpleasantly broken off, with
our friend Thérèse Roger.' Madamoiselle Roger was the singer who had
taken the part of the damsel in *La Damoiselle*'s première in 1893. But
Madame Lerolle-Chausson was wrong; her father was delighted by the
engagement, although at first 'speechless'. He tells Lerolle:

Debussy in 1893, the centre
of attention at Chausson's
home at Luzancy

*I find lovers so utterly captivating, not to say a rarity in our refined
intellectual circle. This announcement is certainly going to set tongues
wagging interminably. I can hear them from here, and I'm happy only to
hear them from here. Personally I'm confident about the outcome; I think
it'll be a very happy marriage, precisely because it's not one that the ultimate
in common sense would approve.*

As for financial 'double dealing' there is little to corroborate such a
charge. Debussy certainly got himself into a mess and was less than
straightforward in dealing with it, but it appears that it was not so
much his finances that were the problem, as the existence of the green-
eyed Gaby. Debussy was up against the strict moral code of a wealthy
middle-class milieu in which he was a complete newcomer.

Mademoiselle Thérèse
Roger, to whom Debussy
became engaged, for a very
brief period, in early 1894

Through Chausson he had gained entrance to some fashionable circles
where he would play and sing Wagner at the piano for large sums, and
perform his own music. One such was the salon of a dominating socialite,
Madame de Saint-Marceaux. 'She's discovered I'm a first-rate talent!'
Debussy wrote to Chausson, refusing to be impressed. 'It's enough to
make you die laughing. But really, you'd have to be a hopelessly weak
character to be taken in by all this rubbish. It's so fatuous!... But at least
I have Lerolle with whom I can come clean.' (But perhaps Madame de
Saint-Marceaux was not herself so fatuous. Her diary for February 1894
records Debussy playing to her some parts of *Pelléas*: 'It's a revelation.
Everything is new, the harmony, the writing, and all so musical.') In this
milieu Debussy and Mademoiselle Roger performed together, and on 17
February 1894, at another concert for the Société Nationale, they gave the
first performance of two of his *Proses lyriques* (*De fleurs*, dedicated to
Madame E. Chausson, and *De soir*, dedicated to Henri Lerolle). The
Marie Vasnier scenario seemed to be repeating itself, although Thérèse

had neither the splendid voice nor the engaging charisma of Marie. But this time the relationship was conducted under the approving eye of Madame de Saint-Marceaux, renowned for her matchmaking. So it seems, despite his protestations to the contrary, that Debussy *was* 'taken in by all this rubbish', for he had his head turned towards the temptations of social respectability.

Financially Debussy was definitely in Chausson's debt, both asking and taking with impunity, but as he wrote in one of his last letters to Chausson, 'my fault was only a certain waywardness in material matters and for that I've been severely punished.' For 'a certain waywardness' one can perhaps read 'careless profligacy' (or 'refusal to take jobs beneath my status as an artist', which Chausson pressed on him) but there is no evidence that he was deliberately dishonest with Chausson over money. His debts certainly played a large part in the ensuing events – and where issues of social class are concerned, money is never far behind – but there seems to have been total transparency on Debussy's part in acknowledging this issue. Undoubtedly he saw his advantage, but this does not amount to 'double dealing'.

Debussy's requests for money could sometimes be blunt ('I'll be brief about it: I need your help once again!'), but so disarming that few could refuse. 'When you come on Sunday,' he wrote to René Peter, 'try to be extremely rich, because if I don't pay my rent, people (or something resembling them) will hang furiously on my doorbell! In any case it's not a question of 50,000 francs and, in passing, forgive me for playing once again the role of "master-sponger". I hope it'll be the last time.' It seems his friends willingly accepted his 'master-sponging', not only because they recognized the extremity of his poverty (as well as his genius), forgiving his inability to use money sensibly, but also because he showed, according to Paul Dukas, 'an exquisite delicacy' as a friend.

On occasion Debussy's requests for funds were left in the air, while he insouciantly allowed the facts to speak for themselves: 'I'm still looking for an apartment,' he wrote to Chausson, 'and Etienne Dupin and I can be found climbing innumerable staircases. On one of them, strange to relate, I even met one of my creditors and the next day had a letter threatening me with all sorts of unpleasant proceedings.' This had been July 1893, just after his stay at Luzancy. A fifth-floor apartment was then found at 10 rue Gustave-Doré, where Bonheur, Satie and innumerable others later came to hear the first renderings of the *Faune* and *Pelléas* at the piano. Chausson helped with the furniture as well as with the rent, and Lerolle gave Debussy a picture for his wall. It was at this point that a dispute about Gaby arose – Gaby of course accompanied Debussy to his new home. Chausson was uneasy about this liaison, but for the present he accepted the status quo.

Debussy was well aware of how his social climbing might be regarded, as he wrote to Lerolle, telling him of his engagement:

> *I have something crazy to tell you! There are plans for a marriage between Mlle Thérèse Roger and Claude Debussy! It's all completely unreal, but that's how it is, and it's happened just like a fairy tale! I've been deeply in love with Mlle Roger for a long time, but it's seemed so impossible that I've just not dared think of it! I beg you not to judge ill of me, I've told Madame Roger exactly the situation I'm in, and that I would wish her daughter to keep her financial independence! As for me, I will always be able to get by. Now Madame Roger would like to see you to talk about me; I thought maybe you wouldn't mind, and that you would do me this little favour? Moreover, I am completely free, my last young lady* [Gaby] *having left one morning in February in order to make something better of her life.*
>
> *Please assure Madame Roger of my best intentions, and of my desire to be worthy of all that she has done for me! And I would ask you to keep this just between ourselves! But truly, I feel a desperate need to dedicate my life to someone, and I think Mlle Roger will fulfil it. And come and talk, for there are things I can't confide to a cold sheet of paper.*

Neither Chausson nor Lerolle need any persuading as to his honour and sincerity – for the present. And they even 'know of his reputation given him by his friends', as Lerolle writes to Chausson. 'If he deserves it, then it seems to me he has changed. In any case, he's very nice to us and he adores Thérèse and her mother.' What was this 'reputation given him by his friends'? That recorded by Jacques-Émile Blanche, of being a sensualist, a voluptuary? All of his friends knew of his debts, and they all knew of the existence of Gaby. It is regarding Gaby, however, that Debussy appears to have been not only less than frank, but hopelessly naïve.

Meanwhile, his assurances that his *petite amie*, Gaby, had left 'one morning in February' were taken at face value. But if the straight-laced Chausson was confident about the prospective marriage, the writer Pierre Louÿs, who had recently become an intimate friend of Debussy's, was greatly concerned. He wrote to his brother that Madame de Saint-Marceaux was guilty of 'a grave imprudence in marrying Debussy to a drawing room singer. I am convinced it would be a bad marriage, and I am distressed for my friend's sake.' As it happened, Louÿs proved to be the most clear-sighted of all the protagonists in this business.

Then, on 17 March 1894, Madame de Saint-Marceaux confides to her diary: 'Debussy's marriage is off. There are dreadful mysteries concerning his life. How sad to think that so wonderfully gifted an artist should live in the mire.' It seems she had received information, anonymously, suggesting that Debussy was intent on keeping on his mistress while undertaking his marriage to Thérèse. The 'dreadful mysteries' – otherwise unexplained – are the stuff of rumour now running amok in respectable drawing rooms. It is probable that at this point suggestions were being made that Debussy was not only deceiving Chausson about his personal life, but swindling him as well.

Debussy had no conception of what he was up against. His letter to Chausson from just the day before, in which he speaks of a 'certain waywardness in material matters', shows him to be quite unaware of the opprobrium about to be visited upon him. 'The only distress I felt at your letter,' Debussy begins, 'was to think that you believed such things of me!' Exactly what 'such things' were is never fully explained. He continues:

I've not hidden any of my debts from Madame Roger and I fully intend to tell her that a certain friend is being kind enough to become my sole creditor! In any case there's nothing else I could do. I need a life that's transparent, without any mysterious depths. It's a transformation I'm undergoing and almost as much an intellectual as a moral one. So it's vital you lend me another fifteen hundred francs! *First I must pay some debts, and then I absolutely have to buy a dress for my mother* [for the wedding, fixed for the middle of April]. *Forgive the detail but it's so you can see I really do need the money! I need hardly add that I'm determined to remove this burden from our friendship as soon as possible!… Could I, lastly, ask you to let me have an answer as soon as possible?*

Could such engaging frankness really be hiding a conniving duplicity? Was Debussy pressing his advantage too far? Chausson would surely have stood by his former avowals of trust and friendship – after all, Debussy was only calling on the help that he had always been promised. But three days later, on 19 March, Chausson is more fully appraised of Madame de Saint-Marceaux's information, whatever that may have been. He writes in anguish to Lerolle: 'I haven't been able to think of anything else except this sordid affair since this morning and I'm feeling more and more despondent about it… My first impulse was to write to Debussy. Jeanne [Chausson's wife] prevented me, and she was right.' The friendship and the correspondence between Ernest Chausson and Claude Debussy had come to an abrupt end.

Chausson believed the worst, but others, including Pierre Louÿs, did not. On 22 March Louÿs writes to Madame de Saint-Marceaux in dignified defence of his friend, yet even now 'the rumours… about his past life' are not spelt out, merely denied:

Madame,

The unfortunate telegram which finalized the break, and which has caused my poor friend so much suffering, has certainly been misunderstood: but I recognize that appearances condemn Debussy and I am not surprised people have been scandalized.

But perhaps you will allow me to add that a young man cannot dismiss like a chambermaid a mistress who has lived with him for two years, who has shared his poverty without complaint and against whom he can level no reproaches, other than that he is tired of her and is getting married. In the ordinary way these matters are settled with a few banknotes; it may not be the height of delicacy, but it serves. As you know, this was not a course Debussy had open to him. He felt he had to act with circumspection. It was a question of kindness, and also of prudence, because if treated more harshly she might have sought revenge. So he proceeded slowly. If his engagement had been announced less precipitately, Debussy would have had the time to disengage himself completely, before the day when a formal engagement forced him to put his former liaison behind him. He did not do so, or, if you prefer, he did not know how to do so: and he has been cruelly punished for it.

As for the rumours that have reached you about his past life, I stand as a witness that they are monstrous calumnies, and I think that the honour of a man (I do not speak of Debussy the artist, whom we are not discussing) cannot be wounded by anonymous letters, which are usually the work of a liar and always a coward. I know from personal knowledge that Debussy is incapable of having lived as it is claimed.

I write this in a state of profound sadness, and with an outspokenness which, Madame, I beg you to excuse. I know of nothing more distressing than to see thus dishonoured, in a matter of no more than a week, a man who is loved and greatly respected, who has been starved of good fortune for fifteen years and who sees all the doors closed against him at the moment when it is becoming apparent that he is a genius.

It can be seen at this point just how out of his depth Debussy suddenly became in his new milieu. The 'refined intellectual circle', in Chausson's phrase, might have espoused up-to-date Symbolist ideas, but it was deeply conservative at root – a milieu of old-money and old-family ties. It is impossible to imagine Debussy ever writing such a letter of justification as Louÿs's, or ever manifesting such man-of-the-world smoothness. His own resolve seems to crumble and, after initial protestations, he ceases to defend himself. Madame de Saint-Marceaux records in her diary: 'He came to justify himself, and to persuade me that all the rumours flying around are lies. He didn't manage to persuade me. He must be two entirely separate beings. He has lost all moral sense.' (Clearly she was not persuaded by the suave Louÿs either.) But Debussy's pride reasserts itself, and he comes to see that, for now at least, the 'new life' he had believed was within his grasp – much influenced by a moral idealism that was actually alien to him – was an absurdity.

Chausson had almost certainly over-reacted. There is some evidence that, after a while, Debussy saw him again, possibly through the good offices of Lerolle. 'I've been to see Debussy,' Lerolle writes to Chausson in October, 'who's getting on slowly. He played again for me some passages of *Pelléas* which I know off by heart, and which I love. What a pity he should be what he is, because we have such good times together. With you being away, if I couldn't go and see him any more I should end up being very depressed.'

Nothing is known about Debussy's own reactions to the situation. It is inconceivable that he would just have carried on as if nothing had happened, although he might have given the appearance of doing so. Indeed, piecing together his state of mind during the years that followed, it seems that these events caused a deep and lasting psychic disturbance. Specifically there is only that single remark by Lerolle that same year, that he is 'getting on slowly' – and even this might be a reference to *Pelléas*. The syntax suggests, however, that the reference to the opera which then follows is unconnected, a new thought. So 'getting on' must refer to an emotional recovery.

There is a small gap in Debussy's correspondence, and the few letters to Pierre Louÿs offer no clues. Then he writes to Lerolle at the end of August 1894: 'I think of you too often to apologize for not having replied sooner, and your letter was just the nourishment my life needed. I was feeling bereft of your friendship, and let it be said all the strength and encouragement I get from it.' He then tells Lerolle about progress on *Pelléas*, and implies he has been through a period when he has been unable to work on the opera (no work appears to have been done on *Pelléas* between February and May at the earliest): 'Pelléas and Mélisande at first refused to have anything to do with me, and they wouldn't come down off their tapestry, so then I was forced to play around with other ideas; then they became rather jealous and came and leant over me, and in those pallid tones you know so well Mélisande gently said to me: "Leave these silly things alone… and keep your dreams for my hair. You know there can be no love like ours."' He put the 'other ideas' aside and turned back to *Pelléas* with a will. And he returned to Gaby – if, that is, he had ever truly left her.

6

Self-Portrait by Paul Gauguin
(1889), a painter who
was close to Stéphane
Mallarmé and who
espoused Symbolist ideals.
He rejected Impressionism
as unconcerned with 'the
mysterious level of thought'
and sought parallels
between painting and music

*'I confess I'm no longer thinking in musical
terms, or at least not much, even though
I believe with all my heart that Music remains
for all time the finest means of expression
we have.'*

Claude Debussy

Poetry, Painting and Music 1894-9

In 1894 two important musical events in the life of Claude Debussy began
to establish his name in the wider world. On 1 March a concert devoted
to his works was promoted in Brussels by La Libre Esthétique, one of
Europe's leading organizations devoted to contemporary art. Thérèse
Roger, his fiancée at the time, accompanied him to Brussels, where she
again sung *La Damoiselle élue* and two songs from *Proses lyriques*. Debussy
'got a good going over' from the critics, as he wrote to Chausson, but at
least he was paid attention: 'I don't really see what more I could ask for!'
It was to be a different experience in Paris at the end of the year, when the
press greeted the first performance of *Prélude à l'après-midi d'un faune*
largely with indifference. It seems that Debussy's new work was generally
overlooked in favour of the other contemporary works on the programme,
among them music by Henri Duparc, Saint-Saëns, Joseph Guy Ropartz
and Franck. The conductor Gustave Doret, however, was convinced of
the historic nature of the *Faune*: 'I had arranged that the hall be full,' he
recalled, 'and that the work should not be played only for the usual limited
circle of the Société Nationale.' Afterwards he decided to break the rule
forbidding encores: 'The orchestra, delighted, joyfully repeated the work
it had loved and had imposed on the conquered public.' But in fact it was
not until the next century, after *Pelléas* and fame, that the *Faune* became
other than a piece for connoisseurs. Doret's own recollections had
become a little distorted by time; Pierre Louÿs, while admitting to 'a real
joy', told Debussy after the concert that he was waiting 'for a slightly
better performance; the horns stank, and the rest were hardly better'.

Much had changed in Debussy's life by this time. He had endured
the March scandal, and appeared to have recovered from it, at least on
the surface. In this he was helped by Louÿs, whose friendship from this
point was to be his mainstay for five years. He had also nearly completed
Acts I, III and IV of *Pelléas*. Occasionally he returned to the 'other ideas'
he had spoken of to Lerolle, and which had made Mélisande so jealous;
some of these ideas would become his great *Nocturnes* for orchestra,
completed in 1899.

It is often stated that *Nocturnes* had begun as *Trois scènes au crépuscule* ('*Three Scenes of Twilight*'), a title inspired by Debussy's poet friend Henri de Régnier. In fact, a surviving two-page sketch of the earlier work from 1892 shows little connection with the later *Nocturnes*, although the comparable imagery of the titles might have some significance. Another version is mentioned in a letter of September 1894 to the violinist Eugène Ysaÿe, in which Debussy speaks of 'three nocturnes for solo violin and orchestra', which he saw as 'an experiment in finding the different combinations possible inside a single colour, as a painter might make a study in grey'. Nothing has survived for certain of this version, but it seems likely that the musical material would have been re-worked into the final triptych of 1899. What certainly remained was Debussy's concern with pictorial imagery, behind which lay the practice of the American painter James Abbott McNeill Whistler. The American's own *Nocturnes*, mysterious landscapes and seascapes bordering on abstraction, were greatly admired by the French avant garde of the 1890s, and not least by Claude Debussy.

Debussy's letter to Ysaÿe provides one of the first signs, from the composer's own pen, of what was soon to develop into the indelible

Nocturne, Blue and Silver – Cremorne Lights, by James Abbott McNeill Whistler (1872). Reproductions of Whistler's paintings adorned Debussy's walls in later life, a sign of his enduring faith in his inspiration of the 1890s

label 'Impressionism' affixed to his music – and the popularly accepted notion that his music was related to Impressionist painting. On one level he is simply employing the word 'colour' as a conventional metaphor for orchestral sonority and timbre: his letter refers to the different orchestrations of each piece. However it is in his development of this metaphor, where he draws a specific analogy with the techniques of colour harmony in painting – 'as a painter might make a study in grey' – that we can see a tiny premonition of a new historical moment.

Debussy was a man of his times and, where the arts were concerned, a deeply sensitive and percipient one. He lived in an age obsessed with the interrelation of the arts, partly a consequence of the Wagnerian conception of the 'total art form', but also an idea embedded within the Romantic movement earlier in the century. (It was Schumann who had said that 'the painter can learn from a symphony of Beethoven, just as the musician can learn from a work by Goethe.') The irony is that by the time he was being called an Impressionist, the visual art movement from which it sprang had already been superseded. Debussy had a keen visual imagination and a profound love of painting, but, with the exception of Degas, he did not especially revere the Impressionists themselves.

Although the roots of Impressionist painting lay in the Realist school of Gustave Courbet, in practice, especially in the work of Pissarro and Monet, the painters sought to release their art from static representation, from the object, in order to capture the transient, the fleeting, the essentially fluid nature of experience. Mallarmé, an ardent champion of cross-arts fertilization, was one of the first to detect this tendency in the Impressionists. In his seminal essay on Manet and his followers he wrote: 'Nothing should be absolutely fixed, in order that we may feel that the bright gleam which lights the picture, or the diaphanous shadow which veils it, are only seen in passing.' Later however, during the period of his Tuesday gatherings in the 1890s, Mallarmé became the friend and supporter of several painters, such as Redon and Gauguin, who opposed the Impressionist aesthetic, or at least considered that it went not nearly far enough. Gauguin claimed that the Impressionists sought for things only 'at the visible level and not at the mysterious level of thought. For them the dream landscape, created as a totality, does not exist.'

For the painters of the 1890s, for the Symbolists and Nabis (Prophets), music was the key to this 'dream landscape'. Influenced by Mallarmé –

Boulevard des Italiens
by Camille Pissarro
(1897). Debussy's music
is popularly connected with
Impressionism, although
in fact he had far closer
affinities with the Symbolists
and Post-Impressionists

who believed in a regeneration of poetry through its identity with music – the Post-Impressionist painters sought the Symbolist ideals of 'suggestion' and the 'inexpressible'. For Redon 'the art of suggestion exists more freely, more radiantly, in the excitations of music, where it reaches its fullest power.' It was the leader of the Nabis, Maurice Denis, Lerolle's friend and a close acquaintance of Debussy, who searched most determinedly for a path beyond Impressionism. Denis's account of the period made much of Debussy's influence:

> *His music kindled strange resonances within us, awakened a need at the deepest level for a lyricism that only he could satisfy. What the Symbolist generation was searching for with such passion and anxiety – light, sonority and colour, the expression of the soul and the frisson of mystery – was realized by him unerringly; almost, it seemed to us then, without effort... We perceived that here was something new.*

It was also Denis who asserted that every work of art was 'the impassioned equivalent of a sensation experienced' – a remark of striking relevance to Debussy's music.

The avant-garde painters of the 1890s were a familiar part of the composer's milieu. Denis, as we have seen previously, drew a coloured illustration for the first edition of *La Damoiselle élue*. Redon sent Debussy an engraving after the work's première in April 1893, to which the composer responded with a copy of the score inscribed 'To this rare artist'. In the cafés Debussy frequented he met Henri de Toulouse-Lautrec, and through Mallarmé he knew one of the poet's most devoted followers, Paul Gauguin. It was at the time of the composer's first plan for his *Nocturnes* in 1894 that he met Whistler at Mallarmé's Tuesday evening gatherings; this was when he made his Whistler-like allusion to 'how a painter might make a study in grey.'

Further confirmation that Debussy became consciously occupied with visual parallels in his music at this period comes from a curious set of three piano pieces, which he wrote towards the end of 1894 and enti-tled *Images* ('Pictures') – the first instance of the generic title that was to become so characteristic of him. (A possible visual allusion in the title *Arabesques*, for the two piano pieces from 1890, can be discounted. The title merely alludes to a genre of piano music – Schumann's – just as the other pieces Debussy was writing at exactly the same time, in an urgent search for money, refer to famous traditions of the piano repertoire: *Ballade, Mazurka, Valse, Tarantelle*, and, in 1892, *Nocturne*.) These *Images* must also have been among the 'other ideas' Debussy spoke of to Lerolle in August 1894, which relieved his struggle with *Pelléas*. The middle *Sarabande*, first published in an arts magazine in 1896, would become the second piece in his *Suite pour le piano* of 1901 (with small but trans-forming alterations). The original version directs that it should convey the atmosphere of 'an old portrait'. The third piece employs the well-known tune *Nous n'irons plus au bois* (to be used again in *Jardins sous la pluie* from *Estampes*) and contains an instruction worthy of Satie: 'Here, one can hardly distinguish the harps from the peacocks fanning their tails, or peacocks imitating harps (whichever you prefer!) and the sky smiles down on summery dresses'. These *Images*, only shadows of what his piano style would later become, remained unpublished until 1977. Debussy dedicated the manuscript to Lerolle's seventeen-year-old daughter, Yvonne, of whom Renoir did a portrait at the piano.

With Closed Eyes, 1890, by Odilon Redon – an artist from Debussy's circle who described himself as a 'musicalist' painter

If Debussy's allusion in September 1894 to 'a study in grey' was a premonition, then so was critical reaction to the concert – the 'good going over' as Debussy called it – promoted by La Libre Esthétique in Brussels earlier in March. The event took place in the same gallery as an exhibition devoted to the latest movements in painting, including the Nabis, Symbolists such as Gauguin, Redon and James Ensor, as well as some of the original Impressionists, including Pissaro, Renoir and Alfred Sisley. Also on display was the striking poster art of Toulouse-Lautrec and the latest innovations in the decorative arts becoming known as Art Nouveau.

None of this need matter – after all, Debussy did not choose to have his music played surrounded by paintings – were it not for the subsequent history of musical commentary which had its starting point here. The critic Maurice Kufferath wrote of the *Proses lyriques*: 'At times the result is pure cacophony. If this were not done for a wager, one must seriously consider that it points to a defect of the auditory sense, similar to the defect of sight which is responsible for the distorted vision of certain painters.' He also wrote of the 'musical *pointillisme*' of the String Quartet, a work which he found both compelling and bizarre, and of its 'copious floods of rich, sustained harmonies that evoke the memory of

the gamelan… It is more like a hallucination than a dream. Is it a work?
One hardly knows. Is it music? Perhaps so, in the sense that the canvases
of the neo-Japanese of Montmartre and its Belgian suburb may be called
paintings.' (It was well known that Japanese colour prints greatly influenced Impressionists and Post-Impressionists alike, and that Brussels,
dubbed a 'suburb' of the area of Paris where most painters lived, led the
way in promoting contemporary art.)

So Modernism, until then dominated by visual art and labelled
'Impressionist' whether it was or not, had come to Brussels in the form
of music. In such a setting as La Libre Esthétique visual comparisons
between Debussy's music and the most innovative movements in contemporary visual art were inevitable. Yet this was before Debussy had even
begun to give his compositions descriptive titles, before his *Nocturnes*,
his *Images* or his *Estampes*, his *Nuages*, *Mer*, *Brouillards* and *Jardins sous
la pluie*. In fact the works chosen for the Brussels programme were either
in the form of 'pure' music (the String Quartet), or they were inspired
by poetry. At this stage visual analogy was not in the least Debussy's
doing, although it is quite possible that the 'other ideas' he spoke of a few
months afterwards were provoked by his experience in Brussels.

Critics, in their efforts to understand Debussy's music, were struggling
to find a new language, just as they had nearly two decades earlier with
the first of the Impressionist painters (indeed the very word 'impressionist' was an attempt at defining the until then indefinable). 'They all
have more or less cross-eyed minds,' one commentator had proclaimed
of the painters, just as Kufferath, the Brussels critic, would later accuse
Debussy of 'a defect of the auditory sense'. By the 1890s it had become
widely accepted, if not applauded, that a seismic shift had taken place
in visual art; some now glimpsed a similar process in the music of Claude
Debussy. Kufferath's bewildered response simply reflected the impression
that Debussy's music made on most listeners at that time: after acknowledging its 'very unusual qualities', and its 'wonderful refinement of tone-
colouring', he then confessed to 'a curious impression of discomfort,
a strange uneasiness such as one feels on waking after a nightmare'. One
critic of the *Faune*, as bewildered as most at its being 'almost outside of
all tonality' (hence without stability, hence the repeated references to
hallucinations and nightmares), nevertheless urged his readers to 'pay
tribute to all innovators without discrimination. M. Debussy is doubtless among these.'

It seems that the language of visual art criticism was becoming the most natural discourse with which to deal with Debussy. (Such cross-arts analogies were not new: Baudelaire had written in his Salon review of 1846 of the 'melodious' qualities of paintings when viewed from a distance, when the effect of colour took precedence over subject-matter.) Even the Académie Française had accused the young Debussy of a 'vague impressionism, one of the most dangerous enemies of truth' in its report on his Prix de Rome composition *Printemps*. And Saint-Saëns, an implacable opponent of everything Debussy stood for, dismissed the *Faune* as 'pretty... but as much like a piece of music as the palette a painter has worked with is like a painting'. This was exactly the criticism levelled at the Impressionist painters: their works were not finished paintings so much as impressions that had scarcely left the palette.

But for the composer Paul Dukas, one of the most discerning of Debussy's champions, it was literature, and above all poetry, that was

Henri Lerolle's two daughters, Christine and Yvonne, painted in 1897 by Renoir. The setting is Lerolle's music room, where Debussy performed Wagner at the piano. In the background are paintings by Degas

the greatest influence on him. In February 1901 Debussy would write
to Dukas in response to a wide-ranging article his friend had just written
on his music, including a critique of the orchestral *Nocturnes – Nuages*
and *Fêtes* had been first performed in Paris in December 1900; *Sirènes* was
not heard until the first complete performance in October 1901. Debussy
thanked Dukas for his 'practically unique act of empathy'. Dukas had
elaborated his perception of Debussy's debt to poetry, of his 'collaboration with Baudelaire, Verlaine, or Mallarmé', and his creation of a
musical language 'so rich, so persuasive, that it sometimes reaches the
eloquence of a new word'. This drew from Debussy a letter of unaffected
gratitude, in which he made the seminal statement: 'To you I confess
I am no longer thinking in musical terms.' He was referring to his own
struggle to forge a new language of musical expression, and to escape
from the dullness and conventionality of so much of the music that surrounded him: 'I find the actual pieces, whether they're old or modern...
so totally poverty-stricken, manifesting an inability to see beyond the
work-table. They smell of the lamp, not of the sun.' In a remarkable
repetition of his frustrations articulated to Poniatowski eight years earlier,
it was again Charpentier who drew his ire, the Charpentier of *Louise* –
one of the greatest box-office sell-outs of the era. 'In short, these days
especially, music is devoid of emotional impact. I feel that, without
descending to the level of the gossip column, or the novel, it ought to
be possible to solve the problem somehow.' The clear implication was
that the solution might be found in other than 'musical terms'.

If Debussy was not thinking in musical terms, then where did he
believe the solution lay? Perhaps in the procedures of poetry and of
those poets that Dukas had mentioned. But he had already given
himself to literature over the previous decades, so this would hardly
have been a new solution. What of the 'alternative means of expression'
Satie was supposed to have urged upon Debussy some years earlier:
'Why not make use of the representational methods of Claude Monet,
Cézanne, Toulouse-Lautrec and so on? Why not make a musical
transposition of them?' This foreshadows the analysis made by Dukas,
the crucial difference being that Satie listed painters rather than poets.
But in his comments on the *Nocturnes*, Dukas for the first time went
beyond literary analogy, as he was bound to considering the work's
visual provenance:

What I am trying to define as one of the distinctive features of Debussy's personality is subordinated no longer to the thinking of poets, but on impressions which are 'entirely decorative', to use the composer's words. Indeed, in the first part [Nuages], in which the 'décor' consists of the slow passing of clouds against an unchanging sky – of their slow progression ending in 'an agony in grey softly tinged with white' – we realize that music is not meant to express to our senses such a meteorological phenomenon. True, it alludes to it, by means of sumptuous, continually floating chords, whose rising and falling progressions bring to mind the movements of aerial architecture. There is a hint of imitation. But the final meaning of the piece remains, nevertheless, symbolic, and however different it might seem from the earlier pieces written by this composer, this Nocturnes has something in common with them: it communicates one analogy by another analogy, by means of music, all the elements of which, harmony, rhythm, and melody, seem, in some way, to fade away in the ether of the symbol, and to be reduced to a weightless condition. And we can add, as always with Debussy, that this music justifies its subtlety precisely by its musicality.

The analogy in question is Debussy's own – '*Une agonie grise*' (literally 'an agony in grey ') – the words he had used in a programme note for the first performance of *Nuages*: 'The title *Nocturnes* is meant to designate… all the various impressions and the special effects of light that the word suggests. "*Nuages*" renders the immutable aspect of the sky and the slow, solemn motion of the clouds, fading away in *une agonie grise*, softly tinged with white.' With Debussy's analogy in mind, Dukas was at pains to make a fine distinction: rather than aiming to be a direct representation of clouds, the music conveyed the *symbolic* meaning of clouds. It is a convoluted argument but it lay at the heart of the contemporary debate about the meaning of art and the opposing natures of Symbolism and Realism. Dukas suggested that music itself was a symbol, employed in the service of another symbol, clouds (which represented for Debussy '*une agonie grise*'). Thus his music communicated 'one analogy by another analogy'.

It did not escape Dukas, nevertheless, that *Nuages* was also concerned with 'special effects of light', with colouristic phenomena. In fact Debussy's programme note was fully consistent with his comment from several years earlier on the *Nocturnes*, concerning 'how a painter might make a study in grey'. And inevitably commentators at the time of the première of the *Nocturnes* called them 'pictures in music': 'They recall the strange, delicate, vibrating "*Nocturnes*" of Whistler,' wrote Alfred Bruneau, 'and like the canvases of the great American painter, they are full of a deep and poignant poetry.'

Debussy's programme note would have left his listeners in no doubt of the analogies they were expected to draw. He continued:

Fêtes *gives us the vibrating, dancing rhythm of the atmosphere, with sudden flashes of light. There is also the episode of the procession (a dazzling fantastic vision) which passes through the festive scene and becomes merged in it…* Sirènes *depicts the sea and its countless rhythms and presently, among the waves silvered by the moonlight, is heard the mysterious song of the Sirens as they laugh and pass on.*

This note probably did more than anything else to confirm the general notion, then gaining currency, that Debussy was an 'Impressionist'. Curiously the other contemporary label, 'Symbolist', in origin a literary one, did not adhere. Debussy himself said very little about it, apart from his famous dismissal of both labels as 'terms of abuse'. But he was always highly secretive about the process of his imagination, or at least found it so fused with the actual moment of creation that he was largely uncon- scious of it. But scattered remarks in his letters and journalism offer fascinating clues, such as his Baudelairean perception of 'the mysterious correspondence that exists between nature and the imagination'. And at the time of the *Nocturnes* he wrote to his composition pupil, Raoul Bardac: 'One must never be in a hurry to write things down. One must allow the complex play of ideas free rein: how it works is a mystery, and we too often interfere with it by being impatient.' With characteristic consistency he returned to this advice a few years later, to the same pupil, but now with a significant expansion on the need for patience: 'Gather impressions. Don't be in a hurry to write them down. Because music has this over painting, that it can bring together all different aspects of colour and light at the same time. It's a truth rarely noticed, though it's so simple.'

So impressions are gathered as part of the artist's progress through life, from many sources. They are internalized, and do not require the urgent representation required of a painter in his eager quest to capture reality. For Debussy the landscape of the mind was sufficient. 'I have innumerable memories,' he wrote a few years later when composing *La Mer*, 'and those, in my view, are worth more than a reality which, charming as it may be, tends to weigh too heavily on the imagination.' He alluded to this internal landscape in the letter to Dukas of 1901, and specifically to the landscape that should exist in the minds of listeners, who should not be expected to *think* but to *listen* (Debussy's emphasis): 'It would be enough… if they felt that for a moment they had been dreaming of an imaginary country.'

This is the anti-intellectual side of his character, born from his life-long opposition to preconceived structures and formulae, to overworked and cliché-ridden musical procedures. (He dreamed, he once said, 'of a kind of music whose form was so free it would sound improvised'.) This is the real meaning that lay behind his confession that he was thinking in other than musical terms. All around him he was aware of poetry and painting that was breaking new ground, exploring new forms and new modes of experience. But music seemed dead, trapped in worn-out conventions. And still his own *Pelléas* seemed no nearer to being performed.

In the second half of the 1890s Debussy had found himself in a creative impasse. The failure to get his opera performed dominated these years, and in the period from its completion, in 1895, to when it was accepted by the Opéra in 1901, he had finished only three works of substance – and the only large-scale one, the *Nocturnes*, with the greatest difficulty. Between 1897 and 1899 he wrote some of his finest songs, the three *Chansons de Bilitis*, on texts by Pierre Louÿs, and two of the *Trois chansons de Charles d'Orléans* for unaccompanied choir (nos I and III).

The burden he carried was twofold: when he told Louÿs in January 1895 that 'finishing a work of art is rather like the death of someone you love', he was describing the natural reversal experienced by all creative artists once a major project is completed. He could see it coming with *Pelléas*. But once his opera was finished that year, and as the years followed on, he began to realize that the project was far from complete, and that in a fundamental respect it was an effort without issue. His masterpiece remained unknown beyond a tiny circle of friends, and only then through the composer's own woefully incomplete rendering at the keyboard: a masterpiece without orchestra, without singers and, even more crucially, without the stage which was its *raison d'être*. His life slowly became bogged down by the apparent non-existence of what he had created.

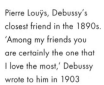

Pierre Louÿs, Debussy's
closest friend in the 1890s.
'Among my friends you
are certainly the one that
I love the most,' Debussy
wrote to him in 1903

During this period he found support from Pierre Louÿs, one of the
most important friendships of Debussy's life. 'We might wonder,' wrote
Lesure, 'who Pierre Louÿs really was: the friend of Gide, Valéry and
Wilde, the frequenter of women of easy virtue in the Latin-quarter, the
erotic photographer, the hellenist, the bibliophile, the composer of
popular songs?' Louÿs was a novelist and poet of considerable brilliance,
who achieved notoriety with *Chansons de Bilitis* – erotic prose poems
purporting to be a translation of a newly discovered Greek text – and
who made his name, and for a time his fortune, with his equally erotic
novel *Aphrodite*. He was also a man of immense charismatic charm.
Paul Valéry wrote: 'Louÿs had an irresistible influence on me, when I
was in his presence, of quite extraordinary power, almost like that of a
woman – but even when he wasn't there I felt it to such an extent that
I had no desire to analyse why or how this was achieved, which made
it all the more astonishing.'

This also seems to have been Debussy's experience. For the composer throughout most of the 1890s – overlapping for a short time with his earlier friendship with Chausson – Louÿs was mentor, mainstay and intimate friend. Debussy relied on him for the deepest needs of affection and moral support, and hid from him nothing. Louÿs, meanwhile, was a man of the world and an inveterate pleasure-seeker. He travelled widely, often absenting himself from Paris for prolonged periods, which added to Debussy's sense of isolation. 'Once again I am mortified at feeling you so far away,' Debussy wrote to him in despair in 1897, 'so irredeemably far that I couldn't summon up the strength even for the simple task of writing to you. I felt it wouldn't go as it should – the words friends speak face to face can't be put on paper.' However, in many ways Louÿs connected the unpractical and socially awkward Debussy to the outside world, as well as simultaneousy protecting him from it. Louÿs also freely lent and gave money, yet, as Lockspeiser has said, 'money never seems to have been a subject of dispute or ill-feeling'.

The highly individual and often opposite characters of the two men intertwined to produce the kind of friendship which was itself creative: they nourished each other, while their respective artistic lives took largely unconnected paths. Numerous collaborative projects were begun, but all were abandoned apart from the *Chansons de Bilitis* (a setting of three of Louÿs's poems), and a small theatrical escapade based on a fuller text of *Bilitis*, for which Debussy hurriedly supplied some musical interludes. He was unhappy with this incidental music and although a performance was given it remained without a complete score; parts went missing, and it was never published in its original form. At the end of his life he recast some of the music as the *Épigraphes antiques* for piano (he wrote duet and solo versions), and only then because of an urgent need for a new work to keep his publisher happy.

His problem with collaboration was principally an artistic one: little of Louÿs's writing struck a chord with Debussy in compositional terms. In the case of *Bilitis* the composer was highly selective, seeing at once that certain themes and images – hair, the Syrinx myth, Naiads (river nymphs) – would serve his own creative instincts. And a song setting is hardly a collaboration in the true sense. Debussy firmly resisted Louÿs's plea, in the autumn of 1898, that a performance of the three songs should accompany a lecture that was to be given on the prose poems. In his letter of reply Debussy is flattering about 'the fearsome and seductive

Bilitis', but his gentle refusal to take part displays an acute awareness of dramatic essentials in relation to music and theatre:

> *Tell me now, what would my three little songs add to the straightforward reading of your text? Nothing at all, my dear fellow; in fact I'd say the result would be a clumsy dispersal of the audience's feelings. Really what's the point of making Bilitis sing either in the major or in the minor, considering hers is the most persuasive voice in the world? You'll say 'Then why have you set it to music?' But that, my dear Pierre, is another question… It's for a different occasion; but believe me when I say that if Bilitis is there, let her speak without accompaniment.*

Herein lies the seed of their gradual estrangement. The gulf between their respective artistic credos is revealed in some comments Louÿs makes, with exasperation one feels, but without the fullest understanding of the revolution Debussy was undertaking, in a letter from July 1896: 'Your mistake (if you're making one) is to believe you're a musician accessible exclusively to the elite, whereas you've everything necessary to be the favourite musician of the man in the street.' Louÿs is, of course, partly correct: Debussy could have turned his musical genius in any direction, and he could certainly have courted popular appeal (just as he did with his Prix de Rome cantata, *L'Enfant prodigue*); but Debussy refuses even to argue the point. He amusingly retorts that he has received a letter signed P. Louÿs of which he doesn't understand a word. 'It's vital we discover the person who is using your handwriting without your ideas.'

A comparison between the incidental and incomplete *Bilitis* music and the three *Chansons de Bilitis* reveals the difference between a composer only half engaged with the creative process and one engaged to the depths of his being. The incidental music, for two flutes, two harps and celeste, is fresh and delicate, but with nothing like the intensity of response that marks out the songs. Again, it is a total engagement with the pith of a text – texture, rhythm and meaning – that characterizes Debussy's song settings and enables him to produce music of such incomparable expressiveness. The piano writing is immeasurably more subtle – lighter textured, more of the instrument – than in any of the solo piano pieces he had written up to this point. The incidental *Bilitis* music reproduces Louÿs's eroticism unerringly, but it remains as *frisson*, merely erotic. The *Chansons* reveal the meaning behind eroticism, *frisson* is transcended and revealed as feeling. The three songs depict a drama in miniature: the awakening of adolescent love, tremulous consummation, and a colder reality. This is Debussy's art at its finest, where without apparent effort he appears to embrace the world.

The extant Debussy-Louÿs correspondence reveals the continuing existence of Gaby in Debussy's life. In July 1894, only four months after the break with Thérèse Roger, we learn of Gaby's presence in Debussy's flat. It is midnight, and Debussy wryly observes to Louÿs – then away in Algeria pursuing a sixteen-year-old girl – how he is himself 'on holiday in the rue Gustave-Doré, protected by the dark foliage of semi-quavers in the middle of which move Pelléas and Mélisande', adding as a post-script, 'Gaby sends her smile to you.' And a few years later, letters detail the events leading to the final rupture with Gaby. In January 1897 she writes to thank Louÿs for his gift of bananas (again he is travelling in North Africa). She is lonely and misses Louÿs as much as Debussy does; indeed it now seems that only through Louÿs do they find any stability in their relationship. Then in February comes an episode, related by Debussy to Louÿs in an ironically melodramatic style, concerning a letter Gaby discovered in his pocket, 'which left no doubt as to the advanced state of a love affair, and containing enough material to inflame the most stolid heart. Whereupon – Scenes – Tears – a Real revolver and *Le Petit Journal* there to record it all.' Despite his apparently detatched irony, Debussy admits to being 'knocked sideways' and laments Louÿs's irre-deemable absence. But the following month the heroic Gaby is still to be found with Debussy, again sending Louÿs 'her nicest smile'.

The relationship with Gaby was falling victim to Debussy's already fragile mental and emotional state, at the root of which was his sense of artistic and personal failure. He was crying a lot, he writes to Louÿs in March 1898. His friend's departure, again, from Paris compounded his misery. 'I can't explain further, and as a friend you will understand the rest.' He complains of his lack of direction with the *Nocturnes* – 'those who claim to write masterpieces while in tears are incorrigible liars' – and he mentions suicide, which, despite his ironic tone (even now), he sees as a serious option: 'I assure you I am not trying to impress you with fine words, and that there are times when I'm afraid of losing the little that has ever been good about me.' A further distraught letter from Debussy follows, in which he again speaks of his loneliness and his inability to face 'the struggle against absurd impossibilities'. This only reaches Louÿs

Tragique épilogue d'une querelle politique

Mᵐᵉ CAILLAUX, FEMME DU MINISTRE DES FINANCES, TUE A COUPS DE REVOLVER
M. GASTON CALMETTE DIRECTEUR DU " FIGARO "

on his return to Paris; and he at once sends a letter designed in the most sensitive manner to ameliorate Debussy's suffering, beginning with a nice allusion to the portrait of Debussy by Marcel Baschet he had just seen when passing through Rome: 'not very far from that of M. Ingres, and in an exquisite place. I assure you I was moved when I saw you over there.'

It is an arresting portrait, capturing a particularly Italian look that Debussy cultivated at that time of his youth, more Florentine perhaps than Roman. One notices the hair low over the brow – the young man ever sensitive to his protuberant forehead – and the silken moustache and beard that the painter has taken such care to execute; and the manner in which he has lavished so much attention on the composer's ear. Contemporary photos confirm the accuracy of this detail, as well as the skill with which Baschet has caught the distant expression of Debussy's eyes. 'I had the immediate feeling,' Louÿs continued, 'that of those three hundred portraits [of Prix de Rome laureates], two or three would be remembered later, and you would be one of them.' Talk of suicide, he tells him, is absurd:

> *You don't have the slightest excuse for such nightmares – because you are a great man, do you understand what that means? Others have hinted at it. Me, I'm telling you. And you might perhaps believe me if I add that I've never said such a thing to anyone else. Whatever problems you might have, that thought must surmount everything. You must carry on with your work, and you must make that work known, two things which you refrain from doing and which ought to be everything to you. Living is not giving music lessons, it is doing everything in your power to get* Pelléas *performed. You consider practical steps as being beneath your dignity, and you might well be very wrong; because the important thing is for you to be able to work, and you will only work if you have what is necessary around you.*

The portrait of Debussy mentioned by Louÿs, now in the Musée National du Château at Versailles. It is by Marcel Baschet, one of Debussy's fellow Prix de Rome laureates, painted in Rome in 1885

Much more, therefore, lay behind Debussy's mental state than 'complications of a sentimental nature' (his own characteristically understated description, in a letter to his publisher Georges Hartmann). However, it seems certain that the love affair discovered by Gaby a year earlier had continued, and it was this which was the immediate spur to his anguish, uncovering an acute lack of fulfilment and a bitter frustration. He was, yet again, losing himself in an affair that was coming to nothing. It seems Alice Peter, the sister-in-law of Debussy's friend René, was the lover in question – to her is dedicated *La Chevelure*, the second of the *Chansons de Bilitis* – although nothing more is known of this relationship.

Because of Debussy's capacity to recover from such crises, it is easy to underestimate their severity. The historical view is also complicated by his habitual ironic detachment, arising from his fear of exposing his inner emotions as well as from a remarkable degree of self-knowledge. Ultimately it was these characteristics that enabled him to recover stability, although Louÿs's presence and support at this moment were undoubtedly crucial to him. Louÿs's biographer, Robert Cardinne-Petit, claims that at some point – perhaps it was now – Louÿs prevented Debussy from destroying the manuscript of *Pelléas*. The story was supposed to have come directly from Louÿs.

This, then, is the background to the long period of creative difficulty that Debussy experienced following his completion of *Pelléas* in 1895. It also puts into perspective the single most important personal event that then ensued – his sudden marriage, in October 1899. An undoubted rebound from his depression, it was to end in disaster and led to the final withdrawing of Claude Debussy behind a screen of prickly taciturnity, from which he rarely emerged for the rest of his life.

7

Debussy with his first wife
Lilly and composer Paul
Dukas, around 1901

*'An artist is in the main a detestable interior
kind of man, and perhaps also a deplorable
husband.'*

Claude Debussy

Lilly Debussy 1899–1905

Towards the end of the 1890s Debussy's finances were, as ever, precarious. This was despite the foresight of the publisher Georges Hartmann, who since 1894 had taken on the publication of Debussy's work under the imprint Fromont and paid him an advance of 500 francs a month, a generous sum. 'He was sent to me by Providence,' Debussy wrote to Louÿs, 'and he played his part with a grace and charm rather rare among philanthropists.' Debussy's many letters to Hartmann during this time show a genuine gratitude, and an amusing willingness to please. Notably the composer never addresses his publisher as 'dear friend' or 'dear Hartmann', but always as Monsieur Hartmann. The following comes in April 1898, six weeks after his crisis of depression:

> To say everything in a few words, I am weighed down by worries. I'm hoping to calm down the screams of these people thanks to the sum of money you are promising, but then the 'Term's Rent' will come to the fore and it will be the same song and dance all over again. Since I've no taste for prostitution, I'm wondering by what trick I can escape this mess. The few lessons I was giving to pay for my daily bread left for the seaside, without a single thought for my domestic economy, and all this is more melancholy than the whole of the Chopin ballads.
>
> Without attempting to draw a parallel between myself and Balzac, not having the scope of that literary cathedral, I have at least in common with him permanent money worries and a total ignorance of what is called savings', and I think that if a marvellous piece of luck hadn't made it possible for me to meet you, I would be reduced to doing the most awkward jobs, and Pelléas would still be in those murky regions where people wrongly believe genius is hiding.

It is in a letter to Hartmann, from the first day of January 1899, that Debussy gives news of Gaby's final departure. As usual, the undoubted seriousness of this event is lightly drawn: 'My life has not been going well: first I've moved [to 52 rue Cardinet], then Mlle Dupont, my *secretary*, resigned her position. It's all extremely troubling, and though one's a musician, one is no less for that a man. You have every reason to complain, as you won't be receiving a visit from either me or the three *Nocturnes*; I only hope your kind heart will retain some sympathy for me.'

But within a few months he was assiduously courting another, Rosalie (Lilly) Texier. She was not entirely new in his life; the two had met the previous year, at which time he had found her pretty but 'affected', according to René Peter. She modelled clothes. It seems that when in May 1899 Louÿs announced his forthcoming marriage, Debussy must have felt he had to take urgent hold of his own life. 'One day we learnt that Claude and Lilly had got married,' related Peter. 'Perhaps the fact that Claude no longer appeared to love Gaby made Lilly feel she was free to act?' But Peter was not party to many aspects of Debussy's life – he was not at his wedding in October, when Louÿs and Satie were two of the witnesses; neither was he aware of the tortuous months from early May when Debussy had begun to pursue Lilly relentlessly, and she had attempted to keep him at bay.

Many of Debussy's letters to Lilly over this period are little known. They are passionate, tender, spontaneous, and they scarcely conceal a frank carnality. He speaks of her slim body, her pretty clothes, and her kisses. 'Claude is barely cured from the ravages of your dear little mouth,' he writes on 24 April. He is also touchingly ludicrous in his avowals of eternal fidelity, his implausible threats of suicide (she was at one point refusing to see him), and his (apparently) innocent sentimentality: 'your letter arrived this morning,' he writes on 29 May, 'with that delicious thought you had of saving a little corner of it for my lips, and the whole of me is thanking you for this idea, as pretty an idea as you are yourself.' As in his correspondence with Chausson, the dramatic irony is painful. Witnessing him opening his heart, and trapping there this steady, pretty and limited twenty-five-year-old from the provinces – ten years his junior – we are left uncomfortably aware that we are catching him out:

> *I assure you that you don't need to frown threateningly when you write: what if I did not love you any longer, or what if I ever stole away? That would be something! I am not curious, but I would love to know how I could ever 'steal away'? Because when all's said and done, you have to admit that, very obviously, I do everything I can to do just the opposite…*

It seems to have been a hundred years since I last saw you. Please be so kind
as to tell me exactly when I shall see you again. If you stole a minute from
me, I'd bear you a grudge until death. These unbearably long days have
served to persuade me of the one thing I already know so well: I love you
and will love you endlessly.

Debussy is here quoting from Act IV scene 4 of *Pelléas*, the point where
Pelléas expresses fear of his undeclared passion for Mélisande: 'I've been
playing like a child near something of whose existence I had no idea. I've
been playing in a dream around the pitfalls of destiny... It seems at times
at least a hundred years since I last saw her.'

In 1899 Debussy must have been aware that for him life was now imitating art, and that in one respect he wanted it to: he needed to find
Mélisande in reality. (Madame Gérard de Romilly, one of Debussy's
piano pupils, recalled that Lilly was then 'at the height of her beauty.
She had delicate features, surrounded by fair hair, she appeared to be the
very incarnation of Mélisande.') Both the fictional and the real relationships were bound to come to grief, considering the extreme imbalance
between the parties: as types, Pelléas and Lilly were far too innocent to
be able to control such complex partners.

In the middle of June Lilly is still resisting, and on the 17th Debussy
writes to her what must have been one of the most persuasive letters of
his life:

I am no longer a young man, and I need to settle my life for good. If
I haven't done it so far, it's because I haven't found someone I really loved
and that I trusted enough. So, I found you again, and the love I had secretly
felt for you, before, was able to develop with a passion which soon became
exclusive and almost wild, I think I don't need to insist on this. Now, no
more than you, would I want you to continue with your job, and my firm
intention was to tear you away from it as soon as possible. The love I have
for you neither can nor wants to be content with just our seeing each other
on joyful occasions. I wanted to immerse myself in your life completely and
to try and make you happy, not only through my tenderness, but also through
my devotion and care which would surround your life at every moment.

At the present moment I earn a living, no more, and if I can offer to you,
all the same, to share it without fear, it's certainly no fortune I'm offering!
And you would have to love me enough to bear a little mediocrity for a couple

of months. That said, I understand perfectly your worries about your future, but how am I to understand the worries you have about my love? There are things which don't lie, and if you say, quite rightly, that you were betrayed once before, how can your feminine instinct not tell you that you can entrust yourself to me without any fear of betrayal! I would have been so proud and happy if you'd said quite simply, 'Claude, I want to share your life for ever, I've enough trust in our love to know that neither you nor I will hurt it.'

There is no doubt that the happiness he so keenly sought came to pass; it lasted about three years.

Debussy had to give a piano lesson on the morning of his wedding, despite his income from Hartmann, to pay the expenses. His pupil that day, Madame Romilly, later set down her recollections, in a manner worthy of a scene from Emile Zola:

Lilly was waiting at the bottom of the stairs to our apartment, sitting on a bench, until the lesson was over, so they could take a wedding ride on the open top of a bus! They got out at the Jardins des Plantes, round which Debussy dragged himself – he hated walking. Then with his parents, who had turned up for the occasion, they went and had dinner at the Taverne Pousset. The meal was paid for by the fee for my lesson, and everyone went home on foot because there wasn't enough money left to take the bus. Debussy had terrible trouble getting home; he was exhausted by the day and particularly by this 'forced footing'.

Lilly's part in the eventual disintegration was unwitting, Debussy's deliberate. Their story might have been different had they not lost their baby in August the following year, a tragedy for any young couple, but quite probably the fundamental imbalance of their relationship would have remained unalterable. Debussy came to see this clearly, Lilly did not. Her relentless emotional blackmail of him at the end, as we shall see, became the mirror image of his relentless pursuit of her at the beginning. Whatever the other imbalances, there was certainly an equality of wills.

It was not long after his marriage that Debussy began to write for the celebrated arts journal *La Revue blanche*. His stock was rising and he embraced his new task with excitement, delighted to be associated with a journal at the cutting edge of the avant garde. In the previous decade Mallarmé and Verlaine had written for this magazine, Lautrec had designed the publicity posters, its art criticism was influential and it had published prints by such as Manet, Pierre Bonnard and Denis. On the front cover of the 1 April 1901 edition the name Claude Debussy was displayed in bold type. 'What you will be finding here are my own sincere impressions, exactly as I felt them,' the new music critic proclaims, and he immediately gives his readers a taste of the kind of barbed comments they are to expect: 'Once and for all: Meyerbeer, Thalberg and Reyer – they are men of genius. But that's as far as their importance goes.' Debussy in these columns was to offend many egos and vested interests, thereby storing up a fund of ill will that would be returned with interest once *Pelléas* reached the stage. It was for *La Revue blanche* that he created his crusty and outspoken alter ego Monsieur Croche.

In May 1901 Debussy received the overwhelming news of *Pelléas et Mélisande*'s acceptance by the Opéra-Comique. One of his first thoughts was to inform Pierre Louÿs, in a short, delighted missive that contained a sad note of realism: 'As you still are – my old friend Pierre! I don't want you to hear from a third party that *I've a written promise* from M. A Carré [the manager of the Opéra-Comique] that he will stage *Pelléas et Mélisande* next season. But is any of this a reason for you not deigning to tell me you're back in town?' Their respective marriages had conspired against their former intimacy, as had Debussy's repeated failure to produce any music for innumerable collaborative projects. None the less Debussy kept Louÿs constantly informed of his opera's progress.

The conductor was to be André Messager, now the musical director of the Opéra and an old ally of Debussy. 'The singers read through *Pelléas* at my house,' recalled Messager. 'Debussy played his score on the piano, singing all the roles in that deep, cavernous voice of his which often meant transposing lines an octave down, but whose delivery grad-ually became irresistible. The impression produced by that music on that occasion was, I believe, unique. To begin with there was a kind of mis-trust, a resistance, then an ever closer attention, with the emotional temperature rising until the last notes of "Mélisande's death", which fell amid silence and tears. At the end all of us were carried away by excite-ment, burning to get down to work as soon as possible.' Mary Garden recalled the same scene, with more colourful additions:

The front page of an edition of *La Revue blanche* from 1895, designed by Henri de Toulouse-Lautrec. Debussy wrote several columns for this celebrated magazine from April to December 1901

As he played the death of Mélisande, I burst into the most awful sobbing, and Mme Messager began to sob along with me, and both of us fled into the next room. I shall never forget it. There we were crying as if we had just lost our best friend, crying as if nothing would console us again. Mme Messager and I returned to the drawing room just as Debussy stopped. Before anyone could say or do anything, he faced us all and said:

'Mesdames et messieurs, *that is my* Pelléas et Mélisande. *Everyone must forget that he is a singer before he can sing the music of Debussy.* Oubliez, je vous prie, que vous êtes chanteurs!' *['Forget, I beg you, that you are singers.']*

Then he murmured a quick 'Au revoir' *and without another word he was gone.*

The Scottish soprano
Mary Garden as the first
Mélisande in 1902

It was this scene, the death of Mélisande in the final act, that Debussy
had been so eager to see and hear on stage, and which finally moved him
so profoundly:

> *The character of Mélisande has always seemed to me difficult to perform.*
> *I had tried to convey her fragility and distant charm in the music, but there*
> *were still her gestures to be decided. One false move during her long silences*

could have ruined the whole effect, even have made her incomprehensible. And above all, Mélisande's voice, which I had dreamed of as being so tender, how was that going to turn out?...

At last came the fifth act – Mélisande's death – a breathtaking event whose emotions cannot be rendered in words. There I heard the voice I had secretly imagined – full of sinking tenderness and sung with such artistry as I would never have believed possible. Since then it is this artistry which has caused the public to bow in ever increasing admiration before the name of Mary Garden.

There was a last-moment panic, among many before the first night, when Messager realized the music in between scenes was not long enough to facilitate scenery changes. 'Debussy had to return to work,' he recalled, 'grumbling and raving, and I went to see him every day to snatch away the notes he had written between one rehearsal and another; that is how he wrote the wonderful interludes which provide such a moving commentary on the action.'

The public dress rehearsal was subject to a typically Parisian tumult. Mary Garden's Scottish accent was delightedly ridiculed, and the child Yniold's rendering of '*petit père*' (Act III, scene 5) greeted with derision. In addition, the word 'bed' at the end of the same scene, when Golaud attempts to get Yniold to spy into Mélisande's bedroom, caused virtuous indignation and caught the eye of the censor. (This scene, even today, is profoundly discomforting.) Maeterlinck, in a display of jealous and philistine stupidity, was partly responsible for setting up the hostile reaction. He had wanted his mistress, Georgette Leblanc, in the leading role, and had attempted to mount legal proceedings against the composer. He also went to his flat, according to the same Leblanc, to beat him with his cane: 'Debussy was sitting peacefully in a chair,' she relates, 'while Madame Debussy ran desperately to her husband clutching a bottle of salts.'

Among the discerning, and the young in particular, there was no doubting that a major artistic event had unfolded. Ravel, it was claimed, attended every one of the first thirty performances. Some critics, like André Corneau, caught at least something of the originality of Debussy's procedures, at the same time giving voice to the difficulties that were inevitably experienced by those familiar with traditional opera: 'You will search in vain through the two hundred and eighty-three pages of the

score for any fragment of melody. Your beloved romances are nowhere to
be found. The characters do not declaim and they avoid singing. They
speak what they have to say in a summarily notated melopoeia. It is to
the orchestra alone that the task of expressing everything is reserved, or
to put it better, of making everything felt.'

The comment on the orchestra is discerning (even Strauss, otherwise
disparaging, praised the opera's 'delicate harmonies, exquisite orchestral
effects, in very good taste'). But the claim that there is an absence of
singing, 'a summarily notated melopoeia,' is hardly valid considering the
intense lyricism of many of the scenes. Yet the vocal writing is certainly
characterized to a large extent by a concern with the inflections of speech,
and in an interview for *Le Figaro* on 16 May Debussy showed he was content to overturn the traditional conception of what melody should be:

> *My wish was that the action should never be halted, continuing uninter-*
> *rupted. I wanted to dispense with parasitical musical phrases. On hearing*
> *opera, the spectator is accustomed to hearing two distinct sorts of emotion:*
> *on the one hand the musical emotion, and on the other the emotion of*
> *the characters – usually he experiences them in succession. I tried to ensure*
> *that the two were perfectly merged and simultaneous. Melody, if I dare say*
> *so, is anti-lyrical. It cannot express the varying states of the soul, and of life.*
> *Essentially it is only suited to the song that expresses a simple feeling.*

As a credo of Modernism, this could not be more revolutionary. It ranks
with the statements and practice of Mallarmé on the abstract nature of
poetry; with the undermining of the cherished alexandrine – the twelve
syllable line, which had such a hold on French poetry until Verlaine and
Régnier; and the *vers libre* (free verse) in the poetry of Laforgue. It ranks
with the startling utterances and practice of the Impressionist painters
a generation or more earlier, of Pissaro, Monet and Cézanne (all of
whom were then still alive); and with the pronouncement of Denis
on the essence of painting: 'A picture – before being a horse, a nude or
an anecdotal subject – is essentially a flat surface covered with colours
arranged in a certain order.' The painters, especially, were seen to be
challenging the foundations of western tradition, and it was now perceived – not only in the milieu of the avant garde, but by the wider
public, and soon internationally – that Claude Debussy was doing the
same. It was a simple step to assume some kind of influence, even collu-

sion, especially in an age which sought interrelation between the arts to the point of obsession.

Through the success of *Pelléas* – which was almost immediate, despite inevitable and often malicious disparagement – Debussy gained the recognition that he both dreamed of and dreaded. He became a celebrated and controversial Modernist, and his life as well as his music entered the public domain. He had his portrait painted by the fashionable Jacques-Émile Blanche, and was awarded the Légion d'Honneur. Despite himself, he found that he was joining the establishment, much to his parents' delight – they who had waited so long – and to his friend Erik Satie's disgust. He did not, however, find the sought-after riches.

Debussy turned forty on 22 August 1902. On the surface his relationship with Lilly seemed secure – friends commented on the happiness radiating from their apartment at the time of *Pelléas*'s première. It was Debussy's friendship with Louÿs that was more obviously waning. In June 1903 Louÿs sent him an inscribed copy of his new book *Sanguines*, a volume of short stories. Debussy was deeply touched: 'It's outrageous that I've not seen you for over a year, it's almost as if you'd died. Of all my friends you have been the one I've loved the most.' He promised to

Claude and Lilly Debussy in 1902 as a happily married couple

send him some music. 'It's sad, even so! You send me your book and
I reply with a score. But all that's just a shadow [or still life – *une vie
morte*]. How much I would prefer that good old hand-shake, but alas!
I can now only imagine it. But I am still your very devoted, but ever
ageing, Claude Debussy.' A few days later Debussy sent him an inscribed
score of *Pelléas*, after which they continued to exchange occasional
letters, but '*les felures*' ('the cracks', in Debussy's term) remained.

After the première of *Pelléas* Debussy was faced with the need for
finding a new path – in the full public glare. Solo piano music had started
to draw him again, for the first time since his unpublished *Images* of
1894. In 1901 came *Suite pour le piano* but, as with the String Quartet from
1893, such dependence on 'pure' musical structures was not the direction
in which he wanted to go. Then came the remarkable return to visually
conceived piano pieces, *Estampes* ('Prints'), completed in July 1903.

The contrast between these two sets of piano pieces, the *Suite* and the
Estampes – each a triptych – could not be more marked. The *Sarabande*
from the *Suite* (actually the revised second movement from the 1894
Images) is an elegaic restatement of the old dance form. The *Prélude*
and *Toccata* are magnificent virtuoso pieces, boldly displaying a tactile
pianism that Debussy knew so well from his days as a piano student
under Marmontel. In style the *Suite* arises from the music of Bach (Roy
Howat has found moments of 'whimsical pastiche' of J S Bach's A
minor organ Prelude and the Prelude from the E major Partita for
violin), as well as the harpsichord music of François Couperin and
Jean-Philippe Rameau, transformed by a confidently colouristic
harmonic vocabulary.

Estampes, however, breaks new ground, not least in its concern with
visual metaphor. Debussy even gave meticulous instructions for the
design and colour of the front cover, his 'cover mania' as he called it.
A Parisian music lover turning the leaves of the exotically titled pieces
would have at once caught the allusion to the fashionable coloured
wood-block prints of Japanese art. Each piece is conceived as a highly
focused (not, it should be noted, impressionistically blurred) picture
from an album, or a print on a wall, complete with precise descriptive
title: '*Pagodas*', '*Evening in Granada*', '*Gardens in the rain*'. Three
locations – the Orient, Spain, and France – are transposed into sound
through simple conventions of musical style: *Pagodes* employs the five-
note scale which, to a western ear, at once signals oriental music (as if

A woodblock print from Hokusai's *Rare Views of Japanese Bridges*, c. 1834. Japanese colour prints were much admired in Debussy's milieu and he owned several, acquired easily from Parisian shops dealing in objets d'art

played by the gongs and metallophones of the gamelan); *La Soirée dans Grenade* the ubiquitous habañera rhythm of Flamenco and the strumming of guitars; and *Jardins sous la pluie*, unmistakably to the French, is built from two French nursery songs cleverly woven into piano figurations which, as in *Suite pour le piano*, suggest Bach. *Estampes* is Debussy's essay in the musical picturesque, a transposition of the formal, clearly defined designs of printmaking into music. The result suggests, in the manner of a Japanese print, the picturesque without sentimentality, a stylized impression without cliché. Debussy explores in these pieces a range of colour and resonance that, for the first time in his piano music, looks ahead into the twentieth century and towards the music of Olivier Messiaen.

Other piano music was forming around this period: the three magnificent pieces that comprise the first book of *Images (Reflets dans l'eau, Hommage à Rameau, Mouvement)*; the tragic *Masques* paired with the exuberant and magical *L'Isle joyeuse*; and the little known *D'un cahier d'esquisse ('From a Sketchbook')*. This last piece, so close in mood to *La Mer* (as well as thematically close), fitted Debussy's aim to create a piece that sounded improvised, and that 'would seem to have been torn out of a sketchbook.' Roy Howat has demonstrated how *Masques* and *L'Isle joyeuse* may have been intended as the outer pieces of yet another piano triptych planned during this period, which failed to take shape. *D'un cahier d'esquisses* provides the ideal central movement for creative pianists wanting to resurrect this plan (as it was perhaps originally intended). All three pieces benefit enormously from such a combination.

Pitched suddenly into the limelight by the success of *Pelléas*, Debussy rapidly became exhausted by the turmoil it created, and by what he came to lament as the never-ending cycle of performances. Again he felt in danger of creative limbo. The piano pieces he wrote could not fend off this feeling for long; in some respects, as he cast around for large-scale projects to get to grips with, they were no more than (sublime) recreation. His plan for a set of orchestral *Images* was a long way from realization (not begun until 1905, these *Images* took him eight years to complete).

And again he was fighting off creditors. Hartmann had died suddenly in April 1900; the 500 francs a month had abruptly ceased and Debussy's new household was put under severe strain. Hartmann's estate had demanded the return of all advances, and just at the time of the *Pelléas* première Debussy was being prosecuted. Fromont, the publisher under whose imprint Hartmann had operated, offered to buy back all the composer's work from Hartmann's heirs. Debussy escaped the courts, but he was no less a pauper. It is truly remarkable, under such circumstances, that he was able to compose at all, let alone lead a dignified life. There is no doubt that he and Lilly suffered extremely from this situation, which gnawed at the fragile foundations of their relationship.

He spent the summer and early autumn of 1903 at the home of Lilly's parents at Bichain in Burgundy. He corrected proofs for Fromont, and finished *Estampes* for his friend Jacques Durand, who was soon to become his exclusive publisher. He was also involved with his *Rapsodie* for saxophone and orchestra. This he never orchestrated, and it was not performed until 1919 in an orchestration by the composer Jean Roger-Ducasse. 'The idea did not interest me greatly,' Debussy tells Louÿs – feeling uneasy, as always, with commissions that for financial reasons he felt compelled to accept. The *Rapsodie* proves again, however, that he was almost incapable of composing anything idly. It is a work with an eastern flavour (he had at first considered calling it '*Moorish Rhapsody*', then '*Arab Rhapsody*'), superbly crafted, and only overlooked today because Roger-Ducasse's highly effective orchestration is deemed inauthentic.

The Moorish melodies in the exactly contemporary *La Soirée dans Grenade* come from the same area of Debussy's imagination, perhaps provoked by Louÿs's repeated sojourns in Algeria and southern Spain. 'The countryside is not boring at all, you see?' Debussy tells him, trying to extol his own ability to be inspired by Bichain. 'The answer lies in not believing that the sun which sets on the hillsides of Bichain is any different from the one which goes to rest on the pale terraces of Biskra.' But he admits to a certain restriction in his surroundings. 'To make up for it I've also written a piano piece which bears the title " *Une soirée dans Grenade*". And I tell you, if this is not exactly the kind of music they play in Granada, then so much the worse for Granada!'

In fact Louÿs was giving up his restless travelling. From this point until the end of his life in 1925, tragically for one who began with such brilliance, he produced very little – which he blamed on a lack of exotic climes. As Debussy's star ascended, Louÿs's waned. His travelling had partly been necessitated by the need for warmer winter climates to escape a habitual bronchitis, but it seems he also craved constant stimulation to ward off an inner vacancy, and that his illnesses were partly psycho-somatic. Like Debussy he was constantly tormented by financial prob-lems, despite enormous success, and he was equally averse to writing to commission – however much he might advise such a path to his friend. He too idealized the Symbolist dream of creating for the select few. It is curious that the two should have gradually lost contact, but from the evidence it does seem that Debussy's complaint was true, that the other's 'door was firmly closed' to him, when it was 'open and welcoming to others'. Perhaps Louÿs could not face his own creative decline with Debussy present.

In Debussy's country retreat at Bichain (from where even now he tells Louÿs that he misses Paris 'when I remember you're still there'), his own creative demon forges ahead. He is still struggling to bring to birth another operatic project, a setting of Poe's tale *The Devil in the Belfry*. 'The scenario is more or less complete, and I've more or less decided the colouring I want to use,' he tells Messager. 'After that come the many sleepless nights and a large quantity of hope.' Hope it was to remain. But during this summer an unexpected new path emerges, a direction which until now he has not mentioned but which he instinctively knows will take him at last beyond *Pelléas* and the *Nocturnes*. In the same letter to Messager he speaks of 'three symphonic sketches' concerned with his devotion to the sea, 'to which you'll reply that the Atlantic doesn't exactly wash the foothills of Burgundy! And the result will be one of those hack landscapes done in the studio! But I have innumerable memories, and those in my view are worth more than a reality which, charming as it may be, tends to weigh too heavily on the imagination.' Within a matter of months Debussy's new creative path – foreseen, planned in detail, meticulously executed – is to be followed by a new path in his personal life, hardly foreseen, certainly (until the last moment) without a coherent plan, and executed in the messiest way possible.

'How often music takes me like the sea,' Baudelaire had written, employing an implicit sexual image of direct relevance to the imaginative impulses behind Debussy's great sea symphony. We might see *La Mer* as the catalyst for the disruption that now sweeps through his personal life – the human consequences of the exhilarating creative freedom that produces *La Mer*. Returning to Paris in October, Debussy meets again the mother of Raoul Bardac, the composition pupil to whom he had been giving lessons intermittently since 1901. In some respects Madame Emma Bardac was another version of Marie Vasnier, although considerably more cultured – a *femme du monde*, a singer (both Maurice Ravel and Fauré had dedicated songs to her), and the hostess of a regular salon in a fashionable quarter of Paris. Like Marie she had married at seventeen, had children, and moved in circles where a certain amount of marital infidelity was accepted within strict laws of comportment. She had had a serious affair with Fauré in the early 1890s, and inspired his song cycle *La Bonne Chanson*.

If Mary Garden is to be believed (whose lively and unreliable memoirs read at times like a salacious romance), matters were made easier for Debussy to conduct his affair when Lilly, in an attempt to ameliorate her husband's natural reclusiveness, encouraged his attendance at Madame Bardac's salon. Mary Garden also claimed that Debussy was 'obsessed with love' for herself, and that he declared it exactly at the time he was beginning his affair with Emma Bardac. Lilly Debussy is supposed to have declared, highly implausibly, on hearing from Mary Garden of Debussy's avowal: 'I think you are the only woman in the world I would give Claude up for.' Clearly, in the light of subsequent events, Lilly did not extend her generosity to Emma Bardac.

It was not until the following summer of 1904 that the crisis came to a head. On 19 July Debussy writes to his wife, 'I have a serious fault

in that I don't explain myself enough.' It was a classic understatement.
He begins to explain, but fails to mention that he is at that moment
with Emma Bardac:

An artist is in the main a detestable interior kind of man, and perhaps
also a deplorable husband. Put another way, a perfect husband often produces
a pitiable artist. It's a vicious circle. You will say, in that case, why should
we be married? However it's possible to reply to such a question, I sincerely
believed I could make you happy by asking you to entrust your life to me!
But alas sometimes I've had to doubt it, especially when you've told me things
which have distanced us – and the anger these things have caused me has
been a great cause of regret.

This letter does not have his usual signature, 'Your Claude', but is simply
signed 'Debussy' – obviously he is hoping Lilly is reading the codes.
(However, in a letter to her from only a few days earlier he had signed
himself, 'Yours passionately, tenderly, Claude.' It seems he was unconsciously transferring the intensity of his new passion, momentarily, onto
his wife.) In a letter nearly a month later, having seen Lilly only once in
the interim on a brief visit to Bichain, he finally arrives at the point –
but even now he fails to mention Emma. He tells Lilly he is on the way
to London from Dieppe with Jacques-Émile Blanche. (It is a curious
coincidence, with echoes of the Marie Vasnier episode nearly twenty
years earlier, that once again Blanche and the port of Dieppe should be
co-opted on to the stage of Debussy's love affairs.) He was in fact with
Emma in Pourville, just along the coast, having spent a week with her
in Jersey. 'Now, forgive me for what is coming next,' he writes to Lilly:

Perhaps I should have told you during my journey to Bichain, but I
couldn't find the time nor perhaps the necessary courage. First let me tell
you that I feel for you the deepest fondness possible, and this makes even
more distressful what I think is honest to tell you today. I have the clearest
conviction after those days spent away from you, during which I was able
for the first time to think calmly about our life, that while having loved you
very much, I've never made you as happy as I should. I also remember
those tiresome moments when you asked me to give you back your freedom.
We are no longer children; so let us try and disentangle ourselves from this
whole thing, discreetly and without bringing people into it… And if I have

this irresistible need to be alone, [it] is because, please understand this, I am
banging my head against things in you which I find distressing and because
I could no longer work like I wanted, with that nerve-wracking worry I had
in me about not knowing where I was going.

Of all the excuses offered for ruptured relationships, the need for being
'alone', when the new lover is already well installed, must rank as the
most common.

Just as in the Thérèse Roger episode ten years earlier, Debussy had
no conception of the odium that he was bringing on his head by leaving
Lilly. He saw it in simple terms and even believed Lilly would too. The
situation was made truly tragic when, on 13 October, Lilly attempted
to shoot herself, an action which was inevitably held against her husband.
Her act proclaimed her as the victim, as she felt herself to be, and Debussy
was struck dumb in the face of it. This time there was no Pierre Louÿs
on hand to defend him. Indeed, there is a distinctly unpleasant tone
in the letter Louÿs wrote to his brother George when the scandal broke,
in which, referring to Lilly having shot herself in the chest, he disdained
to refer to Debussy by name: 'The husband has gone off with a jewess,
something over forty, Madame S. Bardac. I believe you know Bardac,
or at least I think he came once to your office. He's very used to his wife
running off, and he smiles when asked about the latest men in her life:
"She just treats herself to the latest fashion in musicians, but it's I who
have the money. She'll be back."'

According to Mary Garden, who afterwards visited Lilly in hospital,
the bullet entered under her left breast, where there was 'a dark round
hole'. Lilly was fully conscious when Debussy found her, and once
Debussy had ascertained she was not going to die he made no attempt
to see her again – as Mary Garden observed, 'when he was finished,
he was finished'. When the newspapers learnt of Lilly's act, a few weeks
later, Debussy's celebrity meant that the story was soon reprinted in New
York. His friends and associates were appalled and their embarrassment
acute; many could not bring themselves to see him, and he lost several
friends for good. (Among those who remained were Robert Godet, Paul
Dukas and the tirelessly faithful Erik Satie.) It was far worse for Debussy's
reputation that Madame Bardac was perceived to be rich, well-connected
and Jewish to boot (after all this was in a Paris only recently riven by

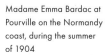

Madame Emma Bardac at Pourville on the Normandy coast, during the summer of 1904

l'affaire Dreyfus, the root of which was anti-Semitism – Pierre Louÿs was in the anti-Semitic, anti-Dreyfus camp).

Up against the culture, intellect and wealth of Emma Bardac, Lilly quite simply did not stand a chance. In addressing his wife as 'poor little Lilly' Debussy was not far off the mark, yet he did her a profound disservice by treating her as a sweet kind of child, however genuine and attractive was the unaffected tenderness he once displayed towards her. But by 1904, at forty-two, he had at last come of age. He had moved on, and upwards.

Emma Bardac divorced her husband on 4 May 1905. Debussy's divorce from Lilly was granted in August, and the settlement in Lilly's favour meant that he had to pay her considerable sums of money for the rest of his life. In October he and Emma moved into a secluded house in the fashionable Avenue du Bois de Boulogne across the other side of the city from his old haunts. On 30 October Emma gave birth to their child, Claude-Emma (Chouchou). The life of a composer continued its course – in November, just at the time the newspapers were carrying his marital scandal around the world, Debussy's modest work *Danses,* for string orchestra and harp, was given its first performance. (He had completed the two dances the previous April as a commission from the instrument maker Pleyel for their newly invented chromatic harp.) In a review, Emma's former lover Fauré suggested that the two dances revealed 'a great many of those same harmonic idiosyncrasies that are at times unusual and attractive and at other times merely unpleasant'.

Debussy and Emma seemed in no haste to get married, and it was not until January 1908 that they became husband and wife. The artist's soft hat was soon to be replaced by a gentleman's bowler.

8

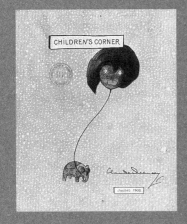

The front page of *Children's Corner*, 1908. Debussy insisted: 'The red on the cover must be an orange-red... for the cover, a light grey paper scattered with snow.'

'Music is a free art, a wellspring, an art of the open air, an art comparable to the elements – the wind, the sea and the sky.'

Claude Debussy

Images 1905-12

Debussy wanted the image of a wave on the front cover of the first edition
of *La Mer*, taken from a colour print on the wall of his study, *The Hollow
of the Wave off Kanagawa*, by the Japanese artist Hokusai. Along with
the title, *La Mer*, and the vividly descriptive names of each movement –
De l'Aube à midi sur la mer (*'From Dawn to Midday on the Sea'*), *Jeux
de vagues* (*'The Play of the Waves'*), and *Le Dialogue du vent et de la mer*
(*'Dialogue of the Wind and the Sea'*) – this simple act reinforced a conception of music as metaphor. 'In the beginning of things, the imagination
created analogy and metaphor,' Baudelaire had written in his review
'*Le Salon de 1859*'. 'The imagination decomposes all creation and with
the wealth of materials amassed and ordered according to rules whose
origins can be found only in the deepest recesses of the soul, it creates
a new world.' This vivid formulation of the processes of artistic creation
had a profound impact on subsequent developments in Symbolist and
Modernist art – and where visual art led, in the half-century or so immediately following Baudelaire's death in 1865, poetry and music soon
followed. Baudelaire returned to the theme in his celebrated critique
of Delacroix, and here might be found the seeds of Debussy's own
imaginative concerns: 'The whole visible universe is nothing but a
storehouse of images and signs, to which man's imagination will assign
a place and relative value; it is a kind of pasture for the imagination to
divest and transform.'

Debussy's first use of the term 'Images' had been for the unpublished
piano pieces of 1894; but it seems to have become an idea that informed
more than just the works he finally called *Images*, as the clearly descriptive
intent of the *Nocturnes*, *Estampes* and *La Mer* indicates. It also seems that
a triptych format was integral to his creative conception (*Ibéria*, the greatest of the orchestral *Images*, is itself in three parts).

A grand project for two series of *Images*, each containing six pieces in
groups of three, was drawn up by Debussy for his publishers Fromont
in July 1903, probably spurred on by his completion of *Estampes*. Visual
metaphor was occupying his mind – a series of triptychs generically

Opposite, the design for the
front cover of *La Mer* was
based on a woodblock print
by Hokusai that Debussy
owned

entitled 'Pictures' would appear to be a logical extension of a triptych of 'Prints'. The project had first taken shape as early as December 1901, for the pianist Ricardo Viñes (who was to give the première of the *Suite pour le piano* one month later), had noted in his diary that Debussy had played him 'two of the twelve piano pieces he intends to compose, six for two hands and six for two pianos'. The two pieces were an early version of *Reflets dans l'eau* (reworked in 1905) and *Mouvement*.

Debussy's suggestion to Fromont was for the following:

1ère série (2 mains)	*2ème série (2 mains)*
I. Reflets dans l'eau	*I. Cloches à travers les feuilles*
II. Hommage à Rameau	*II. Et la lune descend sur le temple qui fût*
III. Mouvements	*III. Poissons d'or*
IV. Ibéria	*IV.*
V. Gigues tristes	*V.*
VI. Rondes	*I.*

Items IV–VI in the first series he indicated as 'two pianos or orchestra'. The remaining three titles were left blank, sadly never to be written.

In the three sets of *Images* as eventually published, '*Mouvements*' became singular, '*Gigues tristes*' became simply '*Gigues*', while '*Rondes*' became '*Rondes de printemps*'. The first and second series remained as solo piano works; the 'two pianos' idea was discarded in favour of orchestration. The *Images* plan, then, with its characteristically evocative titles virtually in place, came almost fully into focus exactly at the time Debussy was composing *La Mer* – whose triptych of titles was equally as evocative. (The opening movement *De l'Aube à midi sur la mer* drew from Satie the amusingly barbed remark that he liked the bit 'at a quarter to eleven'.) It was several years, however, before the majority of his chosen *Images* were fully conceived as music, or even begun on paper. This gives an intriguing insight into the effects of external stimuli on Debussy's creative imagination, and his habits of contemplation – the way in which, in Baudelaire's phrase, he drew on a 'storehouse of images and signs'. So the question as to which came first in Debussy's mind, title or music (often asked, for example, in relation to the piano *Préludes*), can in most cases be answered with confidence: his visual and aural experience of the external world provided a pasture for his imagination 'to divest and transform' – into music. (He did, however, make small changes to the titles of the outer movements of *La Mer* during the course of composition, in response, it seems, to the way in which the music itself was forming.)

Debussy's advice to Raoul Bardac to 'gather impressions, but don't be in a hurry to write them down' was inescapably a visual, or at least experiential, allusion: experience, after a period of contemplation, can be transmuted into art (Wordsworth famously described a poem as 'emotion recollected in tranquillity'). And Debussy also had this to say, in an interview from 1910: 'All the noises we hear around ourselves can be re-created. Every sound perceived by the acute ear in the rhythm of the world about us can be represented musically. Some people above all wish to conform to the rules; for myself I wish to render only what I hear.' There is a suggestion in the phrase 'the rhythm of the world' that Debussy heard what others did not hear, and even perhaps that he heard in a manner that was beyond 'acute': that for Debussy the momentariness of experience was perceived as sound (but that he was not 'in a hurry to write it down'). This is impossible to judge objectively, but in view of the intensely sensory nature of his music it is a question worth pondering. One is reminded again of Denis's statement that every work of art is 'the impassioned equivalent of a sensation experienced'.

As for his rejection of 'rules' in favour of experience, even this remark has a Baudelairian origin, echoing the poet's suggestion that the imagination obeys 'rules whose origins can be found only in the deepest recesses of the soul', certainly the kind of rules of which Debussy would have approved. Yet it is a characteristic irony that in *La Mer* Debussy came close to the 'rules' of symphonic composition – to musical exposition and development, as opposed to quasi-improvisatory structures. Such processes, however, would hardly have been discernible at a first hearing. Instead, those who had admired his earlier orchestral works heard a complexity of superimposed thematic material and an intricate web of polyrhythms (partly influenced by the procedures of the Javanese gamelan) that appeared heretical: the expected descriptive content seemed to be subservient to calculation. 'I do not hear, I do not see, I do not smell the sea,' wrote Pierre Lalo, in a damning critique of the première in October 1905 (for most listeners today it seems that the opposite experience is the case).

Originality comes at a price, and much of the initially hostile reaction to *La Mer* was due to an inability to follow the composer down new paths. Here was a descriptive work largely without the tried and tested formulae, those conventions of nineteenth-century descriptive music that Debussy largely spurned 'in favour of his own highly individual vocabulary' (as Simon Trezise points out in his commentary *Debussy: La Mer*). This is the answer to Lalo, and Debussy implies as much in his dignified but passionate letter of defence. 'If my idea of music isn't the same as yours, I am none the less an artist and nothing but an artist,' he wrote to him. 'I love the sea and have listened to it with the passionate respect it deserves… The heart of the matter is that you love and defend traditions which for me no longer exist, or at least exist only as representative of an epoch in which they were not all as fine and valuable as people make out; the dust of the past is not always respectable.'

But there were other reasons for the lukewarm reception of this masterpiece. The celebrated composer of *Pelléas* was in disgrace for his marital outrages, and he was to be brought down. Few at the time noted another reason – that the orchestra, under the deeply unsympathetic baton of Camille Chevillard, had not mastered the intricate difficulties of the score. Debussy had feared as much: 'Chevillard is bound to dismember *La Mer* unmercifully,' he wrote to Durand before the work's first performance.

One of the most significant of early comments on *La Mer* was made, almost in passing, by Debussy's close friend of these years Louis Laloy, who in 1909 became the composer's first biographer (in French; there had been an English biography the previous year by Louise Liebich). In an essay from 1908 entitled 'The New Manner of Claude Debussy' Laloy examined the clear presence of symphonic form in *La Mer*, noting that 'the music can, strictly speaking, be explained by itself. This fact in no way diminishes the descriptive power of the music, in fact quite the contrary.' Descriptive music and pure music, he was saying, are not in opposition to each other, 'in fact quite the contrary', for the pure actually *enhances* the descriptive, the 'purely musical' procedures (quasi-developmental, cyclical, structural) of the work embodying the descriptive purpose.

The astonishing rapprochement between descriptive-symbolic intent and musical procedure in *La Mer* even carries over into the language used to comment on it. Take the following account of the work's symphonic

characteristics by the composer Jean Barraqué, written in 1962: 'In *La
Mer* Debussy invented a procedure of development in which the notions
of exposition and development co-exist in an uninterrupted stream, per-
mitting the work to be propelled along by itself without recourse to any
pre-established model.' The imagery of fluidity here is almost certainly
unconscious (Barraqué's aim, like Laloy's, was to describe purely musical
procedures), which makes it all the more significant. Debussy's creative
purpose in *La Mer* was surely to put musical structure at the service of
an 'uninterrupted stream'. His music captures and condenses not only
the passing of time – a stream of consciousness, 'from dawn to midday
on the sea' – but also the notion of the sea 'propelled along by itself'.
Trezise goes further and suggests that Debussy might have found his
model in the structures of narrative (anticipating in musical form, it
might be added, Virginia Woolf's *The Waves*, a 'stream of consciousness'
novel some twenty years later than *La Mer*), which gives rise to 'the
deep-seated sense of unity many have admired in the work'. And unity,
Trezise points out, is never at the expense of the all pervading 'motivic
diversity' of the work: 'As the sea's changing states are explored, new
motivic shapes evolve, some incorporating elements of existing ones,
many freshly minted for the moment at hand.'

   La Mer is not only an impressionistic evocation of the sea, a surface
shimmer; the work is a transmutation of mankind's complex and subconscious responses to the sea, achieved through and within the very pith
of the musical material. As an artist Debussy seizes the experience – the
longing, the fear, the delight, the age-old responses – and sets it down
in his own medium. In this sense *La Mer*, rather than being a departure
from music as symbolism, as some commentators have suggested, is
a further profound exploration of this concept – in line with Baudelaire's
ideas on *les images* and *l'imagination*. For Debussy the sea is already
a symbol. His music is another, a symbol of a symbol, as Dukas had first
said in his critique of the *Nocturnes*.

   It is tempting to see evidence in *La Mer*, as Trezise does, of the emotional conflicts in the composer's life at this period: to see the work not
only as the catalyst of events but as in some way the recipient of the
turmoil. This is especially apparent in the intensity of the third movement, where Debussy's psychological apprehension of one of the most
potent symbols known to humankind reaches its fullest power. It seems
that he perceived the sea as overwhelmingly female – as goddess, mother,

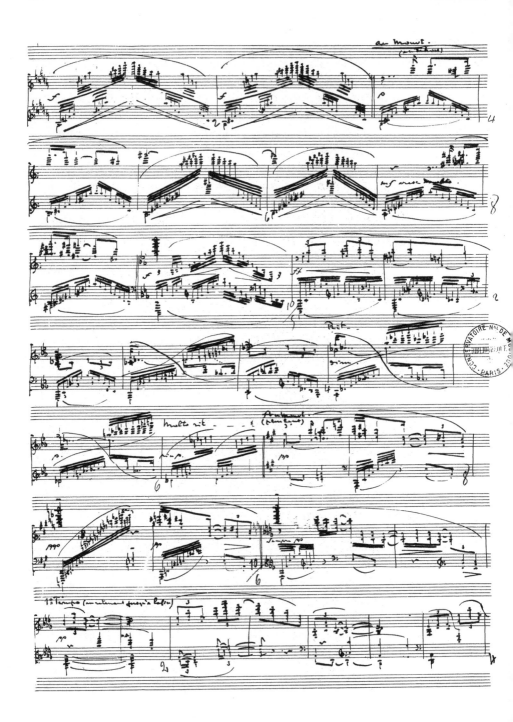

or lover. Several earlier works suggest this: the Verlaine setting *La Mer est plus belle*, parts of *Pelléas*, and *Sirènes* from the *Nocturnes* (in which the fatally seductive voices of the Sirens of Greek mythology appear as a wordless female chorus). And, replete with water imagery, are the two great piano pieces contemporary with the gestation of *La Mer*, the dream-like *Reflets dans l'eau* from *Images* Book 1, and the gloriously hedonistic *L'Isle joyeuse*. The dream world of *Reflets* contains a catharsis in which the sexual symbolism is inescapable, where cascading piano figurations build to a sweeping emotional climax in which sea symbolism is pervasive. In *L'Isle joyeuse*, which Debussy revised and completed during his island idyll with Emma Bardac in June 1904, the joy of sexual fulfilment is sublimated into intoxicating dance rhythms and glorious, orchestrally conceived piano sonorities, complete with allusions to brass and percussion. If this piece, expressly of the sea and the legends associated with it, was supposed to have been inspired by the painting *L'Embarquement pour Cythère* by Watteau – whom Debussy called 'the greatest, the most moving genius of the eighteenth century' – then it clearly burst from the frame. Watteau's painting, in which pilgrims are attending the shrine of Aphrodite, is a gently enigmatic hymn to love; Debussy's music is a paean of praise, a passionate ode to joy that moves beyond decorum. And if the sea is feminine, so too, for Debussy, is music. In June 1903, just prior to his work on *La Mer*, he wrote an article (from which the above comment on Watteau comes) in which he noted that 'those devoted to Art are irretrievably in love with her, and, besides, it is impossible to know how feminine music is.' He adds, with prophetic irony, 'perhaps that explains the frequent chastity of men of genius'.

In a fascinating conjunction of art and life, Debussy's sketchbook that contains parts of the second and third movements of *La Mer* also harbours jottings concerning the traumatic events with Lilly. Debussy was finding an anaesthetic for his guilt in attempting to set the record straight concerning what he saw as Lilly's intense emotional blackmail. In a long and self-justifying list he noted that her proclaimed hunger strike was actually accompanied by four egg yolks a day in her tea, according to her maid; that the suicide attempt on 13 October was preceded by 'four warning letters'; that she shows violence towards the servants. And he writes of 'rows over money, although I'd allowed her more than I could afford (debts) – the subject of bitter reproaches'. (The reference to servants reveals that Debussy's middle-class lifestyle

Opposite, the manuscript of part of *Reflets dans l'eau* from *Images* Book I was already in evidence, despite the financial cost.) 'Constant feigning' he notes, 'for example, says she's never loved me… [and that] she was always in the wrong; took revenge by exercising a daily tyranny on my thoughts, my acquaintances – the material proof [is] my production over these past four years.' So he blames her for his small output of music, forgetting the enormous work he had undertaken to get *Pelléas* on stage. And all of this is set down between the same covers as sketches for his new orchestral triptych.

The première of *La Mer* took place on 15 October 1905, almost exactly one year after Lilly had shot herself. Debussy had completed the score six months earlier, in March, with a dedication to Jacques Durand, although the final draft bears a faint inscription to Emma in Debussy's hand: '*Pour la p.m. [petite mienne] dont les yeux rient dans l'ombre*' – 'for the darling whose eyes laugh in the shadows'. The publisher from here on guaranteed Debussy 12,000 francs a year, having bought the rights to *Pelléas et Mélisande* and an exclusive contract to publish the composer's future works.

Although Debussy found seclusion and comfort in his new home in the avenue du Bois de Boulogne, it was not always the '*isle joyeuse*' for which he might have hoped. At times it was more like a desert island in which he contemplated his own mortality in a wide and lonely space (the house had eighteen rooms). But Emma pampered him, protected him, and bore him a beautiful child. And like the well-bred gentleman that many new acquaintances took him for, he became devoted to the garden, which he had laid out to his own plan. Durand recalled that 'winter and summer, Debussy used to work surrounded by flowers; his study overflowed with them. It was a symphony of colours which used to produce music.' And then there were the oriental objets d'art which he collected and loved: 'The wide table on which he used to work was cluttered with high-class Japanese objects. His favourite was a porcelain toad (named Arkel) which he called his fetish and which he took with him when he moved, claiming he could not work unless it was in sight.' In his letters and surviving photos Chouchou can be seen growing from tiny morsel into little girl, providing her father with further solace. She also provided another creative pasture: he turned his new-found knowledge of childhood into the masterpiece in miniature, *Children's Corner*, dedicated 'To my dear little Chouchou, with gentle apologies from her father for what follows.' All titles were in English, in homage

Claude-Emma Debussy
(Chouchou), Debussy's
daughter from his second
marriage

to the fashionable English-style nursery with which Chouchou was provided, complete with English governess. Nothing could have been further from the world of Debussy's own childhood.

He was, unsurprisingly, deeply conscious of how his relationship with Emma Bardac looked to the outside world. It is curious that with both their divorces granted, in 1905, it took until January 1908 for them to become man and wife. (To his friends, however, he referred to Emma as 'my wife' and 'Madame Debussy' long before they were legally married.) It has been repeatedly stated that Emma's expectation of a large legacy was thwarted when, on account of her liaison with Debussy, she was disinherited by her wealthy uncle; however, Lesure has discovered that she had little expectation of a large legacy anyway. From 1907 she received just 5,000 francs a year.

Life at 80 avenue du Bois de Boulogne became increasingly dominated by an acute shortage of money, although funds had initially been sufficient for the composer to proudly help his parents, both now seventy, to move across the city to be nearer to him. Indeed, funds would have been more than ample had the new couple taken on a less extravagant way of life. The historian Christophe Charle has suggested that 'when Debussy adopted his new lifestyle… he did more than give in to bourgeois conformism – he lost all sense of reality and proportion.' The eighteen-room house they rented was at the upper end of prices for the elite of Paris, at 8,000 francs a year (eight times more than the rent on

Debussy with Emma in 1905

his previous flat in rue Cardinet), on top of which Debussy had to pay nearly 5,000 francs a year to Lilly, the equal of Emma's inheritance. Then there was the cost of servants, a hired car and Debussy's favoured luxuries – culinary treats as well as artistic knick-knacks. He also had considerable debts to pay off, and they mounted for the rest of his life. Durand, however, made him generous advances (and loans without interest), set off against the publishing rights and performances of *Pelléas*. Charle points out that just when *Pelléas* should have eased the financial plight of his first forty years, Debussy 'walked into a new trap by acquiescing in the fallacious prestige of a life too bourgeois for his real income. The historian does not become a moralist in so stating. With the exception of Erik Satie, almost all Debussy's contemporaries were doing the same.'

What could have helped, and such was the expectation and intention, would have been another opera. But for all his considerable work on various projects – notably his dedication to two operas on stories by Poe, *The Devil in the Belfry* and *The Fall of the House of Usher* – nothing achieved completion. After *Pelléas*, innumerable theatrical projects, operatic and balletic, had been suggested, toyed with, taken up and abandoned: projects inspired by yet another version of Tristan, by Orpheus, by the Buddhist story of Siddartha, Verlaine's *Fêtes galantes* (again), Shakespeare's *As You Like It* and *King Lear*, and the *Oresteia* of Aeschylus. Debussy, as usual, worked slowly, meticulously, probing and coaxing his creative demon, doubting his progress, ever watchful not to be seduced by his 'angelic facility'. 'Don't ask me where my work lies,' he told an interviewer in 1911, 'I never know myself.' He was then working on incidental music for *Le Martyre de Saint-Sébastien*, a large-scale commission from the Italian poet Gabriele d'Annunzio. 'Only one aspect of the work is inconvenient: it has to be finished by a stated time. I have a horror of that, and the idea paralyses me. I can think of nothing else.' It was an old refrain. To some, this smacked of idleness. Debussy, guiltily, sometimes saw it this way too, and just occasionally in his splendid surroundings he drifted into *ennui*, that classic state (only ever identified by a French word) which so often features in the *fin-de-siècle* consciousness: fatigue, boredom, heaviness of spirit and a wearily cynical eye cast over the more active members of society. But Debussy was saved from these excesses by his tenacious perfectionism and his abiding sense of humour. In 1906 he had written to Emma's son Raoul: 'I won't say anything about what I'm

writing – there's not much of it, and what there is I don't like. For want of
a better excuse I blame it on the weather.' That year the only piece he
completed was the tiny *Serenade for a Doll,* which was to become part of
Children's Corner. 1905 had not been much better, although at least he
was able to see published his *Images* Book 1 for piano. Of these last pieces
he wrote to Durand: 'Without false vanity, I think [they] work well and
will take their place in piano literature to the left of Schumann and to the
right of Chopin.' Posterity has proved him correct.

In *Images* Book 1 he exploited the full resources of the piano in the
manner of the greatest composers of the nineteenth century, and he
incontestably enriched the repertoire in the process. In fact the first piece,
Reflets dans l'eau, is pianistically Lisztian in conception, combining the
pictorial techniques of such a piece as Liszt's *Les Jeux d'eaux à la Villa
d'Este* – in which an image of water is made ever present to the imagination through shimmering arpeggios and tremolandos – with what
Debussy called 'the most recent discoveries in harmonic chemistry'.
Hommage à Rameau is a work of meticulously controlled structural
tension, in which the mysterious opening monody gives birth to a
dynamic musical drama of cathedral-like proportions. The fluid
arabesques of *Reflets dans l'eau,* where pulse is absorbed and neutralized
by the enveloping textures, are replaced in *Hommage à Rameau* by a
technique of block-chordal writing in which pulse is explicitly articulated – so the unfolding of time, expressed through the flexible and sensual
rhythms of a saraband, becomes the core of a richly evoked homage
to the past. *Mouvement* is brief but no less dramatic in effect. Its subject
matter is movement itself, a perception of time now as implacable
rhythm: the result is an exultant, wheel-like motion whose manic spin-
ning is controlled by strict, almost mechanical, metrical divisions.
(Debussy instructs that the music should be played 'with a fantastical
but precise lightness'.)

The pressures of international celebrity drove Debussy into further
seclusion. Adulators, imitators and the voices of conservatism whom
Debussy had satirized in his critical columns – all combined to place
him in a state of mental and, at times, physical siege. He rarely went out
other than for occasional visits to his publisher, or to call on his book-
seller or antique dealer. These were the years of 'Debussyism', which
reached its height in the period 1908–10. At times it seemed his devotees,
the 'Debussyists', irritated him the most: 'They're killing me,' he declared

to René Peter. Debussy had a horror of being seen as the leader of a 'school', but such was the situation being pressed upon him by those eager to refute the disparagement of his music by conservative critics. In 1910 a collection of articles was published under the title *Le Cas Debussy* which purported to show once and for all that Debussy's music was merely the product of fashion and was of unlasting value. His repeated denials that he represented a new school of composition were seen as hypocrisy, for the writers contended that he had in fact become the representative of 'perhaps the most intransigent [school] one had ever known in music'. As for his 'originality', it existed only in negativity, in 'that which [his music] is not': 'Take out rhythm, melody and emotion and you will just about have it. What remains can have its charms: a sort of diffuse harmony, a murmuring and subtle monotony, still quite capable of pleasing delicate ears.'

On the personal front an abiding achievement was the love he received, and gave, not just to his own daughter but to his stepchildren – the composer Raoul and his sister Hélène, always known as Dolly. His stepdaughter, who lived with her mother and Debussy for six years, recalled how intimidating he could be to those who didn't know him, but how his 'closed' manner 'concealed a painful sensitivity and a disposition which was on the contrary full of warmth towards those to whom he had given his friendship... He was very young at heart, at times seeming like a child; he had a great sense of the comical, but sometimes (rarely, I am happy to say) he could have violent fits of temper when his thundering shouts terrified me.' She also recalled Satie's visits, which she awaited with impatience, 'so unexpectedly comical was his [Satie's] way of expressing himself and his repartee in conversation. His attitude to Debussy was both curiously humble and lacking in spontaneity, in spite of a terribly malicious look from behind his pince-nez.' And of her mother she said: 'She was small and pretty with auburn hair and topaz-coloured eyes. What is more she had an incomparable charm, to which nobody could remain insensible, even during the last years of her life... When Debussy felt too lonely, while he was working, he was in the habit of sending to my mother, from one floor to another, wonderful little notes, full of love and tenderness. "This unique charm of yours" are the words with which he finishes one of them.'

But it was not always like this. Dolly's memoir concealed (or was ignorant of) the darker sides of Debussy's life. His relationship with

Emma was far from idyllic. This is not to say that her recollections, or those of her brother Raoul, are inaccurate. In later years both wanted to leave a record of the great man about whom the world seemed so misinformed. Rich in detail, Raoul's memoir deserves quoting at length:

Certainly his happiness had sometimes been compromised by problems of a financial nature, which had forced him to modify some details of the interior furnishing and to undertake a number of tours. But these were the only clouds on his horizon. The life he led there was not one of luxury (because his taste was not luxurious nor aimed towards the good things of life), but of comfort and extreme refinement, devoid of showy gestures. His day-to-day happiness depended on the satisfaction of little habits within an atmosphere of love and devotion…

Among his literary purchases there was always a large number of English books and magazines. He was very taken with the way they looked and would get them translated for him either by his wife, or by my sister. Debussy was devoted to various objects, silent but faithful companions, which decorated his work-table: very simple pens made of reeds and always of the same make, special blotters, a pot for tobacco, a cigarette box, the toad Arkel, a model of a sleeping Chinaman and so on. People have referred to Debussy as being very much of a gourmand. He was in fact more of a gourmet, but infinitely so – with unction, none the less stopping short of voracity or excess. He loved the things he found good – as he loved the things he found beautiful – but without the slightest trace of vulgar gluttony. He was fond of his whisky, which he used to drink every evening around ten o'clock, served in his special graduated decanter, and of his tea, which he drank only out of his teacup…

But the great, the supreme and constant passion of his life was always music, which he loved for its own sake and which he could not bear to see brutalized, or cheapened, or made the vehicle of empty pomposity. He had never imagined that it would lead him to fame, and had expected even that he would remain more or less unknown. He loved music in its entirety, and responded to its most diverse manifestations, as long as it was true music…

Debussy used to compose slowly, forcing himself, as he used to say to me, to eradicate all parasitical development and to replace it by a musical line which reflected the nature of his ideas and the path that they took, a line which allowed these ideas air… But once the shape of things was clear in his mind, then Debussy used to write quickly and easily: his facility in this respect testifying to his possession of a métier that was as amazing as it was unobtrusive.

If Debussy loved his home, he could also be ironical about 'the smart "cocktail" *habitués* of the neighbourhood, 'this avenue du Bois de Boulogne, smelling of Brazilians and Americans'. His inner conflicts were those of the artist, but they were also entirely human in an everyday, prosaic sense. He loved and needed his family, but often felt hemmed in. As early as October 1907, before he married Emma, he was complaining in a letter to Laloy, 'is it the fault of this corner of Paris? Is it that I'm just not suited to the domestic life?' In 1909 another associate from the *Pelléas* days, the conductor Henri Busser, noted in his diary: 'Long visit paid to Debussy in his private house in the avenue du Bois de Boulogne. He seems bored to be there!'

Then in 1910 comes a severe crisis with Emma, and a time of personal problems far more acute than Raoul Bardac's naïve 'clouds on his horizon'. Debussy writes to a friend in March of 'a dangerous turning point in my life', an ominous phrase he had used just before his departure from Lilly. ('Life has its dangerous turning points,' he had written to Lilly on 16 July 1904, 'and in my case they're complicated by the fact that I'm both an artist – what a business! – and your husband.') Debussy had begun a new liaison. In letters throughout the summer Debussy writes of his turmoil to his friends, without ever naming its cause. He writes of dejection, an absence of sunlight (a recurrent image, with echoes of the symbolism of *Pelléas*), and in a letter to Durand in July of how 'those around me refuse to accept that I could never live in the everyday world of things and people. Hence the irrepressible need I have to escape from myself, and go off on adventures which seem inexplicable because no one knows who this man is – yet maybe he's the best part of me!' This is the side of him, he implies, which makes him an artist. 'Anyway, an artist is, by definition, someone used to living among dreams and phantoms. It's pointless expecting the same man to follow strictly all the observances of daily life, the laws and all the other barriers erected by a cowardly, hypocritical world.' This sounds like a guilty excuse for his actions – just as he had grasped at excuses in his letters to Lilly – but it is also a diagnosis, and takes us to the heart of his creative personality.

Nothing is known of this affair apart from its effect on Emma, whose anguish was severe, and who considered leaving. An undated letter (postmarked 1910) reveals that some time during the summer she went so far as to make an appointment with a lawyer, but then drew back from the brink:

Debussy's paperweight, which he christened Arkel after the old king in *Pelléas et Mélisande*

Maître, *please accept my most sincere apologies, but the lamentable*
state in which I find myself, both morally and physically, would prevent
me in any case from attending the appointment which you have so kindly
granted. I am still hesitating, I am waiting… To leave the one who
inexplicably causes me so much suffering will be heart-breaking. But,
sadly, I have grounds enough for such a decision.

Debussy drew back from the brink too. By the end of the year he is again
sending Emma's greetings in letters to friends, and on a conducting trip
to Vienna and Budapest in early December he writes to her in the fondest
manner, without once alluding to the earlier traumas. It was perhaps
inevitable that the crisis was resolved. His health was failing – he was
showing the first signs, undiagnosed as yet, of the cancer that was to
develop fully a few years later – and the support structure that had built
up around him since 1905 (without his complete acquiescence one feels)
proved far more difficult to break than anything he had ever known
before. He had a child, stepchildren, comfort, protection. However
much he protested, he knew Emma was the focus and mainstay of this
structure, and he again came to see his relationship with her in terms
of love. And financially they survived, thanks to Durand and to the
conducting tours. Durand, a close friend, was also no fool, and knew
what he was backing. By 1910 Debussy was the leading composer of the
day, his compositions constantly performed. (Only the year before he
had joined the pantheon of famous figures photographed by the great
Nadar, as we have seen.) Durand knew what his returns would be in
the end, which is not to say that his hand of friendship, his loans, his offer
of his country home as a holiday house for Debussy and his family, were
not made in a genuine spirit of altruism. But he pressed his composer
hard, and Debussy often wilted under the pressure.

Debussy's letters from December 1910 show the homesick voyager
of old, the same laments as in his Rome days, the same bewilderment
among strangers. He simply hated travelling – or pretended to, for his
writing is lively and full of humour. He makes fun of foreign names,
he can understand no one, musicians intimidate him but somehow he
manages to tame them. And through it all he thinks constantly of his
wife and Chouchou, whose photos he takes with him. Despite himself,
Debussy makes a fine travel writer, for he has an acute eye for the telling
detail and a delight in the well-placed generalization. And in all his

letters the childlike side of his nature reveals itself. Recalling his trip a few months later, he writes to Robert Godet:

> *First Vienna: an old city covered in make-up, overstuffed with the music of Brahms and Puccini, the officers with chests like women and the women with chests like officers...*
>
> *Then, Budapest: where the Danube refuses to be as blue as a famous waltz would have us believe. The Hungarians insincere and nice. The best thing there was a gypsy whose real name is spelt Radics, but pronounced Raditche – don't ask why. He loves music far more than many people who have a reputation for doing so...*
>
> *But I've brought back some really beautiful embroidery and some marvellous chocolates sold by a Monsieur Gerbaud, who is a genius in his own way.*

During all the daily stresses of life lived, of financial and personal crises, of strenuous conducting tours, the composer composed, and great works were completed. As an artist Debussy continued to experience euphoria when new projects were taken up, and dejection when projects were abandoned. Two further sets of *Images* reached the public domain, the second set of three for piano (in 1908), and finally after years of unfulfilled promises the *Images* for orchestra (first performed in part in 1910, but not completed until 1913). And some 'images' under a different name were conceived quite suddenly in the eight weeks or so between the beginning of December 1909 and February the following year, the twelve descriptive pieces for piano making up *Préludes* Book I – although it seems that, in the usual way, the plan might have been germinating for some time. Another work, another change of direction: where *Images* Book II had explored the immaterial and improvisatory – seeking refinements of piano sonority and eastern-influenced tonalities far removed from his previous piano pieces – the new prelude format enabled a sharper focus of expression within a deliberate limitation of means. Again it seems as if piano composition came as a relief from the problems of larger-scale writing. 'How much has first to be discovered, then suppressed, before one can reach the naked flesh of emotion,' he was to write to Godet nearly a year later, lamenting yet again his failure to achieve what he wanted operatically from his favoured Poe stories. Luckily for pianists, the concentration of expression he achieved instead in the piano *Préludes* never ceases to appear miraculous.

Estampe, Image, or *Prélude* – all of this piano music has a descriptive intention, in the manner of Schumann's *Kinderszenen* and *Fantasiestücke,* or Liszt's *Années de Pélèrinage.* The first piece of *Images* Book II, *Cloches à travers les feuilles,* was supposed to have been inspired by the sound of bells across the autumnal forests of the Jura region of France. This may have been the case, although Debussy did not personally hear the bells or see the forests – the scene was simply described to him in a letter from Louis Laloy. But Debussy was adept at picking up his imaginative material in this way, as the *Prélude La Terrasse des audiences du clair de lune* indicates. Debussy alighted on this highly evocative phrase from an account in a Parisian newspaper of a royal ceremony in India: the writer described 'the hall of victory, the hall of pleasure, the garden of the sultanas, *the terrace for audiences in the moonlight*'. The *Prélude La Puerta del vino* arose in a similar way, from a picture postcard Debussy received from Manuel de Falla showing the Gate of Wine at the Alhambra in Granada; and the image of *Les Collines d'Anacapri* came, it seems, from the label on a bottle of Italian wine.

The bells of *Cloches à travers les feuilles,* however, are as much eastern in origin as French, for it is clear that Debussy also tapped into his memory of the Javanese gamelan – the orchestra of gongs and metallophones he first heard at the 1889 Paris Exhibition. Indeed, the sonorities of the gamelan, and its multiple melodic strands sounding simultaneously, lie at the heart of much of Debussy's piano writing (and of his own playing too: 'No one else had his gift,' wrote Émile Vuillermoz, 'of transforming a dissonant chord into a little bell, made of bronze or silver, scattering its harmonics to the four winds'). The second piece of *Images* Book II, *Et la lune descend sur le temple qui fût,* displays just these characteristics. The image of the title suggests a mystical past, an ancient temple behind which the moon is setting. Debussy moves away from the intricate counterpoint of *Cloches* and builds his composition from block chords, just as he had in *Hommage à Rameau,* another piece concerned with evoking the past. The rhythmic and harmonic structure of *Et la lune* create an oriental conception of suspended time and motion. The 1889 Exhibition also introduced Debussy to the Annamite theatre from China; while at the Exhibition of 1900 he had heard the gamelan of Bali (which plays in a brighter and more rhythmic style than the Javanese). The gamelan, he wrote in 1895, was able to express 'every shade of meaning, even the unnameable' – a Mallarméan allusion which survives in Debussy's great piano compositions of the following century.

He completed *Images* Book II with another oriental allusion, and one of his greatest and most ebullient virtuoso pieces, *Poissons d'or*. This piece was inspired by a Chinese lacquer panel that Debussy owned, depicting two golden fish against a black background. A golden willow tree bends down to the water, and the fish appear to be swooping as well as floating, the whole blending motion with stasis. Debussy's imagination runs riot – in a distinct preview of early jazz.

The Gate of Wine, one of the entrances to the Alhambra in Grenada, as depicted on a postcard Debussy received from Manuel de Falla. The image inspired Debussy's composition *La Puerta del vino* from *Préludes* Book II

The final set of *Images*, for orchestra, was conceived between 1905 and 1913, a longer gestation than even the orchestral *Nocturnes* (and a testimony to Durand's infinite patience). Debussy himself conducted the première of the complete work in January 1913, although *Ibéria* had already been performed under the baton of Pierné in February 1910, and *Rondes de Printemps* a month later, conducted by Debussy. The opening movement, *Gigues*, employs the Scottish traditional melody *The Keel Row* as its structural reference, while the final *Rondes* refers yet again to the French tune *Nous n'irons plus au bois* (as had the third piece of the 1894 *Images* and *Jardins sous la pluie* from *Estampes*). Such references are purely compositional devices: if external images exist, they remain within the private world of the composer.

The descriptive context of the central *Image* of the set, however, the Spanish triptych *Ibéria*, is made explicit by its three titles: *Par les rues et par les chemins* ('Along the Lanes and Byways'), *Les Parfums de la nuit* ('Perfumes of the Night'), and *Le Matin d'un jour de fête* ('On the Morning of a Holiday'). This was the most easily and fluently composed of the orchestral *Images*, which at once becomes apparent in performance. The fluid, improvisatory manner of its unfolding makes it one of the high points of Debussy's orchestral genius, and it clearly gave him enormous pleasure and satisfaction. It was surely *Ibéria* to which he was referring in some heartfelt remarks to Durand in 1908, when he tried to explain his reasons for the delay in delivery of the *Images*: 'I'm trying to do "something else" – in a way *realities* – what imbeciles call "impressionism", a term as misused as it could possibly be.' Together with his comments in a letter to Caplet in February the following year, after a rehearsal of *Ibéria* that had delighted him, this shows him developing a significant analysis of the nature of 'impressionist' art – whether visual or musical. The transition between the second and third movements, he tells Caplet, sounds '*as if it hasn't been written*' – and he underlines the words to emphasize his point. He means not only that the music has an air of spontaneous improvisation, but that it actually creates an impression of reality. The images he had in mind appear to come to life, he realizes delightedly, 'with people and things waking up… There's a man selling watermelons, and urchins whistling, I can see them quite clearly.'

This remarkable observation is fundamental to our understanding of Debussy's creative imagination – to the Debussyan 'image' – which

we can now see embraces a Realist as well as a Symbolist view of the nature of art. Debussy also happens to be historically accurate with regard to '*realities* – what imbeciles call "impressionism"'. Impressionist painting in France had grown out of the Realist movement, but with greater emphasis on the complexities of light and colour, seeking not a specific but a fleeting reality. The art was to achieve the impression of spontaneous, momentary experience, an image caught in the blink of an eye – to achieve a painting that would appear, to adapt Debussy's phrase, 'as if it hadn't been painted'. Mallarmé, as we have seen, had observed several decades earlier that in Impressionist painting: 'Nothing should be absolutely fixed, in order that we may feel that the bright gleam which lights the picture, or the diaphanous shadow which veils it, are only seen in passing.'

Ravel adored the *Images* for orchestra, and generously proclaimed as much in an article after the first complete performance in 1913. His article gives a glimpse of the constant debate surrounding Debussy's music, and especially the reactions to its so-called 'picturesque' intent. One critic had asserted that it was only 'writers and painters' who still admired Debussy, whereas 'musicians and sensitive listeners' had grown tired of him. Ravel replies:

> *So, you who have felt the remarkable enchantment and exquisite freshness of* Rondes de Printemps; *you, who felt moved to tears by the flowing quality of* Ibèria, *by the profoundly moving* Les Parfums de la nuit; *by the harmonic richness, so original and delicate; by all of that intense musicality; you are nothing but a writer or a painter. And you fully understand the contempt that these terms convey. I too am only a writer or a painter; and with me, Messieurs Igor Stravinsky, Florent Schmitt, Roger-Ducasse, Albert Roussel, and a host of young composers whose output, however, isn't negligible.*

Debussy, constantly moving on (and wearied by the endless misunderstandings generated by the 'Impressionist' debate), finally relinquished the term *Image*, and turned to the tradition of the Prelude. In one respect he was picking up the direction of his *Suite pour le piano* from nearly ten years earlier. In his two books of twelve *Préludes* he again consciously allied himself to the repertoire of the past, with Bach and Chopin – especially with the latter's *24 Préludes* Opus 28. Similarly, his last solo piano collection, *Douze études* of 1915, returned to the genre of the Study and a final homage to Chopin.

The *Préludes* are, nevertheless, central to Debussy's descriptive style, although the titles are all placed at the end of each piece, hidden away in parentheses, as in '(… *Ondine*)'. There is an echo here from the previous century of the Symbolist ideals of suggestion and ambiguity. As Alfredo Casella recalled, it was in just such a manner that Debussy played himself:

> *No words can give an idea of the way in which he played certain of his* Préludes. *Not that he had actual virtuosity, but his sensibility of touch was incomparable; he gave the impression of playing directly on the strings of the instrument with no intermediate mechanism; the effect was a miracle of poetry.*

The descriptive range of the *Préludes* is remarkably wide, combining twenty-four different images of the world of Claude Debussy into one artistic whole in two parts. 'The point of comparison between music and the world lies hidden very deep,' wrote Schopenhauer, whose writing Debussy had read avidly in the 1890s. 'But the effect of music is far more powerful and penetrates far more deeply than that of the other arts; for they communicate only shadows, whereas music communicates the essence.'

So what might be this essence in the *Préludes*? Debussy's suggestions, his titles that are really 'afterwords', add up to a certain view of the world that, as an artist, he needs to communicate – through music. He is of course communicating the life of his mind, of his imagination; the stories and images that have arrested him, the scenes and fragments of poetry, the imaginings of foreign lands. In many ways this is music of escapism – in no sense an escape from the supremely disciplined craft of composition, but from an increasingly disordered everyday life. The composer, certainly by the time he came to write Book II, was a sick man, his finances were in disarray, world chaos loomed. Many of the titles tell either of a yearning for an unrealizable sensual experience (other than in music), or of an identification with childhood, with a lost innocence. In the first category are such pieces as *Les Sons et les parfums tournent dans l'air du soir* and *La Terrasse des audiences du clair de lune*; so too is the evocation of the Greek world, *Danseuses de Delphe*, and the ancient Egyptian, *Canope*. In the second category come the Chouchou-inspired pieces, those images Debussy drew from her picture books such as *Les Fées sont d'exquises danseuses* and *Ondine*; and the clown pieces *General Lavine, Hommage à Pickwick, La Sérénade interrompue* and *Minstrels*. (Debussy delighted in talking with the clowns of the Medrano Circus, and planned a collaboration with the American vaudeville artist known as General Lavine. He also met Charlie Chaplin before the silent movie icon became world famous, greeting him backstage at the Folies-Bergère with the words: 'Monsieur, you are instinctively a musician and dancer'. Chaplin, on being told that he had just been speaking to the famous Claude Debussy, retorted that he had never heard of him.) The magnificent *Feux d'artifice*, which finishes Book II, fits both categories, in its innocent delight in capturing the glory of a firework display and in its awareness of an ineffable magic. In *La Puerta del vino* the escape is to the dangerous passions of flamenco; in *Les Collines d'Anacapri* it is a yearning for the singing and dancing of Neapolitan cafés.

Just one of the *Préludes* is without an associated image, *Les Tierces alternées* from Book II, which is built entirely from the alternating intervals of thirds, as named in the title. Was this the seed for the piano *Études* which were to come two years later – the final rejection of descriptive intent in favour of 'pure music' – or had Debussy by late 1912 already foreseen the path his piano composition would take? In the light of the long germination of most of his projects, I would argue for the latter. Initially trained as a pianist, and steeped in the repertoire from the age of ten, Debussy had long delighted in the art of piano composition for its own sake.

Finally, one is drawn to the *Préludes* and possessed by them for what Claudio Arrau identified as their 'spiritual meaning', what I would call Schopenhauer's 'essence' – that to which only art can give voice. Just as the painters of the epoch saw what had hitherto been unseen, Debussy heard what had been unheard. 'Heard melodies are sweet, but those unheard / Are sweeter,' wrote John Keats in 'Ode on a Grecian Urn' – which could be the perfect epigraph to the Prelude *Canope*. The images and allusions of Debussy's titles, his '*Mists*', '*Fairies*' and '*Fireworks*', were not intended to take the listener outside the music, but into it. The titles were an invitation designed to provoke an intensity of listening. In his *Préludes*, in a voice often subdued, Debussy distilled and communicated

some of the essence of the external world and touched the core of
human experience.

Two events of some importance in the life of Debussy – and for the
history of music – occurred during this period of the piano *Préludes*:
he met Stravinsky, and he came under the fateful influence of Serge
Diaghilev and the Ballets Russes. For Diaghilev he created what was
to be his last orchestral work, *Jeux*. As a box-office ballet it was to fail,
along with several other theatrical projects that Debussy was drawn
into at this time in a desperate quest for money, including *Khamma*,
Le Martyre de Saint-Sébastien, and the notorious choreographing of
his *L'Après-midi d'un faune* by Nijinsky. But although *Khamma* and
Le Martyre remained somewhat outside the main stream of Debussy's
development, *Jeux* was set to become one of the great early Modernist
artworks of the twentieth century.

9

Debussy with his daughter
Chouchou and their dog
in 1916

*'I must content myself with everlasting patience,
which, someone once said, can sometimes be
a substitute for genius.'*

Claude Debussy

Wisdom 1912-18

The mighty figure of Serge Diaghilev dominated the Parisian theatrical world for two decades following the arrival of his Ballets Russes in 1909. Impresario, visionary, businessman, he provided the opportunity for composers, designers, dancers and choreographers to create dance works whose originality and power still echo down to the present day: hence, among many, Stravinsky's *L'Oiseau feu*, *Petrouchka* and *Le Sacre du printemps*, Debussy's *Jeux*, Ravel's *Daphnis et Chloé*, Satie's *Parade*, Manuel de Falla's *Three-Cornered Hat*, Francis Poulenc's *Les Biches*; hence the choreographic genius of Nijinsky, Mikhail Fokine, Leonide Massine, George Balanchine (as well as the dance genius of the first), and the set and costume designs of Léon Bakst, Pablo Picasso, Henri Matisse; hence in 1912 the controversial *L'Après-midi d'un faune*, with designs by Bakst, choreography and dancing by Nijinsky, music (from 1893) by Claude Debussy.

Choreography is the least recordable of all art forms – or at least it was before the development of Benesh Movement Notation in the 1940s and 1950s, and the present age of video. (Film recording has mostly proved to be too generalized). Many great ballets have vanished, legends only discernible in the diaries and memoirs of those who saw them or who took part. But written and photographic records make it clear that Nijinsky – who danced in, as well as choreographed, *Le Sacre du printemps*, Debussy's *Jeux* and the *Faune* – was the first modernist ballet genius of the twentieth century, radically changing the direction and nature of the hitherto gentle art form and ushering in the avant garde. Some of his extraordinary work is revealed in *L'Après-midi d'un faune*, the choreography of which has somehow managed to survive in the repertoire of Paris Ballet, among others; and more recently from the painstakingly intricate reassemblage of *Jeux* by Kenneth Archer and Millicent Hodson, which opened in London in October 2001.

Neither of these early Modernist ballets present a problem today, either in their choreography or in what was once considered to be their mismatch of music and dance. The première of *L'Après-midi d'un faune*,

Vaslav Nijinsky as the faun in the ballet version of *L'Après-midi d'un faune*, 1912

however, in May 1912, which happened to be Nijinsky's first choreographic experiment, was booed. It only became a sell-out once word had got round of its sexual explicitness. The angular, often static poses of the dancers, in profile like the figures on an antique frieze, were considered incomprehensible and completely at odds with the line and shape of Debussy's music. One year later came *Jeux*, whose scenario was equally sexually charged – a *ménage à trois*, with hints of lesbianism. But sexual innuendo did not save it, proving to be so understated as to be barely recognizable (whereas Nijinsky's shuddering orgasm as the faun could hardly be missed). At its première in May 1913 the obscure choreography of *Jeux* was widely derided; few noticed the music.

Debussy was angry, indignant, and as uncomprehending of Nijinsky as the most reactionary of critics. He considered his *Faune* had been hijacked and desecrated, and now *Jeux* had covered him in ridicule. Even before *Jeux*'s première he had feared the worst, and had written an open letter to the newspaper *Le Matin* disclaiming responsibility: 'Before writing a ballet, I had no idea what a choreographer was. Now I know: he is a man who is very strong in arithmetic.' Of course he did know because of his experience over the *Faune*, but had allowed himself, again, to be charmed by Diaghilev. In his letter he explains, compellingly, how he became involved:

> *How was it?... Because one must dine well, and because one day I dined with Serge de Diaghilev, a terrible but irresistible man who could even make stones dance. He spoke to me of a scenario devised by Nijinsky, made up of the subtle 'sweet nothings' which I suppose should always form the basis of a ballet. There was a park; a tennis court; the chance meeting of two young girls and a young man seeking a lost ball; a mysterious nocturnal landscape with that suggestion of something slightly sinister which the twilight brings; some leaps and turns and nimble footwork – in fact all the necessary ingredients to bring rhythm alive in a musical atmosphere.*

The irony in this is that Diaghilev elicited from Debussy one of his most original and enigmatic scores, a masterpiece which unifies intellect and inspiration, harmonic 'chemistry' (Debussy's word) and imagination, in a gossamer-like rhythmic structure that defies analysis. What is more, Debussy wrote it in six weeks, and was even prepared, without protest, to lengthen it slightly at Diaghilev's request. This enabled him 'to get the shape better', he told Durand, and to take the 'intimations of pleasure right to their limit'. Truly the Russian was 'irresistible'. As the conductor Igor Markevich later remarked, Diaghilev was 'the most extraordinary *agent provocateur* of history... an *agent provocateur* of genius, of talent,

of ideas and he had something really extraordinary. He had the way to
provoke in the artist the best of himself.'

Another irony is that *Jeux* really is a ballet score, not only the concert
piece it has since become. Debussy was intrigued by the scenario, and
its implications of sexual pleasure, however disparaging he was of
the usual narrative fare that ballet served up. 'Have you considered
the influence a ballet scenario might have on a ballerina's intelligence?'
he wrote to Durand in January 1912. But in the case of *Jeux* his imagination was caught, and he even proudly admonishes Stravinsky, with
whom he had recently become friendly, for criticizing his title. The title
'Games', Debussy tells him, clearly conveyed the appropriate sexual
shenanigans, 'the "horrors" that take place between the participants'.
Stravinsky had suggested 'The Park'. 'Please believe me, *Jeux* is better,'
Debussy insisted. And to Durand he wrote: 'There are some pretty
difficult things to achieve, because the music has to embody a rather
risqué situation! When it comes to ballet, immorality passes down the
legs of the ballerina and ends up as a pirouette.'

Problems arose partly because Debussy was not a natural collaborator.
He refused to play what he had written to Diaghilev and Nijinsky before
it was completed, 'not wishing to have Barbarians sticking their noses
into my experiments in personal chemistry'; and there was little discussion as to what was expected on stage, other than what was implied in the
initial scenario. Diaghilev, once he had obtained the alterations to the
score that he wanted, was fully satisfied. Debussy, however, when he
gradually realized what Nijinsky was doing with his work, was horrified.

For his score Debussy devised over twenty short motifs that he conceived as a kind of self-generating mosaic of dancing patterns, 'music
which is almost cheerful and alive with quaint gestures', he wrote to
Caplet, for which he needed to invent 'an orchestra "without feet"…
an orchestral colour which seems to be lit from behind, of which there
are such wonderful examples in *Parsifal*.' The Wagner reference is significant: Debussy's creative imagination was caught at the deepest level,
enabling him to override his professed opinion of ballet as 'light and
frivolous'. In the case of *Jeux* his disparagement of the art was aimed
more at Nijinsky, for his letter to *Le Matin* actually shows him fully alive
to the medium. His keen desire 'to bring *rhythm* alive in a musical
atmosphere' recalls a conception of music he expressed six years earlier,
in 1907, to Durand, when he was struggling with the orchestral *Images*.

Deborah Bull, Bruce Sansom
and Gillian Revie in *Jeux*
at the Royal Ballet, Covent
Garden, 2001. The chore-
ography for this production
was a reconstruction of the
Nijinsky original by Kenneth
Archer and Millicent Hodson

'I feel more and more that music, by its very essence, is not something that can flow inside a rigorous, traditional form. It consists of colours and of rhythmicized time.' It was an example of Diaghilev's genius to provide Debussy with another vehicle for putting this into action. *Jeux* is a triumph in this regard, and it was Debussy's own conception of dance that brought it to birth.

Even before Nijinsky's *Faune* and Diaghilev's commission for *Jeux*, Debussy had become entangled with the world of dance, with the egos and impresarios that peopled the world of stage entertainment in its great heyday just before cinema finally took over. Firstly, there had been a tempting proposal from Diaghilev for what Debussy called 'a Russo-Venetian ballet', for which Debussy wrote a scenario in three scenes. This he even published, as *Masques et bergamasques* (after Verlaine's poem '*Clair de lune*') although, as Robert Orledge has pointed out, the scenario related neither to Verlaine nor moonlight. Who lost interest in it first, Debussy or Diaghilev, is difficult to say, but not a note of music was composed.

The dance work that embroiled him next was *Khamma,* a commission from the Canadian dancer Maude Allan in 1910; this dragged on into 1913 and landed Debussy in a morass of financial and artistic complications. The fine music of *Khamma*, with its meticulously crafted architecture and biting, Stravinsky-like harmonic palette, is often overlooked, partly perhaps because Debussy never orchestrated it. It was not performed in his lifetime, although the orchestration was undertaken, with Debussy's consent and encouragement, by Charles Koechlin. Debussy had become so incensed by the machinations of Maude Allan, by changes to his contract and demands for alterations to his score – which in striking contrast to his dealings with Diaghilev, he adamantly refused – that he was relieved to have it taken off his hands. ('It is impossible that you be permitted to arrange this music to suit your own taste,' he wrote in exasperation to Maude Allan in July 1912. 'Thus I composed it. Thus it shall remain.') But despite his withering criticisms of the *Khamma* scenario, of ballet in general and his dancer in particular, he had great pride in the music he struggled so hard to create.

At the beginning of 1911 Debussy was also manically at work on a commission from the Italian poet Gabriele d'Annunzio, this time for incidental music for a grandiloquent five-act drama on the masochistic martyrdom of Saint Sebastian. *Le Martyre de Saint-Sébastien* was to involve speech, dancing and mime, the collaboration of the dancer Ida Rubinstein, the designs of Léon Bakst, the choreography of Mikhail Fokine – and nearly an hour's worth of the music of Claude Debussy. The whole spectacle, when it finally and exhaustedly reached its première in May that year, took five hours (so the music made up hardly a fifth, although it was the longest score Debussy had composed, and in the shortest space, since *Pelléas*). It is almost impossible today to revive this work in its original form, for the text is bombastic and the spectacle embarrassingly outdated. But Debussy's music is not easy to revive either, robbed of its context, for it truly is 'incidental' and hardly works structurally or dramatically on its own, in the way that the music of *Khamma* does.

Debussy wrote to Robert Godet about the project in early February: 'It's much more sumptuous than the poor little Anglo-Egyptian ballet [*Khamma*]. Needless to say the cult of Adonis is combined with Jesus: a very beautiful notion in my opinion.' The last comment is surely heavy with irony. He had earlier told Emma that for him 'the tale says nothing worthwhile'. Debussy had accepted the commission entirely against his better judgement, and, astonishingly, without having seen the text. The result for a time was paralysis, as he himself observed: 'It is not without a certain amount of terror that I see the moment approaching when I will have to write something down.' It is a self-assessment that has a bearing on the work habits of Claude Debussy far beyond *Le Martyre de Saint-Sébastien*.

What is one to make of his artistic principles at this juncture? The fact that his score achieved completion at all (and only with the help of André Caplet, who orchestrated three of the five acts), against a background of failing health and rising panic at not meeting the deadline, is a sign of the extreme gravity of his financial plight. He was locked into a lucrative contract. But the completion of *Le Martyre* also showed his artistic tenacity, and his ability to challenge his own creative parameters. He would have needed an extremely open mind to succeed: *Le Martyre* is the music of an atheist (or perhaps a pantheist) forcefully yoked to mystical Roman Catholicism.

But at the work's first run-through the power of his music asserted itself to such an extent that, according to Émile Vuillermoz who was present, even Debussy 'could not maintain his usual attitude of ironic goodwill, and, quite simply, he wept'. There would have been an element

Ida Rubinstein, drawn by Léon Bakst as she appeared in the first performance of *Le Martyre de Saint-Sébastien* in May 1911

of relief in this reaction. In the event, the work failed: it ran for nine somewhat shoddy, under-rehearsed performances, and was considered, unsurprisingly, overlong and barely comprehensible, though not because of the music. (Satie, by no means uncritical in his admiration for Debussy's art, observed: 'Claude's music was very successful; it saved the situation.') Dietschy points out how the 'vulgar lyricism' and the 'rhetorical exaggeration of the spectacle' served to relegate the music 'to a secondary plain, and rightly so, as far as the text goes, and perhaps even – in its way – as far as the music goes, which was too unassuming, too sincere for this showy context.' As usual Debussy had given every-thing of himself – despite, or maybe because of, his initial misjudgement.

The plans for *Khamma* dragged on during the year of *Le Martyre*, although Lockspeiser is wrong in stating that Debussy's disillusion with it was such that he told Koechlin: 'Write *Khamma* yourself and I will sign it.' The truth is similar but more fascinating. At the end of 1913 Debussy signed a contract for a music-hall collaboration for the Alhambra Theatre in London, entitled *Le Palais du silence* (later renamed *No-ja-li*). He received 10,000 francs on signing, with another 15,000 to come. The date for delivery of the manuscript was to be 2 April the following spring. Typically, by March barely any music had been written; and, desperate to retain his 10,000 francs, Debussy asked Koechlin to visit him to discuss a collaboration for a London ballet. It was then that he suggested to the young composer that he should 'write a ballet for him that he would sign'. Koechlin refused.

But in the event Debussy saved his advance. He offered the Alhambra instead *Printemps*, one of the works from his Prix de Rome days, from 1887, but which had recently been orchestrated by Henri Busser. This work – the very same that had caused the Académie Française to lament a 'vague impressionism, one of the most dangerous enemies of truth' – duly took its brief place, barely acknowledged, as part of London's theatre season: *No-ja-li*, 'Not Likely!', a revue in twelve scenes. Debussy's youthful score, in its newly orchestrated (and choreographed) clothing, now rubbed shoulders, Robert Orledge has related, with such acts as 'Minnie Kaufmann the trick cyclist, and Chinko the Chinese juggler'. It ran for 305 performances. A year earlier at the Théâtre des Champs-Élysées in Paris the unsurpassable *Jeux* had barely survived a fortnight.

One further theatrical escapade occurred at this period when in 1913 Gabriel Mourey pressed him to write incidental music for his three-act

Carlotta Mossetti and
Phyllis Monkman in Part I
of Debussy's *Printemps*
at the Alhambra Theatre,
London in May 1914

play *Psyché*. (In 1907 Mourey and Debussy had attempted a collaboration on the Tristan legend, but despite announcements in the press of its imminent staging, and Debussy's undoubted enthusiasm for the idea, like so many of his theatrical plans it came to nothing.) All that Debussy achieved for Mourey was the solo flute piece, *Syrinx*, originally entitled *La Flûte de Pan* and intended to be played off-stage. Significantly, considering the archetypal nature of the Syrinx myth and the near-archetypal nature of the composer's response – a faultlessly crafted monodic lament evoking the dawn of civilization – Debussy wrote it without any bar-lines, which were not added until the piece was first published in 1927.

Caught up as he was in theatrical dreams and disasters, Debussy's piano compositions once again provided solace. From 1912 came most of the pieces that would be published the following year as *Préludes* Book II. The faint presence of Stravinsky shades their pages – it is this which makes them such a different musical experience from Book I. Indeed, it was Stravinsky, twenty years his junior, who constituted the further challenge looming in Debussy's creative life at this point. Debussy had met him in 1910 after a performance of the young Russian's *L'Oiseau feu* (the opening of which is a frank acknowledgement of Debussy's influence on him). Debussy was deeply impressed, and even more so with *Petrushka* the following year – its influence is clearly present in *Khamma* and, to a lesser extent, in *Jeux*. To Godet he gives an unreserved appraisal of Stravinsky's 'instinctive genius for colour and rhythm… There are no precautions or pretensions. It's childlike and savage.' To Stravinsky himself, in April 1912, he writes of *Petrushka*: 'there's a kind of sonorous magic in it… and an *assurance* of orchestration I've only come across in *Parsifal*.' When his artistic passions were aroused Debussy could be a most discriminating and far-sighted critic, whether of poetry, painting or music.

At this point he is only admiring of the younger man, and perfectly assured of his own 'sonorous magic'. With prophetic discernment he tells Stravinsky: 'You will go further than *Petrushka*, of course, but you should be proud of what this work achieves.' What came next, of course, was *Le Sacre du Printemps*. In the summer of 1912 the two composers played through an early version for four hands at the piano (one is reminded of Debussy's formidable powers of sight-reading – he took the bass, Stravinsky the treble). 'We were dumfounded,' wrote Louis Laloy, in whose house the event had occurred, 'flattened as though by a hurricane from the roots of time.' Debussy wrote afterwards to Stravinsky, 'your *Sacre* haunts me like a beautiful nightmare.' In his creative soul he was unsettled by this music, which appeared to shatter everything he stood for, to negate the concentrated reticence of the Debussyan ethic.

Debussy's own episode with the Ballets Russes reveals a clash of aesthetics, and one of those moments in cultural history when the old has to give way to the new. Debussy's art was hardly old – *Jeux* is as original and as mould-breaking as *Le Sacre*, although considerably gentler – yet the composer's attitudes had been formed in the Symbolist milieu of the 1880s and 1890s, in a culture for which the young avant garde, including Stravinsky and Nijinsky, had little time. It is notable that Debussy felt out of touch with the new directions of visual art, while Nijinsky had found inspiration for *Jeux* from the Post-Impressionist paintings he saw in London (and his acquaintance with the Bloomsbury set, who promoted them). Debussy also had no understanding of, nor interest in, the atonal

Debussy and Stravinsky in Debussy's study in 1910. In the background are two Japanese prints including Hokusai's *The Hollow of the Wave off Kanagawa*, which was used on the cover of *La Mer* (see p 170)

path of Arnold Schoenberg; nor did he appreciate the direction being taken by Satie, despite acknowledging his originality (he might have called him 'the precursor' but failed to take seriously the path that led to Satie's *Parade* in 1917, leading to a brief rupture in their lifelong friendship). And after genuine protestations of admiration for Stravinsky, Debussy clearly found *Le Sacre* a deeply frightening challenge to his own hold on musical values. At the Théâtre des Champs-Élysées it was the notorious première of *Le Sacre* which in May 1913 thrust aside his own *Jeux* after only two weeks. Coming so soon after the failure of *Le Martyre* this must have been very hard to come to terms with.

In 1913 he wrote what was to be his last collection of songs for voice and piano, the *Trois Poèmes de Stéphane Mallarmé*. It had been nearly thirty years since he had set Mallarmé's *Apparition* (in 1884), although the poet had always been one of Debussy's major sources of intellectual and artistic inspiration. Rivalry was aroused here too, this time with Ravel who was writing his own Mallarmé settings exactly at this point, and who, by coincidence, had chosen two of the same poems as Debussy (*Soupir* and *Placet futile*). Debussy was irritated by the constant comparisons between his music and Ravel's – which the current situation was only likely to fuel, awakening again the wearisome controversy over 'Debussyism' and the merits, or otherwise, of the 'school' of composition that Debussy was supposedly leading.

Actually Debussy's reaction to Ravel, while often self-protectively ironical, could be highly discerning. He wrote to Laloy in 1907: 'I agree with you that Ravel is extraordinarily gifted, but what annoys me is the attitude that he adopts of being a 'conjuror', or rather a Fakir casting spells and making flowers burst out of chairs. The trouble is, a conjuring trick always has to have a build-up and after you've seen it once you're no longer astonished.' On one level we might take this as a dismissal of 'effects'. But it also pinpoints a central aspect of Ravel's genius, his capacity to create an art of the 'magical' or 'miraculous'. Debussy was only wrong in believing that Ravel's magic would not continue to astonish.

In 1913 Debussy again turned to themes of childhood in *La Boîte à joujoux*, a children's ballet employing the composer's most intimate knowledge of Chouchou's toybox, and which quotes popular classics and songs in the manner of Satie. His first idea was to stage it with marionettes, but he came to see it would work just as well with children, who would simply employ 'movements, rather than traditional ballet steps', as he told Durand. Orchestration once more defeated him, and although the work never reached performance in his lifetime, Debussy oversaw the publication of a delightful piano score illustrated by André Hellé. (Caplet did the orchestration and the work was first performed in 1919.)

But Debussy was becoming ill. Early in 1913 he had an operation to remove a cyst from his bowel 'that wanted to keep on growing. A pair of sharp scissors have cut it off in its prime; and that's all,' as he wrote to Émile Vuillermoz. He was either concealing the truth or was not told – or possibly at this stage not even the doctors appreciated the seriousness of the situation. His financial pain was even worse. 'I'm paralysed with worry,' he writes to Durand in August. 'If my little Chouchou weren't here I'd blow my brains out.' In September he has to ask him for a loan 'of one or two thousand francs,' admitting shamefacedly that 'I'm afraid that between us it hasn't been a question of "advances" for some time! But I don't know what to do any more.' What he did, apart from promising Durand a two-piano version of *Jeux* (never begun), was to pick himself up once more and embark on a conducting trip to Moscow. He really believed that the scissors had cured him. In the first half of the following year, 1914, before war broke, he took himself to Rome, The Hague, Amsterdam and London. He forced himself to go; financially of course the trips were imperative, but he needed to promote his music too – to conduct it and also protect it. He had become caught up in a hectic world – the pace of the twentieth century was inexorably increasing.

His relationship with Emma maintained its see-saw pattern. To Durand he could be frank about his domestic travails. Some issue had arisen over Emma's health; her doctor had prescribed that she take the waters at Vichy. Clearly funds were not available, for Debussy asks

The list of characters from the first edition, in piano short score, of *La Boîte à joujoux*, illustrated by André Hellé. Debussy's children's ballet is rarely performed and remained unorchestrated during his lifetime

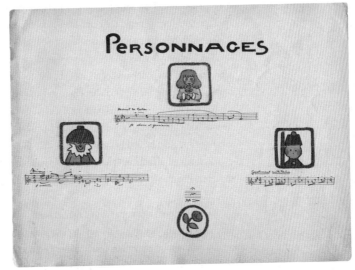

Durand to imagine 'what sort of atmosphere ensued, pregnant with thoughts which are never spoken':

It's unbearable and offensive. Struggling on one's own is nothing! But struggling 'en famille' is terrible! Not to mention the domestic demands of a material comfort one has enjoyed for a long time and which one cannot believe has now become impossible to afford. In my case the struggle is to uphold a point of honour: a crazy one, perhaps, but explicable in the sense that I don't want one day to be reproached for accepting the present situation in order to turn it to my own advantage (there's a fine irony!). Perhaps I'm to blame, because my only energy is intellectual: in everyday life I stumble over the smallest pebble, which another man would send flying with a light-hearted kick! And then I have an innate horror of any kind of discussion.

There is here a resigned criticism of Emma's material demands, along with sensitivity, still, to the question of his motives for marrying her. The formulation of this thought is curiously unclear, however, betraying his deep unease and abiding sense of guilt. He seems to be implying that he only puts up with the domestic torment because he had brought it on himself: it is a point of honour to stick it out, thus proving his motives had not been materialistic. During all this time Lilly too was making her own demands. An ironic comment Debussy makes to Durand in 1916 provides a rare reminder of her continuing presence: 'I've been spared nothing: illness; Chouchou ill; as the last straw Mme Texier ill! It's enough to drive one to suicide at the least.'

But Debussy's view of his second marriage was often expressed from a position of deep depression. His exhausting trips abroad at least had the benefit of taking him out of his enclosed space, and of enabling him to see his relationship with his wife in a different light, in addition to which he was also able to see another side of himself. Separation made him aware of his acute need for love and security, and drew from him heartfelt expressions of affection which he otherwise found almost impossible to utter. From Moscow in December 1913 he writes to Emma:

The rehearsal is just over and in great haste I want to tell you that I love you, that you are my one and only darling and that even so I'm still miserable.
Do you realize that you wrote: 'I don't know how I'll manage not to be jealous of your music'? Don't you think that's enough to upset one's equilibrium

somewhat? First of all, if there were to be any jealousy between you and music, it would be on music's side; if I go on creating it, and loving it, it's because this music, which you are so unfair to, was responsible for my meeting you, loving you and everything. The chances are that if I were never to compose again, you would be the one to stop loving me, because I could hardly rely on the somewhat restrained charms of my conversation or on my physical advantages to keep you by me. And you know how diplomatically music intervenes in those moments of ill-humour which I still tend to be so bad at handling...

Keep loving me! Although I'm such a long way away, pay no attention to the treacherous consolations you're bound to be offered. Tell yourself that Claude is spending a sort of season in purgatory and keep him a place in Paradise, which for him consists only of you.

An ironic tone shades the surface of that final paragraph – Debussy, still fully capable of gallantry towards his wife, is also aware of the rhetorical flourish. As in his letters from London and Vienna several years earlier, his letters from Moscow, even at his lowest point, convey an intense appreciation of the ironies of life, and repeatedly reveal the 'verbal booby traps' (Stravinsky's phrase) of his conversation. 'Someone called Busoni is playing a piano concerto,' he relates, 'which lasts an hour and ten minutes. As you might suppose, he wrote it!'

War engulfed Europe in August 1914. Europe's pain and Debussy's were coinciding. The slaughter of youth in the mud of the Normandy trenches was a negation of the creative instinct, an abandonment of structural cohesion, order and idealism. 'I'm nothing more than a wretched atom hurled around by this terrible cataclysm,' Debussy wrote to Durand on 8 August, 'and what I'm doing seems to me so miserably petty.' All he achieved in 1914, apart from the exhausting conducting tours, was the *Épigraphes antiques* for piano (a rearrangement, with a few lovely additions, of the music he had written for *Bilitis*, back in 1900), and a piano piece for the *Daily Telegraph*'s war anthology *King Albert's Book*, which he called *Berceuse héroïque*. (Small in proportion – 'with no pretensions other than to offer a homage to so much patient suffering,' Debussy remarked – it is immense in impact, though little known.)

His mother died in March 1915 (his father had died in 1910), and feeling his own body and soul wasting away in Paris, in the summer he and Emma rented a house at Pourville on the Normandy coast – where they had spent part of their first summer together in 1904. He wrote to Godet that in Paris he had been barely able to contemplate composition or even the 'familiar sound of the piano, which [has] become something hateful'. But now, in the surroundings of Pourville, his letters quite suddenly begin to sing of the sea and the landscape, and of relief at being away from 'the factory of nothingness' that his study in Paris had become. Arkel the toad is back on his desk, he tells Durand, 'exactly where he belongs; he's as solemn as ever, but seems to like it here.' And the garden delights him in its naturalness, 'with none of the proud orderliness of the gardens laid out by Le Nôtre… a gentle sort of jungle'. Debussy's despair at the war gives way to articulate anger and a passionate defence of French art. 'I want to work – not so much for myself, as to provide a proof, however small, that thirty million Boches can't destroy French thought, even when they've tried undermining it first before obliterating it. I think of the youth of France, wantonly mown down by those Kultur merchants… The music I'm writing will be a secret homage to them.' To several friends he repeats his sense of renewal: 'When I tell you that I spent nearly a year unable to write music – after that I've almost had to re-learn it. It was like a rediscovery and it's seemed to me more beautiful than ever.'

In a white heat of creative energy, during these summer months, he produced some of the greatest works of his life: *En blanc et noir* for two pianos, the Sonatas for Cello and Piano and for Flute, Viola and Harp, and the *Douze études* for piano. Of *En blanc et noir* he wrote to Godet: 'These pieces draw their colour, their emotion, simply from the piano, like the greys of Velázquez, if I may so suggest? Anyway, all the orchestral musicians are at the front line.' The implication is that he might have orchestrated it, but that he is content to limit – and hence concentrate – his palette, in the manner of a painter. So as well as being an allusion to the black and white keys of the piano, the title *En blanc et noir*, with remarkable consistency, is an echo of the analogy Debussy drew over twenty years earlier with 'a study in grey' in painting, when working on his orchestral *Nocturnes*. And there are further allusions to visual art in *En blanc et noir*. Debussy had at first considered calling his new work '*Caprices en blanc et noir*', and at one point had told Durand that he had revised the central movement, as it had become 'too profoundly black, and almost as tragic as a "Caprice" by Goya!' The reference is to Francisco de Goya's etchings *Los caprichos*, renowned not only for their stark

El sueño de la razon produce monstruos from Goya's *Los Caprichos.* Debussy considered the second movement of his *En blanc et noir* to be 'almost as tragic as a "Caprice" by Goya'

exposure of the brutalization of society but for their masterful handling of the black and white medium. It is probable that Debussy also had another series of etchings by Goya in mind, *'The Disasters of War'.* Debussy was toying with visual metaphor and verbal ambiguity as he settled on a title which, this time, clearly evolved during or even after the process of composition. There is a shade of Goya in the final choice of title: even though the first movement of *En blanc et noir* is joyful in a way that seems nothing less than extraordinary – a joy born perhaps of the composer's rediscovery of his art – the tragic character of the second movement remained, inescapably shaded by the disasters of war.

This second movement has an epigraph from François Villon's *Ballade contre les ennemis de la France,* and the music quotes a traditional Lutheran (German) chorale. The irony is deliberate, and Debussy's treatment of the chorale, in counterpoint with the martial sounds of war, starkly conveys what he had described to Godet as 'the naked flesh of emotion'. He tells Durand of his concern with proportion in this movement, which 'makes things clearer and cleans the atmosphere of the poisonous vapours momentarily emitted by the Lutheran chorale – or rather by what it represents, because it's still a fine tune.' The third movement is whimsical and terse, combining a satirical edge with the lightness of a musical Caprice.

The sonatas were to be part of a set of six, although only three were actually written. Debussy turned to the third, the Sonata for Violin and Piano, in 1916, and completed it with great difficulty. He had planned a fourth for oboe, horn and harpsichord, and a fifth for trumpet, clarinet, bassoon and piano. The final sonata was to have combined 'the sonorities I've employed in the others', with the addition of a double bass. 'For many people they won't be as important as a *drame lyrique*,' Debussy wrote, 'but it seems to me they provide a greater service to music!' It is a misconception to regard these works simply as neo-classical; rather they are a homage to the sixteenth-century origins of the sonata as instrumental, as opposed to vocal, music, and a plea for cultural continuity in a world succumbing to violent disintegration. They were conceived, Debussy remarked, 'in the ancient, flexible mould, with none of the grandiloquence of modern sonatas'. The Cello Sonata and the Sonata for Flute, Viola and Harp are remarkable for their structural fluidity; themes appear kaleidoscopically, almost as if improvised, while texture often takes precedence. The expressive drama in these works is deeply affecting: 'I don't know whether it should move us to laughter, or to tears, or both,' Debussy said of the Sonata for Flute, Viola and Harp. The Cello Sonata hovers between heartbreak and nightmare: the piano's urgent cry at the opening sets the scene for what Debussy described as 'Pierrot angry with the moon'. The highly original manner in which he sets the cello against the grain of its famed lyricism – at one point the *pizzicatos* require a kind of strumming – creates sonorities and textures of startling presence, as well as a sense of emotional dislocation.

And then came the piano studies *(Études)*, one of the monuments of twentieth-century pianism, of which Debussy was confidently aware. He dedicated them to the memory of Chopin – whose piano music he had been editing for Durand's new edition, now that German editions were unobtainable. Yet, lacking evocative titles and developed entirely from the deliberately restrictive formalities of piano technique, the format at first masked the music's extraordinary originality – it was several decades before these pieces were considered other than a diminution of Debussy's powers.

With solemn irony Debussy announces, with the title of the first study, a pedagogic intention: *'For Five Fingers – After Monsieur Czerny'.* The repetitive and mechanical piano studies of Carl Czerny are rudely satirized at the opening (specifically Op. 740 No. 1), after which the music abandons itself to joy and sensuality – without ever losing sight of its technical intentions (nor Czerny's Op. 740 No. 1).

Alongside problems of pianistic agility are the intricate requirements of tone production, especially challenging in those slower studies which are concerned with 'finding special sonorities, among them *'For Fourths'*, in which you'll find unheard-of things', as Debussy explained to Durand. One wonders which particular characteristics of this intricate musical creation he had in mind – although it is hardly less extraordinary in its harmonic and sonorous inventiveness than the other eleven studies. *'For Fourths'* overlays suggestions of eastern mysticism with the sensual harmonic richness so characteristic of Debussy's late style, a kind of chromatic ecstasy and a voluptuousness of expression born from his avowed 'rediscovery' of music which seemed to him 'more beautiful than ever'. There is a percussive feel to the piano writing in this piece too, notably in the central section, in which the chains of scintillating fourths for the right hand are certainly 'unheard-of things', especially in a pianistic tradition used to patterns built on thirds, sixths and octaves (all intervals to which Debussy devoted separate studies). But if precedents for such a percussive approach already existed in Debussy's own piano works – for example, in such earlier pieces as *Pagodes, Masques* and *L'Isle joyeuse* – nothing foreshadowed the exultantly savage manner of the final study *'For Chords'*, in which the keyboard is pounded relentlessly in a display of percussive pianism akin to the music of Bartòk.

In his letters Debussy was more forthcoming about the character and progress of his *Études* than about almost any of his music since *Pelléas.* What he spoke little about, however, was the manner in which they were constructed, hardly surprising in a composer who wrote that 'the beauty of a work of art will always remain a mystery; in other words we can never be absolutely sure "how it's made"'. He knew how his own was made, of course – it was just that he refused to disclose his methods. But he was also respectful of his own creative subconscious, so in another sense he did not 'know'. He sought all his life to preserve that element of music which he frankly called 'magic' and which is so pervasive a part of the experience of his piano *Études.* 'They're particularly extraordinary

Debussy with his step-
daughter Dolly in 1916

for their allusive formal qualities,' Messaien has remarked. 'Things are left unsaid, implied, fleeting. All that was very new.'

Just as Chopin's *Études*, near the beginning of the nineteenth century, became the touchstone for the great piano tradition to follow, so Debussy's fulfilled the same function for the twentieth century. Along with *Jeux*, and notwithstanding the Modernist Stravinsky apparently forging ahead of him, this was music for the future. 'I've actually written nothing but "pure" music,' he wrote to Stravinsky in October 1915, mentioning the *Études* and the two sonatas, and betraying his awareness that the descriptive style was past. But in his reborn creative confidence he was able to be generous and open with his rival: 'My dear Stravinsky, you are a great artist!' He dedicated the final movement of *En blanc et noir* to *'mon ami Igor Stravinsky'*.

'I've invested a lot of passion and faith in the future of the *Études*,' Debussy told Durand. 'I hope you'll like them, both for the music they contain and for what they denote.' What the *Douze études* 'denote' is a conception of musical expression that is fundamentally anti-German. In a passionate letter to Robert Godet in October, Debussy developed the idea of resistance that he had originally articulated to Durand earlier in the summer. He now sees that his rediscovery of music was a result of his reaction to the war, which had focused again for him an attitude to art and imagination that had been his lifelong concern:

> *I've been writing like a madman, or anyway like a man condemned to die the next morning. Certainly I haven't forgotten the war during these three months – indeed I've come to see the horrible necessity of it… What a sad lesson for us! I don't just mean the concrete emplacements and the two-way espionage – that's awful I agree. I am talking about the heavy hand laid on our thoughts and our structures, and accepted with a careless smile. That's the serious damage, impossible to forgive and difficult to repair because it's inside us like tainted blood…*
>
> *So, what about French music? Where are our old harpsichordists, who produced real music in abundance? They held the secret of that graceful profundity, that emotion without epilepsy which we shy away from like ungrateful children.*

In that last sentence Debussy, '*musicien français*' as he now signed himself, was providing his own epitaph.

It was not yet the end, although subconsciously Debussy must have known he really was the 'man condemned to die'. Towards the end of 1915 he returned to his beloved Poe project, *La Chûte de la Maison Usher*, which he imagined was nearing completion. Then quite suddenly in December 'it all got worse, so they operated,' as he related to Godet. This time it was not a simple matter of snipping with scissors, but against the odds he survived for more than two years. In October 1916 he managed to turn to his Sonata for Violin and Piano, although he found it woefully hard to complete. The fragility of this beautiful swansong attests to his attenuating state, but he mistakenly considered the work of poor quality.

For most of the time now his pain and his sense of indignity were grievous. To the end, in a manner no less than heroic, and further proof of the tenacity in the face of adversity that he had shown throughout his life, his letters retain his characteristic tone of irony, self-deprecation, humorous self-knowledge – and hope. To Godet in December 1916: 'Naturally, I don't take this poor tattered body for walks any more, in case I frighten little children and tram conductors. But if they could see inside my head! Still it's not important, there are ruins that are best hidden. And even if I'm old [he was only fifty-four] I can't yet expect people to get a historical thrill out of looking at mine.' At the end of this letter he returned to facts: 'What an existence! I'm exhausted by chasing phantoms but not tired enough to sleep. So I wait for tomorrow, for better or for worse; and it starts all over again. In a cowardly way my thoughts return to the morphine I used to take. It made me feel ill, but like a shell at the bottom of the sea. I expect I've bored you enough?'

But Debussy still believed in his renewal – his Violin Sonata was not yet finished. To Emma at Christmas he wrote, 'Forgive me for loving you – Wait for me.' The following year, 1917, he even returned to another favourite project, a collaboration with his friend, the poet Paul-Jean Toulet, on *As You Like It*. In March he wrote what was to be his last piano piece – a tiny, ironic reminiscence of Baudelaire that he offered his coal merchant as payment for the highly precious and rare commodity, in war time, of coal. He gave it the title *Les Soirs illuminés par l'ardeur du charbon* – 'Evenings lighted by burning coals' – a line from Baudelaire's *Le Balcon*, which he had set in 1888. In February he had written to Fauré, lamenting 'the cold, the end'. After several pleas his coal merchant produced the goods and went home happily with twenty-three bars of authentic Debussy.

This year also saw his mini-collaboration with the pianist Marguerite Long; while convalescing in Saint Jean de Luz in the French Basque region he gave her a few piano lessons, which she ingeniously expanded into a book of reminiscences. This was a brief summer of remission. Dukas had found him 'in very good spirits' in August, just before he left Paris, and Emma thought 'he was in better shape than he has ever been'. Debussy's own optimism affected all those around him.

In September he took to the concert platform for what would be the last time, in a performance of his Violin Sonata. The writer Suarès, who had so percipiently taken the measure of this artist at the time of the première of *Pelléas*, was again witness. The summer hope was fading. What had once been the disturbing, living intensity of Debussy's gaze, so remarkable on a first meeting, was now no more:

> *I was struck, not so much by his thin and wasted appearance as by his air of absent-mindedness and by his profound lassitude. His complexion was the colour of melted wax and ashes. In his eyes there was no light of fever but the gloomy reflection of dark pools. There was not even any bitterness in his shadowy smile: one saw rather that he was tired of suffering. His round, supple, plump hand, a rather strong episcopal hand, hung heavy on his arm, his arm on his shoulder, his head on his body and life on his head... When he sat down he gazed slowly at the audience, blinking rapidly, in the manner of those who wish to see without being seen and who look furtively at what they can only half apprehend. He was devoured by pudeur, as an artist often is who feels disgust and almost a sense of shame at his suffering. It was even said that he encouraged the disease by pretending it did not exist.*

By early 1918 hope had vanished altogether. In March Jacques Durand visited him for the last time. The previous night Debussy had been so weak that he was unable to reach the shelter of his cellar, for by this time the enemy's long-range guns had come within reach of the avenue du Bois de Boulogne. Emma and Chouchou had stayed with him in his bedroom all night. He now told Durand that he had only hours to live. 'When I began to protest,' his publisher recalled, 'he signalled that he wanted to embrace me, then asked me to pass him a cigarette, his last consolation.' Claude Debussy died on 25 March 1918. As he lay dying, the artist who had devoted his life's work to forging a musical language unsullied by Teutonic influence heard the sounds of German explosions.

Epilogue

There is a certain symbolic significance in the fact that Debussy, and for a while his musical reputation, did not survive the war. The immediate future, within his own circle, lay with Stravinsky and Satie, and outside it with the music of Schoenberg and Webern. Debussy's 'sonorous magic' could not possibly suit the stark, cynical exhaustion of the post-war world. There had been a cataclysm beyond anything that Europe had ever experienced, and artists everywhere had to face the realization that contrary to Keats's famous phrase, beauty was not truth, nor truth beauty – that these were simply constructs of the human mind, not eternal laws. To assert that 'music is not just the expression of a feeling, it is the feeling itself', as Debussy had in the 1890s, was no longer tenable. Artists were faced with making art not with traditionally sanctioned matter, but with anti-matter.

Even before the war, Modernist European artists had been well aware that 'expression' had to be reinvented, deconstructed, in response to new scientific discoveries as well as to harsh and often brutal political and social realities. The machine reigned supreme – in painting the Italian Futurists had worshipped it, as well as initially glorying in war itself. Cubism had deconstructed form and perspective, while Orphism, as its name implied, had tried yet again to evoke the abstract nature of music, this time in conjunction with Cubist characteristics. It was a Futurist painter and composer, Luigi Russolo, who before the war anticipated *musique concrète* by several decades, when he invented various noise machines and composed pieces for them (e.g. *The Meeting of Aeroplanes and Cars* of 1913–14). Debussy alluded to Futurist music in a review of 1913 for *SIM* magazine, refusing to take it seriously, and as early as 1909 he had prophetically, although ironically, remarked to the music writer Georges Jean-Aubrey that 'one doesn't need to hear the song of the nightingale – the song of the trains is much more in tune with modern artistic preoccupations'. Satie also used noise objects, such as a typewriter and a siren, in his 1917 score of *Parade* – no doubt one of the reasons for which Debussy failed to commend the work.

It is interesting in this regard that both Ravel and Stravinsky showed a keen interest in Russolo's experiments when 'noise concerts', as they were known, first came to Paris in the early 1920s – as did Darius Milhaud, Arthur Honegger and Edgard Varèse.

But gradually it came to be recognized that Debussy's art was by no means only concerned with his avowed reverence for 'the vibrant beauty of sound itself'. In their different ways Messiaen (a pupil of Dukas) and Boulez (a pupil of Messiaen) showed how rhythmic, structural and formal issues lay at the heart of Debussy's concerns. 'It is time to burn the mist off Debussy,' Boulez once proclaimed, and he proceeded to do just that in his polemic as well as from the conductor's rostrum (and in his own works, which lie across the poles of Webern and Debussy). For Messiaen, who understood Debussy's colouristic procedures probably better than anyone, Debussy was nevertheless 'one of the greatest rhythmicians of all time'. But whereas for Boulez *Jeux* and the *Douze études* were the seminal works, for Messiaen it was *Pelléas et Mélisande* and the *Nocturnes*, where Debussy is 'in love with the sound, in love with the chord'. Messiaen, at ten years old (in the year of Debussy's death), had been introduced to the score of *Pelléas* by his teacher who thereby 'placed a veritable bomb in the hands of a mere child'.

Now, at the beginning of a new century and a new millennium, Debussy is hugely in the ascendant. His position as a colossus of western music has emerged through the mist; against the industrial might of endless interpretation and reinterpretation, of analysis and deconstruction, he holds his ground and appears to grow all the larger. Our interest in his life is part of this process. To be curious about the life is to be curious about the art, which somewhere has to connect or there would be no art at all. Biography might be seen as a kind of performance, an interpretation, a means by which disparate and arbitrary elements of a life are gathered, put through a process of selection, and reassembled with, one hopes, feeling, expression and a sense of structure. Biography is the original score and the performance of it. It is also the narrative that takes place in the minds of those who read it. Debussy, the artist who lives on in his music and in the edifice of commentary that has been built around it, can only trust that his interpreters – writers, readers and performers – will be faithful.

Appendix: Why I Wrote *Pelléas*

This insightful note from Debussy, written in April 1902 at the request of Georges Ricou, the manager of the Opéra-Comique, further illustrates some of the points made by the author – and Debussy himself – throughout the book. Particular themes that are alluded to here include Debussy's struggle to write music for the theatre, his views on Wagner, and the creation, revisions, realism and orchestral setting of *Pelléas and Mélisande*. Footnotes in the passage direct the reader back to relevant pages in the main text.

My acquaintance with Pelléas *dates from 1893. Despite the enthusiasm of a first reading, and perhaps a few secret ideas about possible music, I did not begin to think seriously about it until the end of that year (1893).*

For a long time I had been striving to write music for the theatre, but the form in which I wanted it to be was so unusual that after several attempts I had almost given up the idea. Explorations previously made in the realm of pure music had led me toward a hatred of classical development, whose beauty is solely technical and can interest only the mandarins in our profession. I wanted music to have a freedom that was perhaps more inherent than in any other art, for it is not limited to a more or less exact representation of nature, but rather to the mysterious affinity between Nature and the Imagination.[1]

After some years of passionate pilgrimages to Bayreuth, I began to have doubts about the Wagnerian formula, or, rather, it seemed to me that it was of use only in the particular case of Wagner's own genius. He was a great collector of formulae, and these he assembled within a framework that appears uniquely his own only because one is not well enough acquainted with music. And without denying his genius, one could say that he had put the final period after the music of his time, rather as Victor Hugo summed up all the poetry that had gone before. One should therefore try to be 'post-Wagner' rather than 'after Wagner'.[2]

The drama of Pelléas *- which despite its atmosphere of dreams contains much more humanity than those so-called documents of real life -*

seemed to suit my purpose admirably. It has an evocative language whose sensibility is able to find an extension in the music and in the orchestral setting.[3] I also tried to obey a law of beauty that seems notably ignored when it comes to dramatic music: the characters of this opera try to sing like real people, and not in an arbitrary language made up of worn-out clichés. That is why the reproach has been made concerning my so-called taste for monotonous declamation, where nothing seems melodic ... First of all, that's not true. In addition, a character cannot always express himself melodically: the dramatic *melody has to be quite different from what is generally called melody ... The people who go to listen to music in the theatre are really like those crowds whom one sees gathered around street musicians! There you can have your emotions-in-melody for a couple of sous! You can also be sure of a greater degree of attention than is usually found among the patrons of our state theatres, and you will even find a greater wish to understand - something totally lacking in the above-mentioned public.[4]*

By a unique stroke of irony, this public which demands 'something new' is the same one that is bewildered by, and which jeers at, anything new or unusual, whenever someone is trying to break away from making the customary hullabaloo. This may seem hard to understand, but one must not forget that with a work of art an attempt at beauty is always taken as a personal insult by some people.[5]

I do not pretend to have discovered everything in Pelléas, *but I have tried to forge a way ahead that others will be able to follow. These are the fruits of my experience, which will perhaps release dramatic music from the heavy yoke under which it has lived for so long.*

Pelléas *was completed for the first time in 1895. Since then I've reset parts of it, modified it, and so on. It represents some twelve years of my life.[6]*

[1] See pages 64–8, 140

[2] See pages 41–4, 76, 80–1

[3] See pages 106–8, 111, 115

[4] See pages 155, 158

[5] See pages 85–6

[6] See page 116

Classified List of Works

Dates in parentheses are those of composition. The abbreviation 'fp' denotes first public performance; details are given where known.

Stage Works

Hymnis, comédie lyrique to poems by Théodore de Banville, incomplete (scene 1, part of scene 2, scene 7) (c. 1882); opening song *Il dort encore* published in *Sept Poèmes de Banville* in 1984

Rodrigue et Chimène, opera, text by Catulles Mendés, vocal score with piano reduction, incomplete (parts of Act I, Acts II and III) (1890–2). fp of vocal score (reconstruction by Richard Langham Smith, with Paul Roberts, piano) London, February 2 1987; fp of staged work (reconstruction Richard Langham Smith, orchestration E. Denisov) Lyon, 1993

Pelléas et Mélisande, opera in five acts, text by Maurice Maeterlinck (1893–5); additions in 1898; further additions and orchestration in 1900–2. fp Paris, 30 April 1902

Chansons de Bilitis, 'tableaux vivants' to poems by Pierre Louÿs, for two flutes, two harps and celeste (1900–1); full score and celeste part lost, reconstructed by Pierre Boulez in 1954 and Arthur Hoérée in 1971; recomposed as *Six épigraphes antiques* for piano in 1914. fp Paris, 1901; fp of Boulez version 1954 (also see Piano Solo, Piano Four Hands and Two Pianos)

Le Diable dans le beffroi, opera, text by Claude Debussy (after Edgar Allen Poe), incomplete (sketches for two tableaux), (1902–12)

Le Roi Lear, incidental music after William Shakespeare, incomplete (seven sections sketched)

(1904); two sections completed and orchestrated by Roger Ducasse, published in 1926

La Chute de la maison Usher, opera, text by Claude Debussy (after Edgar Allen Poe), incomplete (vocal score of Prologue, scene 1 and part of scene 2) (1908–17). fp (revised and orchestrated by Juan Allende-Blin) New Haven, 1977

Khamma, 'légende dansé', choreography by William L. Courtney and Maude Allan (1911–12), orchestrated by Claude Debussy and Charles Koechlin. fp Paris, 1947

Le Martyre de Saint-Sébastien, 'mystère', incidental music to a drama by Gabriele d'Annunzio (1911); orchestrated by Claude Debussy and André Caplet. fp Paris, 1911

No-Ja-Li (originally entitled *Le Palais du Silence*), ballet to a scenario by Georges de Feure, incomplete (sketches for Prelude and scene 1) (1913–14)

Jeux, 'poème dansé', choreography by Vaslav Nijinsky (1912–13). fp Paris, 1913

La Boîte à joujoux, 'ballet pour enfants', choreography by André Hellé (1913); orchestrated by Claude Debussy and André Caplet from Debussy's sketches; piano score published in 1913. fp Paris, 1919

Flûte de Pan, incidental music for solo flute to a text by Gabriel Mourey (1913); published in 1927 as *Syrinx* for flute. fp Paris, 1913 (also see Chamber/Instrumental)

Orchestral

Symphony in B Minor (1880); arrangement of one movement for piano four hands published in 1933

Intermezzo, after Heinrich Heine, for cello and orchestra (1882); published in 1944; also arranged for piano four hands

Triomphe de Bacchus, suite (lost) after a poem by Théodore de Banville (1882); arrangement of one movement for piano four hands published in 1928

Première suite ('Fête', 'Ballet', 'Rêve', 'Bacchanale') (c. 1883); also arranged for piano

Printemps, for female chorus and orchestra (1887); original score lost; arrangement for piano four hands published in 1904; orchestrated in 1912 by Busser, under Debussy's direction. fp Paris, 1913

Fantaisie for piano and orchestra (1889–90). fp 1919

Prélude à l'après-midi d'un faune, after a poem by Stéphane Mallarmé (1892–4); arranged for two pianos in 1894. fp Paris, 22 December 1894

Marche écossaise sur un thème populaire (1891–1908), version of piano original (1891). fp Paris, 1913

Deux gymnopédies (nos 1 and 3 from Erik Satie's *Trois gymnopédies*) (1896)

Nocturnes ('Nuages', 'Fêtes', 'Syrènes') (1897–9). fp Paris, 1901

La Mer, three symphonic sketches ('De l'Aube à midi sur la mer', 'Jeux de vagues', 'Dialogues du vent et de la mer') (1903–5); arranged for piano four hands in 1905. fp Paris, 1905

Danse sacrée et danse profane, for chromatic harp and strings, (1904); arranged for two pianos in 1904. fp Paris, 1904

Images ('Gigues', 'Ibéria', 'Rondes de printemps') (1905–12). fp 'Ibéria', 'Rondes de printemps', Paris, 1910; fp of complete work Paris, 1913

Première rapsodie, for clarinet and orchestra (1911), version of clarinet and piano original (1910–11). fp Paris, 1911

La Plus que lente (1912), version of piano original (1910)

Berceuse heroïque (1914), version of piano original

Rapsodie for alto saxophone and orchestra (1919), version of alto saxophone and piano original (1901–8); orchestrated by Roger-Ducasse from Debussy's sketches. fp Paris, 1919

Songs for Solo Voice
(with piano accompaniment unless otherwise stated)

Ballade à la lune, text by Alfred de Musset (1879)

Madrid, princesse des Espagnes, text by Alfred de Musset (1879)

Aimons-nous et dormons, text by Théodore de Banville (1880)

Caprice, text by Théodore de Banville (1880)

Nuit d'étoiles, text by Théodore de Banville (1880)

Rêverie, text by Théodore de Banville (1880)

Beau soir, text by Paul Bourget (c. 1880)

Fleur des blés, text by André Girod (c. 1880)

Les Baisers, text by Théodore de Banville (1881)

Souhait, text by Théodore de Banville (1881)

Triolet à Phylis (Zéphyr), text by Théodore de Banville (1881)

Les Baisers d'amours, text by Maurice Bouchor (1881)

Chansons tristes, text by Maurice Bouchor (1881)

L'Archet, text by Charles Cros (1881)

Les Papillons, text by Théophile Gautier (1881)

Les Elfes, text by Leconte de Lisle (1881)

La Fille aux cheveux de lin, text by Leconte de Lisle (1881)

Jane, text by Leconte de Lisle (1881)

Rondeau: Fut-il jamais, text by Alfred de Musset (1881)

Rondel chinois, text unknown (c. 1881)

Tragédie, text by Léon Valade (c. 1881)

Fête galante, text by Théodore de Banville (1882)

Les Lilas, text by Théodore de Banville (1882)

Pierrot, text by Théodore de Banville (1882)

Les Roses, text by Théodore de Banville (1882)

Séguidille, text by Théophile Gautier (1882)

Sérénade, text by Théodore de Banville (1882)

Flots, palmes, sables, text by Armand Renaud (1882)

Clair de lune, text by Paul Verlaine (1882)

En sourdine, text by Paul Verlaine (1882)

Fantoches, text by Paul Verlaine (1882)

Mandoline, text by Paul Verlaine (1882)

Pantomime, text by Paul Verlaine (1882)

Musique, text by Paul Bourget (1883)

Paysage sentimental, text by Paul Bourget (1883)

Romance: Silence ineffable, text by Paul Bourget (1883)

Coquetterie posthume, text by Théophile Gautier (1883)

Chanson espagnole, text by Alfred de Musset, for two equal voices and piano (1883)

Églogue, text by Leconte de Lisle, for soprano, tenor and piano (c. 1883)

Regret: Devant le ciel, text by Paul Bourget (1884)

La Romance d'Ariel, text by Paul Bourget (1884)

Romance: Voici que le printemps, text by Paul Bourget (1884)

Apparition, text by Stéphane Mallarmé (1884)

Deux romances ('L'Ame évaporée', 'Cloches'), text by Paul Bourget (1885)

Barcarolle, text by Édouard Guinand (c. 1885)

Ariettes, paysages belges et aquarelles ('C'est l'extase', 'Il pleure dans mon coeur', 'L'Ombre des arbres', 'Chevaux de bois', 'Green', 'Spleen'), text by Paul Verlaine (1885–7); published in 1888, republished in 1903 as *Ariettes oubliées*

Cinq poèmes de Charles Baudelaire ('Le Balcon', 'Harmonie du soir', 'Le Jet d'eau', 'Receuillement', 'La Mort des amants'), text by Charles Baudelaire (1887–90)

La Belle au bois dormant, text by Vincent Hyspa (1890)

Fêtes galantes ('En Sourdine', 'Fantoches', 'Clair de lune'), text by Paul Verlaine (1891)

Trois melodies ('La Mer est plus belle', 'Le Son du cor', 'L'Échelonnement des haies'), text by Paul Verlaine (1891)

Les Angélus, text by Grégoire Le Roy (1892)

Proses lyriques ('De Rêve', 'De Grève', 'De Fleur', 'De Soir'), text by Claude Debussy (1892–3)

Chansons de Bilitis ('La Flûte de Pan', 'La Chevelure', 'Le Tombeau des naïads'), text by Pierre Louÿs (1897–8)

Nuits blanches, text by Claude Debussy (1898); two songs of a projected five, originally intended as a second set of *Proses Lyriques.* fp by François Leroux and Noël Lee, Paris, 1991

Berceuse pour 'La Tragédie de la mort', text by René Peter, for unaccomanied soprano (1899). fp by Dawn Upshaw, London, 1992

Dans le jardin, text by Paul Gravollet (1903)

Trois chansons de France: 'Le Temps a laissié son manteau', text by Charles d'Orléans; 'La Grotte', text by Tristan L'Hermite; 'Pour ce que la Plaisance est morte', text by Charles d'Orléans (1904)

Fêtes galantes ('Les Ingénus', 'La Faune', 'Colloque sentimental'), text by Paul Verlaine (1904)

Le Promenoir des deux amants ('La Grotte' [from *Trois chansons de France],* 'Crois mon conseil', 'Chère Climène', 'Je tremble en voyant son visage', text by Tristan L'Hermite ('La Grotte' 1904; others 1910)

Trois ballades de Villon ('Ballade de Villon à s'amye', 'Ballade de Villon feit à la requeste de sa mère', 'Ballades des femmes de Paris'), text by François Villon (1910)

Trois poèmes de Mallarmé ('Soupir', 'Placet futile', 'Eventail'), text by Stéphane Mallarmé (1913)

Noël des enfants qui non plus des maisons, text by Claude Debussy, for children's chorus, two voices and piano (1916)

Choral and Vocal Orchestral

Daniel, scene 1 and part of scene 2 of cantata for three solo voices and orchestra, text by Émile Cécile (c. 1881)

Le Printemps, for female chorus and orchestra, text by Compte de Ségur (1882); vocal score published in 1928 as *Salut printemps,* with piano arrangement. fp Paris, 1928

Choeur des brises, sketch for soprano and three female voices (c. 1882); extract published in 1950

Invocation, for male chorus and orchestra, text by Alphonse de Lamartine (1883); vocal score published in 1928 with piano four hands arrangement. fp Paris, 1928

Le Gladiateur, cantata for three solo voices and orchestra, text by Émile Moreau (1883). fp of vocal score Paris, 1928

Diane au Bois, vocal score of part of Act II, scene 3 and scene 4, text by Théodore de Banville (1883–6). fp broadcast on BBC Radio 3, 1968

L'Enfant prodigue, 'scéne lyrique' for three solo voices and orchestra, text by Édouard Guinand (1884); orchestrated in 1906–8. fp of vocal score Paris, 1884

La Damoiselle élue, 'poème lyrique' for soprano, female chorus and orchestra, text by Dante Gabriel Rossetti, translated Gabriel Sarrazin, (1887–8). fp Paris, 1893

La Saulaie, for voice and orchestra, incomplete, text by Dante Gabriel Rossetti, translated Pierre Louÿs (1896–1900)

Trois chansons de Charles Orléans ('Dieu! Qu'il la fait bon regarder!', 'Quand j'ai ouy le tabourin', 'Yver, vous n'estes qu'un villain'), for four voices a capella ('Quand j'ai ouy le tabourin' 1908; others 1898). fp Paris, 1909

Noël pour célébrer Pierre Louÿs, pour toutes les voix y compris celle du people, text by Claude Debussy (1903); unpublished

Le Jet d'eau (1907), version of vocal original (1887–90)

Trois ballades de Villon (1910) version of vocal original

Petite cantate, for soprano, baritone, chorus, bells, piano (1907); unpublished

Noël, for tenor, chorus, bugles, piano (1914); unpublished

Ode à la France, sketch for soprano, chorus and orchestra, text by Louis Laloy (1916–17); orchestrated by Marius-Françoise Gaillard in 1928. fp Paris, 1928

Chamber/Instrumental

Nocturne et scherzo, for cello and piano (1880)

Premier trio, for piano, violin and cello (1880). fp (in arrangement for violin and piano) 1882

Premier quatuor, for string quartet (1893). fp Paris, 29 December 1893

Rapsodie, for alto saxophone and piano (1901–8)

Première rapsodie, for clarinet and piano (1909–10). fp Paris, 1911

Morceau à déchiffrer pour le concours de clarinette de 1910, for solo clarinet (1910); published as *Petite pièce* for clarinet and piano. fp Paris, 1910

Syrinx, for flute, 1913 (also see Stage Works)

Sonata for cello and piano (1915). fp Paris, 1917

Sonata for flute, viola and harp (1915). fp Paris, 1917

Sonata for violin and piano (1916–17). fp Paris, 1917

Piano Solo

Danse bohémienne (1880)

Ballade slave (c. 1890); re-published in 1903 as *Ballade*

Deux arabesques (c. 1890)

Mazurka (c. 1890)

Rêverie (c. 1890)

Suite bergamasque ('Prélude', 'Menuet', 'Clair de lune', 'Passepied') (c. 1890); revised and published 1905

Tarantelle styrienne (c. 1890); re-published in 1903 as *Danse*

Valse romantique (c. 1890)

Nocturne (1892)

Images (1894); three pieces, first published in 1977 as *Images oubliées*

Suite pour le piano ('Prélude', 'Sarabande', 'Toccata') (1894–1901); the 'Sarabande' is a revised version of the second of the *Images* of 1894

Images I ('Reflets dans l'eau', 'Hommage à Rameau', 'Mouvement') (1901–5)

D'un cahier d'esquisses (1903). fp Paris, 1910

Estampes ('Pagodes', 'La Soirée dans Grenade', 'Jardins sous la pluie') (1903). fp Paris, 1904

L'Isle joyeuse (1903–4). fp Paris, 1905

Masques (1903–4). fp Paris, 1905

Morceaux de concours (1904); based on a sketch from the unfinished opera *Le Diable dans le beffroi*

Children's Corner ('Doctor Gradus ad Parnassum', 'Jimbo's Lullaby', 'Serenade for the Doll', 'The Snow is Dancing', 'The Little Shepherd', 'Golliwogg's Cakewalk') (1906–8). fp Paris, 1908

Images II ('Cloches à travers les feuilles', 'Et la lune descend sur le temple qui fût', 'Poissons d'or') (1907). fp Paris, 1908

Hommage à Haydn (1909)

The Little Nigar (1909)

Préludes I ('Danseuses de Delphes', 'Voiles', 'Le Vent dans la plaine', 'Les Sons et les parfums tournent dans l'air du soir', 'Les Collines d'Anacapri', 'Des Pas sur la neige', 'Ce qu'a vu le Vent d'Ouest', 'La Fille aux cheveux de lin', 'La Sérénade interrompue', 'La Cathédrale engloutie', 'La Danse de Puck', 'Minstrels') (1909–10)

La Plus que lente (1910)

Préludes II ('Brouillards', 'Feuilles mortes', 'La Puerta del Vino', 'Les Fées sont d'exquises danseuses', 'Bruyères', 'Général Lavine – excentric', 'La Terrasse des audiences du clair de lune', 'Ondine', 'Hommage à S. Pickwick Esq. P. P. M.C.', 'Canope', 'Les Tierces alternées', 'Feux d'artifice') (1912–13)

Berceuse heroïque (1914)

Six épigraphes antiques ('Pour invoquer Pan', 'Pour un tombeau sans nom', 'Pour que la nuit soit propice', 'Pour la danseuses aux crotales', 'Pour l'égyptienne', 'Pour remercier la pluie au matin') (1914) (also see Piano Four Hands and Two Pianos)

Douze Études (Book I: 'Pour les cinq doigts', 'Pour les tierces', 'Pour les quartes', 'Pour les sixtes', 'Pour les octaves', 'Pour les huit doigts'; Book II: 'Pour les degrés chromatiques', 'Pour les agrèments', 'Pour les notes répétées', 'Pour les sonorités opposées', 'Pour les arpèges composés', 'Pour les accords') (1915). fp Paris, 1916

Elégie (1915)

Pour l'oeuvre du 'Vêtement du Blessé' (1915); fp in 1933 as *Page d'album*

Les Soirs illuminés par l'ardeur du charbon (1917)

Piano Four Hands and Two Pianos

Petite suite ('En bateau', 'Cortège', 'Menuet', 'Ballet'), for four hands (1886–9). fp Paris, 1894

Marche écossaise sur un théme populaire (1891); orchestrated in 1908. fp Paris, 1909

Lindaraja, for two pianos (1901). fp 1926

Six épigraphes antiques (1914). fp (piano duet version) Paris, 1917 (also see Piano Solo)

En blanc et noir (1915). fp Paris, 1916

Further Reading

The most thorough and wide-ranging account of
Debussy's life in the recent literature is only available in
French: François Lesure's *Claude Debussy: biographie
critique*. Lesure's researches into the Symbolist years are
particularly illuminating, incorporated as the first half
of his biography but originally published as *Debussy
avant Pelléas ou les années symbolistes* (Paris 1992). Lesure's
recently published *Claude Debussy – Correspondance*,
discussed in the Preface, is the definitive collection of
Debussy's correspondence, and now replaces all
previous selections. I also give below the most
significant English translations, among them Roger
Nichols' *Debussy Letters* (which draws on, and
amplifies, an earlier selection by Lesure), the mainstay
for English readers and readily available in libraries. I
have also mentioned in the Preface Roger Nichols'
admirable *Debussy Remembered*, a collection of
memoirs compiled and translated by Nichols that are
not easily available elsewhere. Readers might also like
to look at two other books in this series that have
a strong bearing on Debussy: *Satie Remembered* (edited
by Robert Orledge) and *Ravel Remembered* (Roger
Nichols). Finally, some of most recent Debussy
research has discovered the full and fascinating memoir
of Debussy's later years by the American violinist
Arthur Hartmann. Some of the material appeared in
Nichols' *Debussy Remembered*, but now thanks to
tireless American scholarship we have the complete
account, along with a host of letters from Debussy's
wife Emma to Hartmann. The image of Debussy is
fulsomely laudatory, amusing, and slightly ludicrous,
but, as David Grayson says in his introduction,
Hartmann's memoir, despite its colourful (and self-
serving) tone, has the ring of truth.

Debussy's Letters

Cobb, M. (ed.) and **Miller, R.** (trans) *Debussy's Letters
to Inghelbrecht – The Story of a Musical Friendship*
(Rochester, University of Rochester Press, 2005).

Cobb, M.G. '*Claude Debussy to Claudius and Gustave
Popelin: Nine Unpublished Letters*', 19th Century Music,
18 (Summer 1989), 39–48.

Lesure, F. and Herlin, D. (eds) *Claude Debussy –
Correspondance* (Paris, Gallimard, 2005). The complete
collection of Debussy's correspondence, in French.

Lesure, F. (ed.) **and Nichols, R.** (ed. and trans.)
Debussy Letters (London, Faber, 1987). The only edition
of Debussy's letters (extensive but far from complete)
in English.

Debussy and his Works

Austin, W. (ed.) *Debussy: Prelude to 'The Afternoon
of the Faun'* (New York, Norton, 1970). Although
published thirty-five years ago, this remains one of the
most illuminating of all introductions to Debussy's
early masterpiece.

Briscoe, J. R. (ed.) *Debussy in Performance* (New
Haven and London, Yale University Press, 1999).
A collection of essays about the relationship between
Debussy's music and the performers and conductors
who give it voice.

Clive, H. P. *Pierre Louÿs (1875–1925): A Biography*
(Oxford, Clarendon Press, 1978).
An account of the man who was the most important
friend of Debussy's in the 1890s.

Cobb, M. G. (ed.) *The Poetic Debussy* (Rochester,
University of Rochester Press, 1994). A compilation
of all of Debussy's song texts, along with information
on the genesis of the songs, their poets, and with
selected letters.

Dietschy, M. *A Portrait of Claude Debussy,* ed. and trans. William Ashbrook and Margaret G. Cobb (Oxford, Oxford University Press, 1990). An important biography, first published in 1962, full of detail and containing hitherto unpublished facts about Debussy's early life.

Fulcher, J. F. (ed.) *Debussy and His World* (Princeton, Princeton University Press, 2001). Of especial interest in this collection is the essay on *La Mer* by Brian Hart; the two essays on Debussy's Prix de Rome compositions, and on his conservatoire training, by John Clevinger; *Debussy in Fin de Siècle Paris* by Christophe Charle; and *Debussy, Mallarmé and 'Les Mardis',* by Rosemary Lloyd.

Holloway, R. *Debussy and Wagner* (London, Eulenburg, 1979). The definitive account of Debussy's debt to Wagner.

Hsu, S., Grolnic, S. and Peters, M. (eds) *'Claude Debussy As I Knew Him' and Other Writings of Arthur Hartmann* (Rochester, University of Rochester Press, 2003). See preamble.

Jarocinski, S. *Debussy: Impressionism and Symbolism,* trans. Rollo Myers (London, Eulenberg, 1976). The first in-depth study of the subject, and still the most eloquent argument for Debussy's debt to Symbolism.

Lesure, F. (ed.) **and Smith, R. L.** (ed. and trans.) *Debussy on Music* (London, Secker and Warburg, 1977). The collected journalism of Debussy, but just as much a book about him as it contains extensive annotations by Langham Smith.

Lesure, F. *Claude Debussy: biographie critique* (Paris, Klincksieck, 1994). See preamble.

Lesure, F. *Claude Debussy: iconographie musicale* (Geneva, Minkoff, 1980). A collection of photographs of Debussy, his family, friends and associated material. Text in French and English.

Lockspeiser, E. *Debussy: His Life and Mind,* vols. I and II (Cambridge, Cambridge University Press, 1978). By far the most important and detailed treatment of Debussy's life and times available in English.

Nichols, R. *Debussy Remembered* (London, Faber, 1992). See preamble.

Nichols, R. *The Life of Debussy* (Cambridge, Cambridge University Press, 1998). A short account, drawing on the most recent research.

Nichols, R. and Smith, R. L. *Claude Debussy: Pelléas et Mélisande* (Cambridge, Cambridge University Press, 1989). A detailed investigation into the genesis and meaning of Debussy's masterpiece.

Orledge, R. *Debussy and the Theatre* (Cambridge, Cambridge University Press, 1982). Every one of Debussy's numerous theatrical projects, many of which came to nothing, is examined and placed in the context of his overall life's work. This was the pioneering research on this subject and has not been surpassed.

Roberts, P. *Images: The Piano Music of Claude Debussy* (Portland, Amadeus Press, 1996). A survey of Debussy's piano music in relation to visual art and literature.

Smith, R. L. (ed.) *Debussy Studies* (Cambridge, Cambridge University Press, 1997). A collection of articles, many of biographical interest, arising from a Debussy symposium in London in 1993.

Trezise, S. *La Mer* (Cambridge, Cambridge University Press, 1994). A refreshingly broad-ranging examination of *La Mer,* daring to offer a programmatic interpretation alongside more formal analysis, and placing the work against the background of Debussy's turbulent life at the time of its composition.

Trezise, S. (ed.) *The Cambridge Companion to Debussy* (Cambridge, Cambridge University Press, 2003). This wide-ranging and absorbing collection of essays was published after I had completed my own writing, but it explores in depth many of the themes I have touched upon.

Selective Discography

The Debussy discography is extensive, if not overwhelming, so I can only offer a small selection that has
caught my eye, and ear, over the years. Almost all are still
in print, although with today's easy internet access to
archive and out-of-print recordings I have also included
some relative rarities. In the *Pelléas* list I prize the Ernest
Ansermet recording from 1964 (the 1952 version is worth
searching out too, with the inimitable Suzanne Danco),
and the second recording by Pierre Boulez, following his
magnificent collaboration with the director Peter Stein
for Welsh National Opera in 1992 (now on DVD). The
Ansermet and Boulez interpretations could not be more
contrasted, the first delicate and poetic, highlighting the
tenuous, mysterious qualities of the opera; the second
cleaner lined, more awake, drawing attention to the
incipient (as well as the real) power of Debussy's highly
wrought score. Listeners need to tread with care in the
extensive song and piano lists, which offer an enormous
range of interpretations to suit all tastes, as well as as a
large number that are unmemorable. Debussy demands
a very particular voice quality for his songs, as well as an
exquisite subtlety of interpretation, and these two
requirements are hard to come by simultaneously. The
archive recordings of Maggie Teyte, with Alfred Cortot,
set a standard rarely attained by others (although Suzanne
Danco with Guido Agosti comes close). I love Felicity
Lott's Baudelaire songs (with Graham Johnson); and
Dawn Upshaw gives a good impression of Debussy's
mistress Marie Vasnier in her recording (with James
Levine) of the Vasnier Song Book. Among archive piano
recordings, the complete piano works by Gieseking
always stands out, not so much for the sound as for the
ease and beauty of the phrasing. Rubinstein's various
forays into the Debussy repertoire are all worth
searching out; Michelangeli's recordings remain inimitable. For me Boulez is always fine in the orchestral
works – I like Debussy clean and structured, without the
'mist', as Boulez once proclaimed; while the Toscanini

recording with the NBC Symphony orchestra is
compelling Debussy unlike any other. Some curiosities:
Mary Garden singing 'Mes longs cheveux' from *Pelléas*
with Debussy accompanying at the piano; Stokowski
conducting his own orchestration of *La cathédrale
engloutie;* Debussy's early piano arrangements (under
protest, but for necessary financial reward) of works by
Tchaikovsky, Schumann, Saint-Saëns and Wagner,
performed by Daniel Blumenthal and Robert Groslot;
and a remarkable arrangement of 'Minstrels' (from
Preludes Book 1) for cello and piano, performed by
Mischa Maisky and Daria Hovora, which places the
piece somewhere between the string sonatas and music-
hall entertainment. And lastly I must mention another
fine example of the art of piano transcription: Ravel's
arrangement for piano four hands of Debussy's
orchestral *Nocturnes*, recorded by John Ogden and
Brenda Lucas.

Stage Works

Pelléas et Mélisande
Pierre Mollet (tenor), Suzanne Danco (soprano), Heinz
Rehfuss (baritone), André Vessières (bass) Hélène
Bouvier (mezzo soprano), Flora Wend (soprano), Derek
Olsen (baritone); Choeurs et Orchestre de la Suisse
Romande conducted by Ernest Ansermet (1952)
DECCA 425 965–2

Pelléas et Mélisande
Camille Maurane (tenor), Erna Spoorenberg (soprano),
George London (baritone), Guus Hoekman (bass)
Josephine Veasey (mezzo soprano), Rosine Brédy
(soprano), John Shirley-Quirk (bass-baritone),
Gregore Kubrack (bass); Choir of the Grand Theatre
Geneva, L'Orchestre de la Suisse Romande conducted
by Ernest Ansermet (1964)
DECCA 473351–2

Pelléas et Mélisande
Alison Hagley (soprano), Neill Archer (tenor), Donald
Maxwell (baritone), Kenneth Cox (bass), Penelope
Walker (mezzo-soprano), Samuel Burkey (treble);
Chorus and Orchestra of Welsh National Opera

conducted by Pierre Boulez; directed for the stage and screen by Peter Stein
DG 073 030–9 (DVD)

Rodrigue et Chimène (reconstructed by Langham Smith; orch. Denisov) Donna Brown (soprano), Laurence Dale (tenor), Hélène Jossoud (mezzo-soprano), José van Dam (baritone), Jules Bastin (bass-baritone), Vincent le Texier (bass-baritone); Lyon Opera Choir and Orchestra conducted by Kent Nagano
ERATO 4509 98508–2

Le Martyre de Saint-Sébastien (incidental music) Leslie Caron (narrator), Sylvia McNair (soprano), Ann Murray (mezzo-soprano), Nathalie Stutzmann (contralto); London Symphony Chorus and Symphony Orchestra conducted by Michael Tilson Thomas
SONY SK 48240

Orchestral

Prélude à l'après-midi d'un faune
La Cathédrale engloutie (orch. Stokowski) NBC Symphony Orchestra conducted by Leopold Stokowski; with works by Gould and Holst
CALA MONO CACD 00526

Prélude à l'après-midi d'un faune
Images
Printemps
The Cleveland Orchestra conducted by Pierre Boulez
DG 435766–2

La Mer
Chicago Symphony Orchestra, conducted by Daniel Barenboim, presented by Paul Roberts
EUROARTS (NAXOS) Masterpieces of Classical Music, (DVD)

Jeux
Nocturnes
Première rapsodie for Clarinet and Orchestra
La Mer
F. Cohen (clarinet); The Cleveland Orchestra Choir,

the Cleveland Orchestra conducted by Pierre Boulez
DG 439896–2GH

La Boîte à joujoux
Children's Corner (orch. Caplet)
Danse (orch. Ravel)
Danses sacrées et profanes
Fantasie for Piano and Orchestra
La plus que lente
Khamma
Petite suite (orch. Büsser)
Première rapsodie for Clarinet and Orchestra
Rapsodie for Saxophone
Marie-Claire Jamet (harp), Aldo Ciccolini (piano), Guy Dangain (clarinet), Jean-Marie Londeix (saxophone); French Radio and TV Orchestra conducted by Jean Martinon
EMI DOUBLE FORTE (ADD) 5 72623–2

Danse
Images
Ibéria
Marche écossaise
La Mer
Nocturnes
Nuages
Fêtes
La Damoiselle élue
Jarmila Novotna (soprano), Hertha Glaz (contralto); Schola Cantorum Women's Chorus, NBC Symphony Orchestra conducted by Arturo Toscanini
NAXOS MONO 8. 110811–2

Songs

The Vasnier Songbook: 'Pantomime', 'Calmes dans le demi-jour (En Sourdine)', 'Mandoline', 'Clair de Lune', 'Fantoches', 'Coquetterie posthume', 'Silence ineffable', 'Musique', 'Paysage semtimental', 'Romance (Voici que le printemps)', 'La Romance d'Ariel', 'Regret'
Six Forgotten Melodies
Five Poems of Charles Baudelaire
Dawn Upshaw (soprano), James Levine (piano)
SONY 67190

Ariettes oubliées
Fêtes galantes (1st series)
Chansons de Bilitis
Le promenoir des deux amants
3 Ballades de François Villon
Suzanne Danco (soprano), Guido Agosti (piano); with
Fauré's *La Bonne chanson*
AUVIDIS V 4803

Chansons de Bilitis, Fêtes galantes, Proses lyriques (1)
Mes longs cheveux (2)
(1) Maggie Teyte (soprano), Alfred Cortot (piano)
(2) Mary Garden (soprano), Claude Debussy (piano)
EMI 761038–2

Cinq poèmes de Charles Baudelaire
Felicity Lott (soprano), Graham Johnson (piano); with
works by Duparc, Fauré, Bréville, Sévérac, Sauguet,
Capdevielle, Chabrier
HARMONIA MUNDI 6031434

Nuit d'étoiles
Fleur des blés
Voici que le printemps
Mandoline
Cinq poèmes de Charles Baudelaire
Les Angelus
Romance
Les Cloches
Trois mélodies (Verlaine)
Fêtes galantes (2nd series)
Trois ballades de François Villon
Christopher Maltman (baritone), Malcolm Martineau
(piano)
HYPERION A 67357

Vocal Orchestral

La Damoiselle élue
Victoria de los Angeles (soprano); Boston Symphony
Orchestra conducted by Charles Munch; with works by
Berlioz and Massenet
TESTAMENT MONO SBT 3203

Chamber/Instrumental

Sonata for cello and piano
Mstislav Rostropovich (cello), Benjamin Britten
(piano); with works by Schubert and Schumann
DECCA (ADD) 460 974–2

Le Petit Nègre
Petite pièce
Première rapsodie, for clarinet and piano
Rapsodie, for saxophone and piano
Sonata for flute, viola and harp
Syrinx
William Bennett (flute), Nicholas Daniel (oboe), James
Campbell (clarinet), Rachael Gough (bassoon), John
York (piano), Ieuan Jones (harp), Simon Haram
(saxophone); with works by Saint-Saëns
CALA CACD 1017

Piano trio in G (1880)
Florestan Trio; with works by Fauré and Ravel
HYPERION CDA 67114

String quartet
Juilliard Quartet; with works by Dutilleux and Ravel
SONY DIGITAL SK 52554

Sonata for violin and piano
Kyung-Wha Chung (violin), Radu Lupu (piano); with
works by Franck and Chausson
DECCA 460 006–2

Minstrels arranged for cello and piano
Mischa Maisky (cello), Daria Hovora (piano); with
works by Bach, Boccherini, Chopin, Handel, Saint-
Saëns, Schubert, Schumann (on *Cellissimo: Favourite
Encores for Cello*)
DG 439 863

Solo Piano

Deux Arabesques
Ballade
Berceuse héroïque

Children's Corner
Danse bohémienne
D'un cahier d'esquisses
Éstampes
12 Études
Hommage à Haydn
Images – Books 1 & 2
L'Isle joyeuse
Masques
Mazurka
Nocturne
Le Petit Nègre
La Plus que lente
Pour le piano
Préludes – Books 1 & 2
Rêverie
Suite bergamasque
Valse romantique
Fantasie for piano and orchestra
Walter Geiseking; Hessischen Radio Orchestra
conducted by Kurt Schröder
EMI MONO 5 65855–2

Éstampes
Images – Book 2
Préludes – Book 1
Paul Roberts
CLASSICAL RECORDING COMPANY CRC 501–2

Children's Corner
Images – Books 1 & 2
Préludes – Books 1 & 2
Arturo Benedetti Michelangeli
DG (ADD) 449 438–2

Estampes: 'Soirée dans Grenade', 'Jardins sous la pluie'
Images: 'Reflets dans l'eau', 'Hommage à Rameau', 'Poissons d'or'
Masques
La Plus que lente
Préludes: 'La Fille aux cheveux de lin', 'La Cathédrale engloutie', 'Minstrels', 'La Terrasse des audiences du clair de lune', 'Ondine'

Artur Rubinstein, with works by Fauré, Franck, Ravel and Saint-Saëns
RCA 2CD (ADD) 74321 846062

Études – Books 1 & 11
En Blanc et Noir (for two pianos)
Paul Jacobs, Gilbert Kalish
NONESUCH 79161

Préludes – Book 1: Voiles, Des Pas sur la neige, Ce qu'a vu le Vent de l'Ouest, La Fille aux cheveux de lin, La Cathédrale engloutie, Minstrels
Paul Roberts
HAL LEONARD (Amadeus Press) HL 331696 (DVD)

Piano Four Hands and Two Pianos

En blanc et noir
Printemps
Lindaraja
La Mer (arr. Debussy)
Prélude à l'après-midi d'un faune (arr. Debussy)
Diane (arr. Debussy)
Marche écossaise sur un thème populaire
Symphony in B minor
Triomphe de Bacchus
Christian Ivaldi, Noël Lee
ARIO ARN 268128

Nocturnes (arr. Ravel)
John Ogden, Brenda Lucas; with works by
Rachmaninov, Katchachurian, Shostakovitch, Bizet
EMI 569386–2

Arrangements of Works by Other Composers

Tchaikovsky: Excerpts from *Swan Lake*
Saint-Saëns: *Etienne Marcel, Caprice*
Schumann: *Six Études*
Wagner: *Overture: The Flying Dutchman*
Daniel Blumenthal, Robert Groslot
MARC 8223378

Index

Page references in italics refer to
illustrations

**Photographic
Acknowledgements**

Courtesy of Lebrecht Music and
Arts Collection, London 23, 59, 142

©Mike Hoban 112–3

Courtesy of Topfoto.co.uk:
ArenaPAL Picture Library 200–1
©Collection Roger-Viollet 2, 14
©Haringue/Roger-Viollet 32
HIP/British Library 39
The Image Works 119

Courtesy of Pierpoint Morgan
Library, New York 57